GRAND DELUSIONS

GRAND DELUSIONS

The Cosmic Career of John De Lorean

Hillel Levin

THE VIKING PRESS
NEW YORK

Copyright © 1983 by Hillel Levin
All rights reserved
First published in 1983 by The Viking Press
40 West 23rd Street, New York, N.Y. 10010
Published simultaneously in Canada by
Penguin Books Canada Limited

LIBRARY OF CONGRESS CATALOGING IN PUBLICATION DATA
Levin, Hillel.
Grand delusions.
1. De Lorean, John Z.   2. Businessmen—United States—
Biography.   3. Automobile industry and trade.   I. Title.
HC102.5.D4L48   1983   338.7′6292222′0924   [B]   83-47906
ISBN 0-670-26685-X

Grateful acknowledgment is made to Lawrence Institute of Technology for permission to reprint "Know You What It Is to Be an Engineer," by John De Lorean, which appeared in *Tech News*.

Printed in the United States of America
Set in Linotron Caslon 540

Foreword

I first interviewed John De Lorean while on assignment for *New York* magazine in the spring of 1979. Like so many other reporters, I was struck by his charm and intelligence. I was also caught up in his effort, then well under way, to build his own sports car. In preparing a favorable profile, I used no more than our three hours of conversation and his glowing press clips as source information. Before *New York* could run my story, several other De Lorean articles went to print. My editors decided not to be lost in the shuffle and eventually killed my piece.

Two years later, as senior editor of *Monthly Detroit* magazine, I returned to De Lorean in much different circumstances. His first stainless steel, gull-winged cars had already rolled off the assembly line, and I was getting reports from dealers around the country about shoddy product quality. I also received a copy of the prospectus for a new stock offering that significantly reorganized the car company. At just a glance, I could see that the goals he once articulated for the De Lorean Motor Company had drastically changed.

What interested me most, however, were other changes in his personal holdings, especially the De Lorean Manufacturing Company. When I hunted up annual reports for this Michigan firm, filed with the state's Department of Corporations and Securities,

I found a list of other places of business, which included Route #1, Salmon, Idaho. From there I followed a paper trail of lawsuits and court hearings—all leading to an area of De Lorean's past business affairs that had never before been examined by the press.

As I would write in the magazine, the details that emerged from De Lorean's Byzantine empire did not amount to a flattering portrait, but rather one of "a man who has reached too far, perhaps jeopardizing all he has already gained." I gave De Lorean a chance to respond to several disturbing questions about his business conduct raised by my research, and he chose to speak with me on the telephone. Our tense conversation lasted for ninety minutes. He called me again, before the magazine went to press, warning me that I was "doing tremendous injury to the people there in [the] Belfast [Northern Ireland assembly plant]." It was the last time De Lorean was willing to speak to me. The resulting article, which appeared in December 1981, was some 5,000 words long, but I felt I had only scratched the surface of the De Lorean story.

Even as De Lorean's car company unraveled around him, the American press was still reluctant to look closely at the legend he had spun. The time would come, almost one year after my article, when De Lorean's record would be scrutinized more carefully, but it took the auto executive's arrest with over $24 million of cocaine to spark the media's interest.

While De Lorean's involvement with narcotics has made him newsworthy, there is no evidence that he had any long-term relationship with illegal drugs, either as a user or dealer. Instead, his arrest appears to be a jarring coda to a fascinating career—a career that I believe deserves close and thorough examination in its entirety.

John Z. De Lorean remains a sensitive subject for all those who have worked with him. While some people were willing to be interviewed about De Lorean, for a variety of personal reasons, they asked not to be identified by name. I fully appreciate their concerns, and when quoting them, refer to only the generic terms for their positions. Many more sources have given me permission to attribute quotes directly. I'm deeply grateful to everyone who aided my research.

Acknowledgments

Kirk Cheyfitz, the editor of the magazine article I did on De Lorean, remains the guiding force behind this project. In bringing me to Detroit, he restored my faith in the potential of journalism and gave me opportunities that I had never known before in this profession. He continues as my editor at *Metropolitan Detroit*, and I'm proud to call him a friend and teacher.

My thanks also go to the other founders of *Metropolitan Detroit*—Tom Jones, Eric Keller, Jane Rayburn, and Jack Felker—who all put up with my repeated absences at a crucial stage in the magazine's development.

As a novice at book writing I'm greatly indebted to my agents, Paula Diamond and Nat Sobel, who have directed and sustained this effort from beginning to end. I'm also grateful for the considerable aid I received in the development and preparation of the manuscript from my editor at Viking, Alan Williams.

In Detroit, my principal researcher was Mike Morgan. I had further help from lawyer Lawrence C. Burgess.

Contents

· 1 ·
The Shell
1

· 2 ·
Dark Secrets
11

· 3 ·
A Company Man
25

· 4 ·
High Performance
39

· 5 ·
Hollywood
51

· 6 ·
Falling from the Fourteenth Floor
70

CONTENTS

· 7 ·
A Very Brilliant Financial Analyst
88

· 8 ·
Four Bad Deals
101

· 9 ·
100 West Long Lake
140

· 10 ·
Silver Beauty
159

· 11 ·
Forty-five Days
181

· 12 ·
GPD
195

· 13 ·
Belfast
208

· 14 ·
New York
222

· 15 ·
Irvine
239

· 16 ·
The Ethical Car
252

· 17 ·
Out of Control
270

CONTENTS

· 18 ·
Roy to the Rescue
290

· 19 ·
Trapped in a Terrible Tower
308

· 20 ·
Aftermath
320

Index
329

Photographs follow page 100

· 1 ·
The Shell

Forty-three stories above 280 Park Avenue, the smoked-glass doors of the De Lorean Motor Corporation headquarters swung open to an expanse of white marble floor and red upholstered furniture. A brown glass reception desk—long enough for ten secretaries—loomed straight ahead. Once corporate headquarters for Xerox, this penthouse suite now made an impressive setting for a company that had only begun manufacturing and was still far away from turning a profit.

In the fall of 1981, Robert Henkel became a frequent visitor to the De Lorean sanctum. "There was," he says today, "a tremendous excitement in those offices—not just among the executives. Even down to the secretaries and maintenance men."

As executive vice president for the public relations agency of Carl Byoir & Associates, Henkel had the job—within the span of a fifteen-minute promotional film—of transmitting that excitement to all the De Lorean employees, dealers, and potential customers who would never ride an express elevator to the top of the Bankers Trust Building.

He worked mostly with the company's in-house PR staff. Occasionally John Z. De Lorean himself would wander into their meetings. With a smile and a nod, he'd ask what they were up to, and then sit back, in his light blue Pierre Cardin shirt-sleeves, and pensively listen to their explanations. "He struck me as a person with natural curiosity," Henkel recalls. "He wanted to know how we did this or that. He seemed to appreciate the importance of what we were doing, and no doubt he was very creative himself."

It took Henkel a few months to put the finishing touches on an eleven-page proposal for a film he entitled, *The De Lorean Dream: A Reality that Works*. But by the time he submitted the script in December, the dream was already disintegrating around De Lorean. The public relations project went no further. Henkel wouldn't even see payment for his services.

Nevertheless, his stillborn proposal remains a fascinating relic of the De Lorean empire—a typewritten inscription for a latter-day Ozymandias. The last page of Henkel's film treatment follows.

We return now to John De Lorean in his office, standing in front of a worldwide map or some other business graph.

He says something like this: "Our dream is coming true, and justifying the calculated risk we took. Sure, I'm a risk taker. And the people who drive our De Lorean car are probably risk takers, too. People who dare to lead other people. . . . People who live life to its fullest potential. . . . People who enjoy the special exhilaration of making things happen. . . . People who dream of a better world, and do whatever is needed to transform that dream into reality."

John De Lorean is next shown sitting inside his car. He ends by saying, "As hard as I've struggled, I'm one man who can say that my dream has come true. Our difficult efforts have succeeded, life is good, and I'm grateful!"

Then De Lorean closes the car and drives off onto a handsome modern highway with elegant city skyscrapers in the background. Closing music and credits appear over this final radiant scene.

THE SHELL

De Lorean's words in the script were his own—pasted together from speeches he had delivered over the years—and they ring with the blare of Sixties-style pop psychology. Taking risks, daring to lead, making things happen, living life to the fullest: these were the credos of a turbulent, activist decade—probably the most important period in De Lorean's adult life. He would keep his Sixties' sensibilities along with his predilection for long, drooping collars, turtlenecks and bell-bottom pants. He also kept the era's fascination with dreams—not the ones that were cooped up in the bedroom, but the dreams that trembled on the verge of fulfillment for those bold enough to "do whatever is needed to transform . . . dream into reality."

Oddly enough, in the Henkel script as well as in the few ads that De Lorean actually completed, the chief executive's personal success was more prominently featured than his stainless-steel product. This strategy may have helped endow the car with the glamour of its namesake's wealth and power. But the personal sales appeal worked at another level. De Lorean's customers did not only get a car. They also became a part of what De Lorean liked to call his "personal Horatio Alger dream."

In a dream come true, De Lorean would have ended his own story as happily as Henkel closed the film—the modern industrial hero riding his gleaming dream car into the sunset. But on the night of October 19, 1982, less than one year after Henkel finished writing his proposal, the eyes of the world were to see John De Lorean in a very different "radiant scene," one lit by the icy blue glare of photographers' strobe lights. This time he would not be riding off in his own car, but in the backseat of a police car with his hands cuffed behind him.

He was arrested earlier that evening with over $16 million worth of cocaine. In the first few dispatches to beam out over the news wires, he had to take second billing to the narcotic that has become a Hollywood celebrity in its own right, and the headlines read, BUSINESSMAN HELD IN COCAINE DEAL.

But if there were some members of the press who were not aware of De Lorean or his gull-winged innovation, the legal authorities were quick to provide them with the details. They made the car company his prime motive for breaking the law. De Lorean would have gone to any end to save his dream, prosecutors charged, and the drug deal was his last-ditch, Faustian bid to buy back the assembly plant.

It was the climax to a drama that had played for months in hotel-room stakeouts around the country. The select audience—federal authorities with videotape cameras—watched behind two-way mirrors. Some of the cast were indeed actors: agents of the FBI and the Drug Enforcement Administration posing as Mafiosi drug dealers. But the police charge that other performers, such as pilot William Morgan Hetrick, who allegedly smuggled the cocaine into the country, and his indicted accomplice, Stephen Lee Arrington, were not playacting. The sting, the authorities say, was initially staged for the benefit of Hetrick and Arrington. De Lorean was the walk-on who ended up stealing the show. Only moments before the arrest, De Lorean had held up a packet of dope and crowed, "This is better than gold." And he brought down the curtain by pouring wine all around and proposing a toast to one of the great moments in his career.

His battery of high-powered defense lawyers was left with the monumental task of proving that the authorities had preyed on De Lorean's desperation to save his company and lured him into a deal he would never have attempted on his own.

Such legal strategies may keep a man out of jail, but they do little to salvage his good name. They do nothing to blot out the pictures of a rumpled, downcast De Lorean, slumped in the backseat of the police car. No one understands that better than John De Lorean. His public image was his most finely crafted creation. Ironically, his final attempt to keep up appearances would pull them down forever.

Jail, De Lorean liked to tell reporters, was graduate school for many young men in the tough Detroit neighborhood where he grew up. He would add, half jokingly, that he was lucky not to have joined them.

• THE SHELL •

De Lorean's own route to incarceration strayed far from the paths of his childhood friends. Along the way to federal prison on Terminal Island—where he stayed two weeks until bail bonds were raised—he passed through the centers of corporate power and high society in America: from the boardrooms of General Motors to Hollywood, Wall Street, and Fifth Avenue.

These travels were accompanied by a more internal voyage, which started back at General Motors when the brilliant young engineer realized that he'd need more than mechanical sophistication to climb the corporate ladder. His involvement with the company product moved outward—from the gritty detail of the transmission and suspension, to the surface appeal of its gleaming metal shell, and finally to how the whole package was marketed to the masses. The public, he discovered, bought the wrapping—not the contents.

He rose to be the youngest general manager at Pontiac in the history of the division. With his flair for merchandising, he was given the lion's share of credit for changing the image of what had once been "the old lady's car." In the process, he changed his own image as well. By the end of the Sixties, he had gone through extensive facial cosmetic surgery. He dieted half the weight of his six-foot-four-inch frame away and built up the other half with barbells. Even his closest friends were shocked by his obsession with his appearance. He filled his home with mirrors, and in later years he carried a compact so he could check his face in the backseats of cars and blot his complexion with corn starch. He limited his wardrobe to a few styles and colors that most flattered his figure and, some say, he had many sets of the same light blue, high-collared shirt, and dark blue, Italian-cut suit. His efforts at reconstruction went beyond the scalpel, reaching even to his Eastern European roots, which he later denied in interviews.

Much to the chagrin of his General Motors superiors, he also remodeled his life-style. He made an effort to spend more time on the West Coast, making the nightclub scene with Hollywood celebrities and race-car drivers. He divorced his wife of fifteen years, dated movie starlets, and finally settled for a nineteen-year-old as his second bride.

He didn't just marry youth, he incorporated it. Young people, who had long been ignored by Detroit automakers, were buying his fast, sleek Pontiacs and turning the division into a powerhouse. In a time when the media focused on a generation gap, De Lorean jumped to the other side, becoming a vocal defender of youthful protest and an incisive critic of the establishment—even as he climbed higher into the General Motors stratosphere. Never had the Detroit press corps found a top auto executive both so accessible and such good copy. When they pegged him as eventual chief executive material, it was partly wishful thinking.

Yet his departure from General Motors in 1973 did not dismay De Lorean's admirers. For a lesser mortal, it would have been an ignominious development. With De Lorean, it took on the shining armor of high moral principle. His initial explanation laid the blame on his promotion from general manager at Chevrolet to policymaking vice president on the vaunted fourteenth floor of GM's headquarters. In his favorite analogy, he had gone from quarterback "to the guy who owned the stadium," and the cramps from his inactive managerial muscles became unbearable.

But as time went on, the reasons he gave for leaving became more pointed. His most detailed account of the split would emerge with the publication, in 1979, of *On A Clear Day You Can See General Motors*, a scathing attack on the wisdom and morality of GM's management, which he wrote as a first-person narrative with the considerable aid of longtime Detroit automotive reporter J. Patrick Wright. Already embarked on the developmental stages of his own car company, De Lorean tried to stop publication of the book, fearful that the wrath of GM would snuff out his infant firm. Wright finally published the book himself, but De Lorean still garnered credit as a courageous critic. Eventually, the book's place on the best-seller list only added luster to the De Lorean success story.

He did not need the book to bring him publicity. His supposedly gutsy career change and conquest of mid-life crisis was immortalized by Gail Sheehy in *Passages*. Despite his exile from

• THE SHELL •

GM, he remained hot copy for business reporters, always the ideal subject for an interview. He was never too busy for the press. Before an interview was over, he could bring up the Beach Boys, quote Montaigne, or mention the ruminations on human misery by social historian Peter Gay. Just as important, he listened. Like a gracious host, he turned encounters with reporters into casual conversations. The results that reached publication were almost reverential. His stellar achievements at GM seemed to glow even more brightly in retrospect.

If the seeker had been anyone but De Lorean, the quest to start a new auto company might have been written off. But the press was caught up in his dream to produce the "ethical car," and closely followed his search for investors. Ultimately, it seemed as though De Lorean had done the impossible. Against all predictions, and beyond even his own best expectations, he landed over $90 million in start-up money from the British government. Their condition—that he build the cars in strife-torn Northern Ireland—paled next to the magnitude of the windfall.

Even before one of his stainless-steel, gull-winged cars plopped off the assembly line, he already appeared to be climbing to the top of America's corporate, capitalist royalty. His residential estates, apartments, and ranches dotted the country. Their garages were filled with a private fleet of expensive cars. His third wife was an elegant, raven-haired beauty and one of the world's highest-paid professional models. All this, and he still professed a social conscience, and a desire to be a good corporate citizen.

It was all too good to be true.

And it wasn't true.

John De Lorean had not led just a double life. He led a quadruple life. Even as he sealed his deal with the British government and seemed ready to change the face of the automobile industry, his own pristine façade was starting to crumble away. Press clips were not the only chronicle of De Lorean during the Seventies. Court documents in lawsuits filed across the nation told another story, and they ran alongside the laudatory media accounts like photographic negatives.

Miniature auto racetracks; a breakthrough engine-coolant system; a cattle ranch; an auto dealership; a warehouse of CB radios; movie projectors for salesmen: all belong to a motley catalogue of soured deals that ended up in rancorous court battles. In these arenas, John De Lorean was not a lone gunfighter up against greedy corporate giants. His opponents charged that he was the goliath, trampling their precious dreams underfoot. One case carries the strong implication that his relationship with a GM supplier forced his exit from the corporation.

The records show that De Lorean did pay a heavy price to live his dream, assembling an unwieldy string of incongruous properties that sapped his energy and periodically threatened his bank account. It was all he could do to hold his byzantine empire together, while he canvassed for new partners to support his auto venture.

Cited in virtually all of the lawsuits was Roy Nesseth, a huge, six-foot-six, former car salesman. His intimidating performances mark the course of the less-publicized business career of John Z. De Lorean. Nesseth, a man who is alternately charming and offensive, has a record of civil lawsuits that runs through the indexes of Los Angeles courthouses like a page torn from a telephone directory.

De Lorean once described Nesseth to one of his auto-company executives as "a mean man who enjoyed being mean." He told others that Nesseth was a man who could get things done, and he counted on him to extricate the De Lorean name and fortune from investments that went bad. Despite warnings from De Lorean's associates that Nesseth's bullying—and, possibly, illegal—tactics did more harm than good, the two men grew only closer over the years. It was an affinity that mystified some De Lorean friends, but more important, it was a bond that most knew little about. In his world of business transactions, the orbits of De Lorean's satellites seldom intersected.

Only one man besides De Lorean is capable of putting the pieces together: his personal lawyer, Thomas Kimmerly. A mild-mannered tax specialist of slight build and owlish countenance, Kimmerly is the antithesis of Nesseth, preferring to blend into the background instead of taking center stage. The mastermind

THE SHELL

behind the web of De Lorean holding companies and subsidiaries, during the last decade Kimmerly became De Lorean's closest and most loyal business associate. Together, Kimmerly and Nesseth helped mask De Lorean's more embarrassing forays into private enterprise. In any case, the British government, like the media, seemed more anxious to accept the De Lorean myth. Their charity became his undoing.

The car company, like nothing before, tested the power and limitations of De Lorean's delusions. His ability to attract financing, auto dealers, and accomplished executives to his unlikely project revealed the stuff that the industry's pioneers were made of. In the process, he created a whirlpool that sucked in both the British government and his employees. The fact that they brought the company as far as they did—even as they lost faith in De Lorean's legendary prowess—remains a testament to their own determination.

The corporate renegade who had continually tested his superiors at GM suddenly found himself in charge, and there was no one to keep him in check. His expenses skyrocketed and company funds found their way into his personal household. For all the talk of a dream fulfilled, De Lorean's attention wandered off the car and onto other projects. Some of his executives wondered whether he was enriching himself at the expense of the British-backed company—much the same accusation he had once made against GM's brass. If anything, he seemed intent on repeating the litany of managerial errors he'd recited in *On A Clear Day*. His headlong rush to reap a paper profit—the shortsighted business behavior he had once so roundly condemned—doomed his dream to insolvency.

The wreckage of the De Lorean Motor Company is scattered across two continents: from the unpaid bills of a multinational conglomerate in France, to the dashed hopes and dignity of an assembly worker in Belfast, to a small parts-supplier in California. But the ultimate victim of his own delusions was John De Lorean.

In the summer of 1982, when all those around him saw imminent collapse, he—for the first time—saw a reason to invest personal funds in the dream car. The last evangelist in his own church, he still tried to convince auto dealers and investors that somewhere behind the miasma of mounting debt, there had been a stunning success. Even when Kimmerly and Nesseth couldn't find the impossible solution, De Lorean believed that he could summon the miracle, and took matters into his own hands.

Finally, he would find salvation—or so he thought—in a Mafia drug dealer. This was not an investor who cared about an "ethical car company," or an "ethical" anything. De Lorean's pitch could be aimed no higher than greed.

In exchange for his piece in a narcotics transaction that could net $60 million, he offered half his stock in De Lorean Motor Company, Inc. In fact, DMC, Inc. was something quite different from the De Lorean Motor Company. Formed some time before by Kimmerly, it existed as no more than a paper entity—a shell company.

It was the final grand charade.

·2·
Dark Secrets

It took a while, but Michigan Bell finally caught up with John Z. De Lorean. For months, the twenty-three-year-old had plied Detroit in a battered green utility truck, offering merchants advertisements in something he called the Yellow Pages. He made enough money on his first calls to even print up a few copies of his Yellow Pages for the advertisers.

The scam was no news for his close friends at the Lawrence Institute of Technology. The phone company didn't worry him, he laughed. He had just started attending law school at night and had already researched copyright law. Michigan Bell had forgotten to register its Yellow Pages as a trademark. His whole scheme was made in the shade.

Of course, Michigan Bell's lawyers were of a different opinion, and they weren't going to stop with a civil suit. They demanded criminal prosecution as well. The college boy had sold advertising under false pretenses, not only denying Bell its rightful returns but also bilking the misbegotten merchants.

The news about the phony phone books quickly buzzed through Lawrence Tech. The perpetrator wasn't just any member of the 1948 graduating class; if the engineering school had a Big Man on Campus, it was John De Lorean. He wrote a column for the school paper, sat on the student council, made the Lambda Iota Tau honor society and organized the first chapter at the college of the American Society of Industrial Engineers. To top it off, he could do the jitterbug with the best of them, and often did, spinning the prettiest girls at dances. The lanky young man with the unruly shock of hair seemed to have everything else in life at his fingertips. But suddenly, Michigan Bell threatened to bring the big bopper down to earth. In the eyes of some classmates a brilliant career hovered on the brink of oblivion even before graduation.

When John De Lorean returned home from college each night, he needed no reminder of how far he had already come in the world, and of how far he had yet to go. He still lived with his mother and younger brothers on the east side of Detroit in a narrow wood-framed bungalow, crammed between two other small homes. The house was just a few streets from the railroad tracks in one direction, and a few streets from an elevated freeway in the other—stuck in a dingy matrix of flat treeless streets crowded with tiny shingled houses. Bars, gas stations, and bodyshops dotted the main avenues.

When John was growing up, most of the neighbors were of Eastern European stock: still peasants who sowed postage-stamp backyards with vegetable gardens, slaughtered their own pigs, and made their own wine from the vines hanging off their garages. Although they took pride in their small homes, carefully cutting the grass and sweeping their sidewalks, the working-class neighborhood never measured up for their children. It was a place to leave behind.

John was born to Zachary and Katherine Pribak DeLorean on January 6, 1925, the first of four sons. His father was a tall, dark-browed, brooding man who sweated out a living in the foundries of the Ford Motor Company. The next to last of fourteen children in a farming family that lived just west of Bucharest, Rumania, Zachary had come to America alone as a teenager. According to John, before his father found factory work in Detroit, he was a ranch hand in Montana, and a steelworker and policeman in Gary,

Indiana. The latter occupation seems most odd since the elder De Lorean was not fluent in English, but at the turn of the century, the constabulary of industrial cities often hired immigrants to keep order during worker demonstrations.

There was evidently no great affection between father and son. In fact, as John grew older, he became more vague about Zachary's ethnic origins. In early interviews he placed his father's birthplace in middle Europe, and later, in the Alsace-Lorraine region of France. In 1974, while on a trip to an auto factory in central Rumania, De Lorean actually had the chance to visit Zachary's hometown. He was accompanied by two other Rumanians. One, Reo Campian, also grew up on Detroit's east side. "I couldn't understand it," Campian recalls. "Here we were near the village where his father was from and he didn't want to see it. I couldn't understand why he didn't want to go."

De Lorean was not embarrassed by his father's problems with alcohol or marriage. He is brutally frank in interviews and in his recollections for J. Patrick Wright in *On A Clear Day You Can See General Motors*. In the book, he says of his father, "He was a big man at six foot one and 220 pounds and enjoyed a certain amount of physical violence. Not that he was mean, but he got into his share of fights, sometimes after having a few beers with the boys after work."

While he attributes some of Zachary's bellicoseness to his difficulties with the English language, he doesn't say what his father's native tongue was. As he told Wright, "Part of my dad's inclination toward fisticuffs came from a deep frustration caused by his inability to communicate effectively and thereby capitalize on his mechanical genius. He was uneducated when he came to the U.S. and he couldn't speak English. Though he eventually mastered the language, he always spoke with a trace of an accent."

John's grade school records report that primarily Rumanian was spoken in his home. He explains in the book, "I do know that [my father's] frustration with his inability to verbally get out the things that were inside of him eventually led to a serious drinking problem which resulted in the breakup of our home."

De Lorean blames Ford for his father's frustration as well. No matter how well Zachary spoke English, he asserts, management wouldn't have taken him seriously. In a later interview with one reporter he says, "[my father] was one of the more intelligent people I've ever met. Among the corporate executives I've known in my lifetime, and I've known a lot of them, I don't know of a single man who was dramatically more intelligent than my father. But the way the world cast its lot, he was destined to be a common laborer all his life. . . . He led a frustrated life because he felt he had a contribution to make and the mechanism by which he could make a contribution wasn't available to him. Nobody would listen when you're just a little guy down on a foundry floor."

In the book, as he often did in interviews, De Lorean graphically recounts his favorite story about the indignities of working for Ford: how company security men broke into his childhood home one morning and ransacked it in a futile search for stolen tools. He calls the intruders, "Harry Bennett's goons." Bennett was a poorly educated tough who rose, as head of Henry Ford's private police force, to become the second most powerful man in the company. Whether or not his men did break into De Lorean's house, two of John's childhood friends recall that it was Bennett who actually hired Zachary for his foundry job to begin with. Evidently the older DeLorean had come highly recommended by a local political hack who assured the antiunion Bennett that Zachary was "a character with a closed mouth." Certainly his former stint working for the police in Gary couldn't have hurt. It wasn't unusual for Bennett to hire workers. It has been estimated that, for a while in the Thirties and Forties, one out of three men on the shop floor was doing double duty as a Bennett spy.

Whatever De Lorean's later reflections on his father's stunted talent, as a child his affections lay with his mother. She, too, was an immigrant. But she arrived in America from Salzburg, Austria, as a child, and was better adjusted to American life than her husband. When the couple fought, she often took the children and left for long periods to join her family in Los Angeles. The DeLoreans finally divorced after John left high school, but he continued to live with his mother until he first married at the age of twenty-nine.

In *On A Clear Day,* De Lorean calls her "an incredible woman," and most who knew her agree. At times she held down two jobs to support her four sons. She worked longest for General Electric as a tool assembler. Active in the local church, she also found time to garden around her house. Neighbors remember her trellises covered with roses.

The constant shuttling back and forth to Los Angeles made it difficult for John to fit in with the kids from the neighborhood. He tended to hang out with older boys whose fathers worked with Zachary. At one time he earned some money working at a friend's newsstand, although he ended up losing most of the wages to his employer pitching pennies against a curb.

Although most of the parents in the area were hardworking, their American-born children were not as willing to fit into the system as law-abiding cogs in the wheel. Reo Campian grew up around the corner from the De Loreans. He remembers an adolescence filled with random fights and petty lawlessness. Teens would graduate from stealing the tires off cars to breaking and entering homes. "Some people on my block made a living from stealing," he says. Today Campian owns a successful engineering firm, but he adds, "It took some hard work and good luck to get where I did. A lot of my friends wound up in Jackson [Michigan state prison]."

The teenagers Campian knew who got into trouble did so on their own. But one contemporary recalls that there were others who had some help from adults. Even after Prohibition, the mob thrived in Motor City. The government may have permitted alcohol, but taxed it heavily. Canada and cheaper booze lay just a few minutes' cruise over the Detroit River. The smugglers' favorite craft were the pleasure boats they borrowed from the yacht clubs on the city's east side. Often they had street kids riding along in the hold to help load the contraband. Children were also used as runners between their nightclubs—not the safest job at a time when rival gangs were engaged in mutual annihilation.

Henry Ford, the man who choreographed the nightmare of the fathers' working lives, also directed the dreams of their children. He became the prime example of what a little mechanical know-how could reap. Ford was no more than a semiliterate farm boy when he first came to Detroit, and his tinkering would bring him one of the world's greatest fortunes.

John De Lorean was only ten years old when he grappled with his first car in the tiny wooden garage in the alley behind his house. Underneath the steel shell lay dark secrets of grease and iron to be fathomed on endless Saturday afternoons. "It was an old Model T that my dad bought for us for some insignificant amount," he remembers. "We'd take it apart and he'd always have to come out again and put it back together for us."

Of course, boys did not just take apart cars hoping to be a mechanic in a service station. "In those days being an engineer was a big deal," Reo Campian says. "It was a title and it was a good job. That's the sort of thing kids in the neighborhood shot for."

From the start John De Lorean wanted to be an engineer. In interviews and in *On A Clear Day* he represents himself as a poor student in grade school who hung out with juvenile delinquents. "I know about being a street kid," he told a reporter for the *Detroit Free Press*. "I learned about getting in trouble. I thought the whole world grew up like I did."

But De Lorean's neighbors from those days don't think he was as tough a street kid as he says. "I remember him as being studious," says one man his own age who grew up in the house behind the DeLoreans'. "While everybody else was playing baseball, [John] had his books. He wasn't much like the rest of us."

For a boy who was willing to study, Detroit in the 1930s offered unlimited possibilities. Probably no city in America better demonstrated the opportunities of capitalism and democracy: the public school system meshing perfectly with private industry to offer any good student a secure job after graduation.

The first rung on the ladder for aspiring engineers was Cass Technical High School. As De Lorean says, his elementary school years may have suffered from his constant travels to Los Angeles with his mother, but he had to have above average grades to get into Cass—and getting in was much easier than getting out with a diploma.

• DARK SECRETS •

Housed in an imposing seven-story limestone building, Cass offered its predominantly male students practical training in such careers as drafting, mechanical engineering, and electronics. But a liberal arts education ran alongside the vocational classes and the standards in those courses were high as well. "English and math were especially rough," Thaddeus Pietrykowski remembers. An engineer today, he entered Cass the same year as De Lorean. "I was in one algebra class with twenty-four students, and eighteen flunked out. That was pretty typical. They didn't bend over backwards to help you at that school. If you didn't study, you were gone. I believe that in our time only one out of six entering as freshmen ever graduated."

Often Cass students got enough training to go into industry without a diploma. Although he did not continue on to college, Reo Campian, who went to Cass a few years after De Lorean, wound up at a drafting table at Fisher Body. Long after De Lorean had left the school, Campian says, his mechanical drawings were still displayed in the hall. "They were so neat and meticulous, they were like works of art."

De Lorean made his mark at Cass primarily as a student, but his classmates also elected him a class representative and member of the senior council. Among his extracurricular activities were the Radio Club and something called the Star Delta Club, which featured field trips to such places as a radio-station transmitter and telephone company switching house.

In the yearbook pictures, young John stands surrounded by an ethnic melting pot: children named Ryan, Hrit, Palazzolo, Gotkowski, Soo Hoo, and Goldstein. De Lorean was a year younger than most of his graduating class and despite his height, he looks less mature, although very serious with his furrowed brow. His face is soft, with a weak chin, and his head appears disproportionately small on a long neck and gangling body.

College was to be the first of the many radical transformations in De Lorean's personality and appearance that layer his life like geological strata. The Lawrence Institute of Technology was an unlikely place to improve his social skills. Far from the typical college campus, the school was only one ivy-covered Georgian-style mansion down the street from Chrysler's Highland Park headquarters. Hardly ten years old when De Lorean entered in the fall of 1941, the school was started by the two Lawrence brothers, who felt that even in the midst of the Depression the auto industry needed some nearby breeding ground for engineering talent. The brothers' lofty hope was to offer the chance for a degree to all those who wanted one, no matter what their financial status. If students had to work to support a family, they could earn their degree at night. Those who were especially bright and able to pass an entrance exam could earn a full scholarship for day classes.

But the school administrators were wise enough to make Lawrence Tech more than an advanced vocational training center. Although all the students commuted from home, they were offered all the typical collegiate trappings—varsity sports, school bands, newspapers, and fraternities. "Whatever impression you might have of engineering schools and students," says John Fawcett, a professor from De Lorean's era, "it was actually a very informal, tight-knit place. Most of the teachers were on a first-name basis with the students, and I think the students were pretty close with each other as well."

With the start of World War II and the specter of the draft, it was hard, even for engineering students, to take study all that seriously. In his freshman year alone, John De Lorean became the school's most irreverent student spokesman. He immediately plunged into extracurricular activities, starting out with the anemic college band. The group is pictured in a 1942 yearbook wearing Salvation Army–style uniforms. De Lorean had picked up the clarinet in high school and had led his own neighborhood dance band over the summer, and eventually he'd push the college ensemble from Sousa to swing.

But first, the freshman became the band's biggest recruiter. He joined the *Lawrence Tech News* and wrote two columns he called, "Music Makers" and "Men of Note." In the first he'd ask, "Where are the jive hounds around this jernt? The LIT band had dwindled from the thirty-one pieces of Smartie Pshaw's poor man's symphony to the six-man size of Benya Goodman's Sextet (Benny and his five bagels). . . . Gentlemen, Lawrence Tech is a major College that does not have a major dance band. This certainly is not the type of distinction we want. So, let's get out and do something about it!"

The band didn't fare much better, but De Lorean stuck with the biweekly paper, inaugurating a joke column he called, "5 with D." He'd later aptly caption the spot as "a place where old jokes go to die," many on the order of the following: "As a Burlesque queen said when she woke up one morning and found herself fully clothed—'My God, I've been draped.' "

The column was more a showcase for jive talk than humor. "Hey, cat," one party in a story says to another, "you look shot to the sox." Or "I was talking to a pretty girl and trying to dig up jive for this five minute intermission. I said, 'Hurry up Fat Woman, I got a deadline to make.' She said, 'Tell it to me anyhow.' " The story is followed by De Lorean's offer to give "a special course to explain my jokes."

Most of the jokes poked fun at the school administrators and other students. Some were self-deprecating as well. At first he made the author of each column another variation on De Lorean: H. V. De Loreanborn, Ross De Loreanhollen, and so on. But, more important, he used the newspaper to create another John De Lorean. This version was not Rumanian, but in his words, "the leering Frenchman." This John De Lorean was also a hip sophisticate, an insouciant rake and inveterate barhopper. He leads off one column with: "What popular, handsome, dashing Tech student got kicked out of three jernts last night? What can I do for a bruised eye?" He casts himself as the lead in most of his necking jokes as well: "I kissed her. She sighed. I said, 'Don't mention it, the pressure was all mine.' "

His newsprint image may not have been idle boasting. The awkward adolescent had filled out, and his face became longer and leaner. He had the large almond-shaped eyes and dark features of a Hollywood Latin lover. "He was quite a ladies' man," one of his Lawrence Tech frat brothers remembers. "It didn't seem as though he had any problem finding women. But he was very vain about his looks. Whenever he passed a mirror, he glanced over to see himself, or tried to comb down his hair. He was an immaculate dresser, always wearing the most stylish things. I never figured out where he got the money for those clothes."

The spring semester of 1943 was the last De Lorean spent as a civilian. He signed off for the duration with one more joke: "In my spare time I've written a book on how to stay out of the army. Those who wish to secure a copy of this infallible booklet should send twenty-four cents to . . . Pvt. J. Sachelpants De Lorean at Camp Custard. But, seriously, the best way to stay out of the army is to join the navy . . . s'long JD ERC [Enlisted Reserve Corps]."

The next semester, enrollment at Lawrence Tech plummeted from 2,000 to 200. De Lorean spent the duration on uneventful stateside duty. He returned for the fall semester in 1946, and shortly thereafter resumed "5 with D," but the column was to be much more truncated. He had the GI Bill paying his tuition and living expenses, but like his veteran classmates, the twenty-one-year-old was anxious to finish school and get out into the working world.

If studying became more frenzied, social life at the school kept pace. Lawrence Tech's basketball team went big time, playing schools from around the nation. Games were held in the coliseum on the Michigan State Fairgrounds. Afterwards, students adjourned to the nearby Horticultural Building for dances that would go on long into the night, often featuring the best of the big bands—Woody Herman, Gene Krupa, Tex Benecke, Stan Kenton. Although he was going to night school as well, De Lorean didn't miss a dance. "He was the life of the party," the wife of one classmate remembers. "I don't think anybody there could jitterbug like he could."

His fraternity brother has the same memories. "There was something about crowds that turned him on. He always seemed to project himself out front. And he was a fun guy to be around. He liked to laugh and joke. But I don't think he had one best friend. He was one of those sorts who's popular with everyone and not close to anyone in particular."

He also remembers De Lorean living up to the reputation he painted for himself in the newspaper column. "He liked to drink a lot, and he liked to drive his car as fast as he could go. After my brother's wedding, he was pulling out of a long, narrow road and there were some old folks ahead of him going too slowly, so he just bumped up right behind them with his car and started pushing them. Another time I got in his car and as soon as we hit the freeway, he kicked that thing up to what must have been eighty miles an hour. Afterwards he told me he thought he had a blister on his tire and he was testing to see whether it would blow. That was the last time I ever rode in his car."

Nothing about De Lorean's social life disrupted his schoolwork. "He could just thumb through a book half an hour before a test and have the best grades of anyone," his frat brother says. Another classmate, Ted Pietrykowski, adds, "He was a genius. It was that simple. He used to say he had a photographic memory and you had to believe it."

Hurst Wulf, an associate professor at the time, taught De Lorean strength of materials, mechanics, and calculus. "He was one of the best students I had," Wulf says. "I can't think of one better. The whole thing seemed to be effortless for him; to come naturally. I liked to schedule tests on Monday, so the boys could study over the weekend, but De Lorean would think nothing of going to Chicago and getting back just in time to get a perfect mark on the exam."

De Lorean stood out in humanities courses as well. One of his favorites was world economics, taught by Edwin Graeffe. Almost a stereotype of the stiff-backed Prussian, Graeffe proudly bore an old duelling scar raked down the side of his face. Despite his threatening appearance, and the fact that his students had recently fought against his countrymen overseas, Graeffe was among the most respected members of the faculty. He liked to play devil's advocate and De Lorean enjoyed battling him. Having practiced law in Europe, Graeffe encouraged De Lorean to try some legal courses at night school, and he briefly took a stab at them.

But engineering was evidently closer to his heart. Hurst Wulf says, "He always did like engineering best. And he got to be pretty good at it. By his senior year, he figured he could engineer his way out of anything."

One of the few serious notes he ever struck in his *Tech News* column was an elegy to the profession. He starts off with a typical wisecrack: "5 with D: By William De Loreanspeare, 'The Immoral Barge.'" But what follows is evidently, and quite portentously, serious:

> Know you what it is to be an Engineer?
> It is to have a dream without being conscious you are dreaming lest the dream break; it is to be trapped in a terrible tower of pure science. . . .
> It is to live in a mean, bare prison cell and regard yourself the Sovereign of limitless space; it is to turn failure into success, mice into men, rags into riches—stone into buildings, steel into bridges, for each engineer has a magician in his soul. . . .
> It is to make the guns roar, the machines hum, the night resound with such meaningful glory as sparks fly up from hidden plants that nightingales cease song in reverence to listen to the call of golden fountains from afar and revel in the promise of moonswept silver stars. . . .
> It is to give deep springs of water to thirsty travelers, to provide warmth and shelter for the homeless, to add adventure and allay the tedium of lesser men's hours. . . .
> . . . it is to . . . be perpetuated by the delicacy of illusion of distance that too often twilight foretells—
> It is to be a Conqueror and a coward, a King and a captive, a Savior and a slave; it is to be good unto seeming Godlike while contrasting evil incarnate; it is to suffer a throne alone in your terrible Temple of Science while companions roam the city streets and make carefree carnival—
> It is loving and winning only to lose and love again and again, for Engineering is a fanciful Goddess clad in fickle fantasy, form-fitting fortune, and flaming Fool's Gold who recognizes neither disaster nor despair—
> KNOW YOU WHAT IT IS TO BE AN ENGINEER?

De Lorean's purple prose must have struck home with some other students, because he got requests to reprint the column. He would be just as serious with his race for the student council presidency in his senior year. His slogan: "John's Your Man." In his newspaper solicitation his backers declared themselves to be, "the firm supporters of liberal and progressive action. . . ." They go on to distinguish their candidate, oddly enough, by his promises: "You will hear much during this campaign about what the various candidates HAVE done. We prefer to tell you what our candidate WILL do."

Ever the visionary, De Lorean promised to cut off "endless bickering" on the council floor and delegate more responsibility to other officers—actually techniques very similar to the ones he would adopt at GM and his own car company. Whether they would have worked on the council will never be known. While the election brought out the largest percentage of voters in the school's history, De Lorean came in second, 200 votes behind the winner. The *Tech News* analyst had the night-school students turning the tide.

Soon after his loss, De Lorean went into his competition with a bigger opponent, Michigan Bell. Some classmates remember him selling advertising space by mail as well: clipping out ads from the phone book and sending them to advertisers with the message that it was time to renew. He enclosed an envelope with his "Yellow Pages" address.

When an outraged customer tipped off the phone company, Michigan Bell's lawyers picked up his trail and threatened to take him to court. The incident did not surprise De Lorean's friends. "It was the sort of stunt only he could have pulled," his frat brother says. "He always thought big. If we had voted on such things, John would have been voted most likely to succeed and most likely to get into trouble."

Both professors Wulf and Fawcett remember that the younger faculty members at Lawrence Tech couldn't help but be amused. "We weren't that much older than he was anyway," Wulf says. "We didn't think it was much more than a prank. I really didn't think less of him."

Student rumors had De Lorean near expulsion or headed for jail. But instead he turned to the admonishment and aid of Doc Graeffe. He returned all of his ill-gotten gains and, in return,

Graeffe got him off Ma Bell's hook. The whole affair only added some more bite to the appropriately irreverent send-off his editors at the *Tech News* gave him upon his graduation: "Though [De Lorean] has departed to seek his eternal reward, those of us who knew him will draw inspiration from his example. We shall miss his sober countenance and the lofty idealism of his '5 with D' column. . . . We shall always remember his sage remark, 'Eternal vigilance is the price of dishonesty.' "

· 3 ·
A Company Man

One day, not long after he was hired by General Motors in 1956, John Z. De Lorean drove to the sprawling campus of the company technical center to see a special showing of GM's newest models. He arrived to find that he couldn't park near the auditorium. All of those spots were reserved for the top brass in from the headquarters. De Lorean had to settle for a place on the other side of the complex and then run back before they locked the doors. Huffing and puffing, he barely made the start of the show.

De Lorean returned to his office in Pontiac afterward and told a co-worker about the parking pecking order. He would have been upset if he had missed the show, he said, but he understood why the company did those things. "It's one more challenge to work harder, so some day I can have a good spot reserved for me."

Less than ten years after he had graduated from college, the wisecracking "D" had lost the edge to his looks and outlook: no more odes to the joys of late-night drinking. Now he sang the praises of the great corporate system. While other GM engineers had to work several years before they qualified for the coveted bonus pool, De Lorean garnered the fringe benefit the day he was hired as head of advanced engineering for the Pontiac division.

In the process he became one of the youngest executives ever to receive the coveted perk. His age, however, was not be judged by his appearance. He had grown old before his time: his face fleshing out and his eyes sinking beneath dark circles. His shoulders were rounded, and his once-trim figure bulged and softened around the middle. A chain smoker, he no longer had the wind or the time for the clarinet and the jitterbug. Most evenings were reserved instead for homework or a few quiet moments with his wife.

While De Lorean neatly fit into the life-style of the typical GM executive, there was nothing conventional about how he got to be one. Unlike most of his fellow graduates from Lawrence Tech, he didn't head, hat in hand, for the nearest car company. Despite the unprofitable nature of his Yellow Pages business, he was evidently still bitten by the sales bug. In *On A Clear Day You Can See General Motors*, he fails to mention his little escapade with the phone company, but does relate a fling as a life-insurance salesman; a profession he took up, he says, to overcome shyness (something no one ever accused him of in college). After selling $850,000 worth of insurance (a feat most seasoned salesmen could not have matched in those days), De Lorean claims he tired of the job and started pitching for an auto-parts manufacturer.

In later years, De Lorean would express admiration for the selling skills of GM founder William Crapo Durant, who made his first success as a life-insurance salesman, and perhaps De Lorean was consciously taking Durant's career as a pattern for his own. In any case, it would have been hard to ignore the two divergent paths to success lit by Durant and Ford.

In 1887, when Henry Ford rode to Detroit in a horse-drawn carriage, he had little more than an idea about mass-producing a cheap motor car for the "multitudes." Before he was done, his idea melted down mountains of iron ore, dried up oceans of oil, and made America run rivers of asphalt.

In 1908, soon after he turned around the fortunes of the Buick car company, William Durant had an idea about gluing together the great automakers with stock in a holding company he called General Motors. Before the year was out, his idea swirled a blizzard of paper through Wall Street and changed the course of world commerce.

Together, Ford and Durant loom larger than life in the capitalist pantheon—great men with great talents and great flaws. While Ford was a brilliant engineer, he had very little business sense. Durant's acumen was strictly financial. His salesmanship with car buyers, investors, and other automakers did far more for GM than his mechanical ability.

For the young men of De Lorean's era, the god of ambition wore a face split—like some Hindu deity—between the cold, chiseled features of Ford and the soft, puckish visage of Durant.

Ironically, both men were blinded by the brilliance of their original ideas. Ford relied too much on the Model T, shifting gears and diversifying only in the late Twenties to stave off financial ruin. Although Durant's strategy of aggressive agglomeration won out over Ford's monomania, it became his personal undoing. Three times his personal fortune puffed up like a giant, glistening soap bubble only to pop and splatter, leaving slightly oily stains behind. He would die destitute in his hometown of Flint—a bowling alley and a hamburger joint his last two ventures.

Durant's demise did not diminish the respect De Lorean had for him. Years later he'd say in his book, "The breadth of the General Motors Corporation today is due to the imagination and courageous mind of William Crapo Durant . . . whose expansionary philosophy put substance into the corporation and set a precedent for growth after his departure."

Throughout his life, De Lorean lurched between the two opposite poles symbolized by Ford and Durant. In 1950, he was pulled back again to engineering, and with the help of an uncle who worked at Chrysler, he enrolled in the Chrysler Institute. Like Cass and Lawrence Tech, Chrysler Institute was one more boost Detroit offered able young men from working-class backgrounds. The company didn't ask for tuition. In fact, the students—many of whom came from the best engineering schools in the country—were paid. They spent only a few hours in the classroom each day. They spent the rest of their forty-hour workweek in other areas of the company—a rotating sequence similar to a medical internship. After two years, the students received a master's degree in automotive engineering, and more important, a good shot at a job with Chrysler. In De Lorean's day, over 50 percent of the Institute class were still with the company ten years later.

De Lorean was not among them. After working a few months in the tank division, he looked elsewhere. Working for any employer as big as Chrysler was not then his style: "I've always had to see how and what I did integrated with the whole," he later told one interviewer. "That was not obvious to me in a large company."

He turned instead to a much smaller car maker, Packard Motor Car Company—a company that the financial community did not give long to live. But that possibility made De Lorean's move all the more savvy, as one of his later GM colleagues sees it: "If John had started out at GM, he would have had to work his way up the ladder. But at Packard, the senior people were already starting to bail out. Before the company folded John had a chance to come away with a good title."

Packard had other advantages that made it an ideal choice for De Lorean's continuing education. Its small size required the engineering staff to be general practitioners. No one could hide as a specialist on one tiny component of the car as many unambitious engineers could do at the big companies. Since much of Packard's marketing strategy centered on product innovation, the engineers were also given free rein to experiment as they ranged over the company's limited model line.

But by the time De Lorean applied for work at Packard, the older engineers were starting to lose their influence on product development. After working miracles at Hotpoint, Jim Nance was appointed Packard's president with the mission of pulling the company into the new era of auto manufacturing. Nance brought along with him a team of bright young Harvard MBAs who may have had little knowledge of the auto industry, but who were well versed in the latest marketing and finance trends. "It seemed like all of them wore those pointy dark glasses," one Packard engineer, Carroll J. Lucia, recalls.

For the first time in the company's history, Packard engineers had to justify every expenditure, and hard-bitten veterans like Lucia didn't feel equal to the task. "We figured there was no way we'd outtalk the Harvard whiz kids. We finally decided that if we didn't have the charisma to impress management, we should hire charisma."

At that fortuitous moment, De Lorean walked into Lucia's office: a tall, presentable young man with no glasses, but with an easy smile and an impressive, deep-timbred voice. Lucia put him to work on the Ultramatic transmission—among the industry's first automatic transmissions and one more of Packard's pioneering innovations.

"When I hired De Lorean, I was afraid about his ability," Lucia says. "So I told him, 'I'm a little bit old-fashioned. I'll start you at six hundred a month. . . . If you're still here after sixty days, you'll get a sixty-dollar raise.' Well, he really showed me something in sixty days, and it wasn't long before he was next in line after me in Research and Development."

The head of the department was Forrest McFarland, an auto-industry legend as an engineer. Together Lucia, De Lorean, and McFarland worked on the guts of the automobile—the transmission and suspension. Car makers saw a vast potential market in the woman driver and were convinced that only the gearshift stuck in the way. In totally revamping his product line, Packard president Nance pushed hard for a push-button transmission (a system that created insurmountable maintenance problems), and his engineers seemed to have the rest of the industry beaten to the punch.

In 1954, at the age of twenty-nine, with his job secure, De Lorean married Elizabeth Higgins, a pretty blond pixie from a small town in northern Michigan. They met, ironically enough, while she worked as a representative for the phone company. They had their wedding one fall afternoon in the Central Methodist Church, just off Woodward Avenue. For weeks before the event, De Lorean had been pestering Lucia about getting a company car. "I didn't realize what he was so anxious about until I stood there at the ceremony. He wanted to drive off after the wedding in some fancy car. Even in those days, he was out to impress people. But wouldn't you know that after the ceremony he drove off in a brand new Cadillac. He was going to Florida for his honeymoon, and it turns out that he offered to deliver the car down there for some Detroit dealer. I don't know how they ever got back, but while they were there, he met that ballplayer Ted Williams in a bar and evidently they really hit it off. When John got back to work he was on cloud nine."

In *On A Clear Day You Can See General Motors*, De Lorean speaks of the Packard days as among the happiest in his career. Unlike the big companies, Packard permitted him to follow a design from the drafting board to implementation on the factory floor. "I was excited by the work, so I put in long hours and learned more in four years with Packard than I would in any similar time since."

De Lorean goes on to relate that he learned a great deal from the shop workers as well: "If you looked at them the wrong way or dealt with them in any manner other than a man-to-man, professional fashion, they would simply reach under their workbenches without saying a word, throw their tools into the big box and leave."

The craftsman's self-confidence and independence, he declared, would become the hallmark of his own career. "From that experience, in part, I developed my own philosophy: That I would work extra hard at whatever I was doing to become so good at it that I would never have to kiss anyone's fanny to keep my job. And I never have and I never will."

But such claims come as news to his onetime Packard superior, Carroll Lucia. "De Lorean was the biggest brownnoser I ever encountered. It got to the point where the guys who worked with him laughed at it. There was no mistaking what he was doing—it was almost crude. For example, whenever any management big shot was around, De Lorean always got thirsty, so he'd be at the water fountain just in time to introduce himself."

Lucia admits that he wasn't too quick himself to notice the naked ambition. "I was the first guy he felt he had to impress. I could see his potential, but I could also see that this was a guy willing to work twelve and fourteen hours a day on his career.

Most of us will work eight hours. De Lorean had bigger things in mind than most of us.

"For a while there, he'd come over to my house damned near every weekend with his wife, Liz. All he wanted to do was talk shop. He always asked about the best way to get noticed by management. There were only ten engineers in the company, but still that didn't mean that the top brass knew each and every one of them. Meanwhile his wife was in the next room telling my wife how John thought I was such a great guy. Of course, my wife never got the idea that she was supposed to tell me what Liz said. She'd bring it up years later."

The Lucias made the De Loreans godparents for their three children, and Carroll remembers taking John along one afternoon when he was helping his son prepare for the Little League. "De Lorean got on the mound to pitch to my son and he started throwing knuckleballs as if he had pitched all his life. I couldn't hold on to them. It was as though there was nothing too small for him to show off with."

In time the couples' friendship cooled. "Eventually I could see what he was doing," Lucia says. "And besides, it got to be a bore. We didn't have all that much to talk about, and here I was with three young kids and a new house and a lawn to seed and I didn't have time to sit around all day and socialize with the De Loreans."

De Lorean found other engineers to visit on a weekend afternoon, but he continued to take Lucia's advice to heart. Patents, the older engineer told him, were the way to get noticed. "You have some great inventors who don't have any patents because they're not patent-oriented," Lucia explains. "Getting a patent is an art in itself. Of course, all of our patents were assigned to Packard and we didn't get any revenue from them, but as each one came in, the top brass could see your name. Sometimes you had ideas that would never be processed for a patent. Those were usually put in the 'B' file. But if you threw a lot of ideas in the 'B' file it was another way of gaining visibility."

Before De Lorean left Packard in 1956 he had twelve patents granted or pending for the corporation and countless other applications languishing in the "B" file. His patents were not enough to save the company. Nance's expansion plans—especially his merger with Studebaker—inexorably mired Packard in red ink, dooming its Detroit auto production. McFarland became the first key member of the engineering team to leave. Lucia had already been moved to another department, so for a few months De Lorean directed the moribund remnants of Research and Development. But the title didn't hurt. Packard engineers had gained an enviable reputation in the rest of the industry, and the Big Three moved quickly to snap them up.

Lucia and Herbert Misch, Packard's chief engineer, prepared to take over at Pontiac, where management had tapped Semon "Bunkie" Knudsen as new general manager and provided him with carte blanche to turn the ailing division around. To their surprise, Knudsen bypassed Misch for the job of chief engineer, turning instead to an Oldsmobile executive, Elliott M. "Pete" Estes. But Packard was not to be denied representation in the new Pontiac team. Knudsen tapped thirty-three-year-old De Lorean as head of the new advanced engineering department.

Like his superiors at Packard, De Lorean had also been aggressively searching for a new job. Some of his patents caught the attention of top GM engineers who rushed to recruit him. Today, De Lorean says he was just as inclined to join a small auto-parts manufacturer, and he relates his first meeting with Pontiac's outgoing top engineer—"a nice old guy wearing high-top shoes and a suitcoat stuffed with cigars." Determined not to work for any "old ladies' division," De Lorean called Knudsen back to tell him he wouldn't take the job. But Knudsen convinced him to meet Estes, the new chief engineer, before he made up his mind. The two hit it off immediately, and with the assurance that Pontiac was in for an overhaul, De Lorean signed on.

In the minds of some car people, Pontiac was riding to extinction bumper to bumper behind Packard. In 1956 the division's clunky product line held only 6 percent of the market—down from 7.4 percent in the previous year. "I left another car company to join Pontiac about the same time John did," one GM engineer recalls, "and I remember people telling me I was making a mistake to join Pontiac—that GM was ready to disband the whole division."

But GM president Harlow H. Curtice gave Pontiac one more chance with Knudsen, the company's resident miracle-worker, at the helm. Knudsen made his first mark at GM during World War II when he increased production in one tank plant by almost 50 percent. After the war he turned around the Allison aircraft engine division and then Cleveland Diesel.

With Pontiac he faced his greatest challenge. The heart of the problem, as he saw it, lay in the product's fusty image. The public may have regarded the hulking, turtlelike Pontiacs as dependable cars, but there was nothing about the line that provoked any excitement. Market analysts were already gleefully rubbing their hands over projections from the postwar baby boom. By the time those infants came of driving age, Knudsen wanted Pontiac to be loaded with youth-oriented cars. "You can sell a young man's car to an old man," he'd say, "but you can't sell an old man's car to a young man."

Robert F. McLean, an engineer with GM's styling section, remembers Knudsen bursting in one day in 1956, shortly after he became Pontiac's general manager. "There was nothing he could do about the new models or even the next year's models for that matter. But he still wanted to have some imprint on the product to show that there would be a change. In those days, Pontiac had a decoration running along the side that looked like silver railroad tracks. At least he could stop the factories from painting those things on. That horrible Indian-head hood ornament went next."

Knudsen had more fundamental changes in mind than hood ornaments. He wanted to revamp the Pontiac from bumper to bumper, and he assembled the best engineers he could find for the task. To contend with the holdovers from prior regimes, he created a new division, Advanced Engineering, circumventing the veterans, while injecting new blood into product development.

For the new department's chief, moving to Pontiac was a lot like staying with Packard. De Lorean had still sided with "the little guy" against the titans of a larger corporation. The division headquarters in those days were not much more than a cluster of buildings around the main assembly plant on the outskirts of the city of Pontiac, some thirty-five miles from Detroit. While most of the facilities were antiquated, the brick, two-story engineering building had been completed only a few years before. Upstairs were the large open rooms with drafting tables and blueprints. Below were the cubbyholes and shops where union craftsmen turned the engineers' ideas into substance.

Although GM has since become much more rigidly centralized, back in the Fifties, divisions were still like duchies in a feudal ingdom. Over the preceding decades, each had created a separate identity and loyalty—especially among the foot soldiers slogging away in the trenches, and the general managers often had to claw out their share of the corporate turf. No one disputed Chevrolet's dominance, although some executives felt the division went too far to maintain it. Cadillac, with its high-priced, highly profitable products comfortably nestled in a special niche. The fiercest competition raged between Buick, Oldsmobile, and Pontiac. Somehow the real enemies—Ford and Chrysler—got lost in the shuffle. The only blows that mattered for GM divisional executives were delivered against other GM divisions.

Through the years, the company's top management debated whether such internal friction was counterproductive. To dampen the sectarian feelings, they often transferred general managers from one division to another, or after a limited tenure, kicked them upstairs to corporate headquarters. But to a great extent, the rivalries during De Lorean's era were the reflection of the rambunctious men who ran the company. Most of them had battled for their education, their jobs, and finally their positions at GM. There were rare occasions when arguments over such things as fuel efficiency almost brought the top executives to blows.

Bunkie Knudsen was not one to shy away from such arguments. In *On A Clear Day*, De Lorean credits him for being a smooth politician, but Knudsen does not give himself any kudos for diplomacy. "None of us were easy to work with," he says today. "If we wanted anything we had to fight for it, and we had some tough battles. But that was part of the act."

Unlike most of his colleagues at GM, Knudsen had not pulled

himself up from the working class. His father, Bill, had been one of the industry's pioneers, first as Henry Ford's production chief and later as a GM president. But in the words of one of his friends, "However many millions Bunkie may have inherited, he was out to prove he could have earned them on his own." He had no apologies for his own record at GM, and although he didn't have his father's bulky height, the barrel-chested Knudsen had no trouble filling his shadow. In Bob McLean's thirty-five years at GM, he says, "Knudsen was the most aggressive executive they ever had. He got up every morning as though he had to show you something."

Knudsen was able to pass some of that aggressiveness on to his troops at Pontiac—especially the engineers. Their division may have been the runt of the litter, but it was going to be a feisty runt. He had the perfect drill sergeant in Chief Engineer Estes. Despite his volatile temper, the big, beefy Estes could also be a warm and generous leader, quick with compliments and an arm around the shoulder. Estes often spurred competition among his own staff, assigning one project to two different teams. While some of his subordinates resented those tactics, they still delivered. Pontiac engineers often worked on Saturdays and occasionally stayed until dawn. Bill Collins signed on in 1958. He doesn't remember anyone complaining about the hours. "From an engineer's standpoint," he says, "the late Fifties and early Sixties at Pontiac were some of the most exciting years in the history of GM. We seemed to constantly be on the cutting edge of product innovation."

None of Pontiac's engineers shone as brightly as John De Lorean. In short order he became Knudsen's most potent weapon against the other GM divisions. He continued the work he had started on transmissions at Packard—continuing as well to rack up the patents. His redesign of the body frame became the industry standard. And in his boldest stroke, he helped Bunkie through a potentially disastrous bout of corporate intransigence.

By the end of the Fifties, GM's corporate staff was putting pressure on Pontiac to assemble a warmed-over version of the Corvair. The car was the pet project of Chevrolet general manager

Ed Cole, a rival of and eventual victor over Knudsen in the race for GM's presidency. No one questioned the Corvair's nifty body styling, but some voices in the corporation saw safety problems with the rear engine and suspension—flaws that Ralph Nader would later chronicle in *Unsafe At Any Speed*. Pontiac had been anxious to make an entry into the small-car market, but when Knudsen refused to clone the Corvair, corporate management wouldn't give him the funds to manufacture a new creation.

So De Lorean went to work on a potluck special—a unique car that would meld components GM already produced. To get a four-cylinder engine, he took Pontiac's standard V8 and cut it in half. His biggest challenge came in fitting that engine mounted in the front of the car with the underbody of a Corvair. The standard car had a hump down its center to house the transmission running from the engine to the rear wheels. But with its engine mounted over the rear wheels, the Corvair underbody had no need for that hump. Instead of having a solid shaft run from the engine to the rear wheels of his hybrid, De Lorean used a narrow, flexible iron rod that could bend beneath the Corvair underbody. The system became known as the rope drive. The resulting hodgepodge car emerged as the 1961 Tempest.

Even De Lorean, in *On A Clear Day*, would call the Tempest "less than successful," adding, "there was no mechanical problem, but the car rattled so loudly that it sounded like it was carrying half-a-trunkful of rolling rocks." After two years, Pontiac dropped the rope drive. But back in 1961, the Tempest was De Lorean's greatest achievement. His ingenuity put Pontiac in the small-car market at just the right time, and whatever the problems with noise, the Tempest became the division's best-selling car.

De Lorean no longer had to hang around the water fountain to catch the boss's eye. Knudsen quickly became De Lorean's mentor both inside the company and the tight-knit GM social circle in the suburbs of Detroit. "He was the sort of guy you had to take a liking to," Knudsen remembers. "He seemed very enthusiastic about his job and was about the smartest automotive engineer I ever saw in Detroit."

The young engineer tagged along with Knudsen when he went

to corporate meetings downtown, or convened a conference on the first tee of the Bloomfield Hills Country Club. Despite his gruff corporate behavior, Knudsen was still a man of wealth and refinement capable of introducing De Lorean to art, wine, and fancy restaurants. Access to Bunkie's private plane put half the continent at their disposal. "No person had the influence on my life that Bunkie Knudsen did," De Lorean told Gail Sheehy. "It was like exposing a ghetto kid to the finer things of life."

One of Knudsen's greatest passions was auto racing, and soon after he took over Pontiac, he saw a way that the sport could blast Pontiac out of its lethargy. While the rest of the industry shifted to smaller, six-cylinder engines, GM corporate plans left Pontiac languishing last in line for the changeover. If he was going to be stuck with big engines, Bunkie decided they'd be the most powerful on the road. Although the auto companies had decided in the mid-Fifties to limit their support for professional racing, Knudsen wasn't going to let formalities stop him. New engines seemed to go into production only days before the nation's biggest stock-car rallies. By 1958 and 1959, with Fireball Roberts at the wheel, Pontiacs started to show their potential on the racetrack, picking up a handful of Grand National titles. By 1961, Pontiacs took the checkered flag in twice as many NASCAR competitions as any other model.

In many ways, the racetrack became the high-pressure proving ground for the Pontiacs in the showroom. Fuel, engines, aerodynamics: all were shaken out at speeds over one hundred miles an hour. Some of Knudsen's engineers, who had never been to a racetrack before, watched their inventions propel the winner across the finish line. But the expertise did not go just one way. Racing introduced Knudsen to the nongraduate engineers working in the pits.

Long and lean, with sideburns running to the edge of his jaw and a flattened hat that had the brim turned up at the sides, Smokey Yunick was the resident mechanical master of the gypsy-like stock-car circuit. Although he had no formal engineering background, Yunick was an intuitive genius who squeezed more horsepower out of engines than their Detroit progenitors ever hoped for. He first met Knudsen back in 1958 when the general manager surreptitiously supported the Pontiac racing team. "He paid me with a personal check," Yunick remembers. Knudsen soon found that Smokey was too valuable to be left at the racetrack and lured him to Detroit as a high-priced consultant. Walking down the halls of GM's Tech Center in a windbreaker and shorts, Yunick was not very impressed by the engineers in their white shirts and ties. He would feel different about De Lorean. "Just in talking with him, you could see he had a hell of a mind. He knew the car. Not just one piece of it, but the whole car. Most of the others at GM were pelicans, and you know what a pelican is—something that eats, shits, and squawks. In my mind De Lorean was different. He was a hardworking son of a bitch."

4

High Performance

Woodward Avenue shoots out of the Detroit River and slices a straight twenty-five-mile swath through city and suburb. Like a geometrically drawn aorta, it flows with the wealth of the auto industry, and pushes deep into the flat Michigan farmland, leaving housing developments, shopping centers, office buildings, and factories along the way.

No road ever had more synergy with the cars that traveled it. Whether self-propelled or riding on the back of a truck, the automobile was the lifeblood of the thoroughfare and all that had sprung up around it.

But by the early Sixties a steadily growing phalanx of drivers were using their precious four-wheeled possessions for thrills as well as transit. In the late hours of the night, with Woodward lit up like an endless runway, their cars came hurtling back to Detroit. These were sleek machines that had dropped the bulges and fins of the Fifties. Their noses hunkered close to the ground and their haunches were jacked up on thick, oversized tires. At every red light, they sought each other out, pairing up at the intersections. Engines snorted and roared. Metal skins trembled as though they were ready to shake to pieces. With the first flash of green, they leaped into the night, leaving only the high-pitched squeal of their tires and the acrid smell of burning rubber behind.

In time, the very name of the avenue became a verb. For teenagers across the country Woodwarding was the ultimate test of the automobile, and Woodward the ultimate track. The dragsters raced the thickest, straightest stretch of the avenue, from Thirteen Mile Road to Eight Mile Road, through towns named Berkley, Royal Oak, and Ferndale—the blue-collar suburbs that were often their homes as well. The machines that had been the hard, grueling work of the fathers were now their sons' toys—fantastic playthings that could melt all the gas stations, fast-food stands, and stores lining Woodward into one multicolored blur.

Teenagers weren't the only ones Woodwarding. On some nights, a homeward-bound Pontiac engineer sidled up to the hot rods, still dressed in his tie and button-down shirt. Even De Lorean and the gray, distinguished general manager, Bunkie Knudsen, took their marks under the stoplights. If the teenagers laughed at the old men behind the wheel, the Pontiac engineers smiled with the confidence that their company cars would leave the hot rods back at the starting line. As one Pontiac engineer puts it, "We knew the kind of power we had under the hoods."

But the real race was not between the Pontiac engineer and the teenager. If anything, they, along with the stock-car racer, were one mind behind the wheel and one hand on the gearshift, pushing the auto engine as far as it would go.

The Sixties—the go-go years—were to be a boom time for the car makers and America. Pontiac's products seemed just the thing for a nation with high octane in its blood, and the division would "go" faster and more profitably than any other at General Motors. In 1960, Pontiac sold 396,000 cars—its volume second only to Chevrolet's in GM. The day "the old ladies' car" passed Oldsmobile for those honors, Knudsen and Estes sent a marching band down the middle of the assembly plant.

In 1962, when Knudsen stepped up to the top job at Chevrolet, Estes took over as Pontiac's general manager. At only thirty-seven years of age, De Lorean became chief engineer. During his three years in the job, product innovation reached an even more fevered pitch. Although he didn't originate all the changes he later took credit for, De Lorean did manage to bring out the best in the men around him.

"There's no doubt that John was a great leader," Bill Collins says today. Collins took De Lorean's spot in Advanced Engineering and was soon pegged as another De Lorean–style comer in the division. "He worked best with those of us who were the Young Turks at Pontiac. We really wanted to impress him. That's what a leader can do, and John had real leadership qualities—at least with us. He had no patience with the older guys. I remember there was one heavyset engineer nearing retirement who used to smoke a lot of cigars. John just didn't like the looks of the guy, and one day he went up to him and said, 'I don't want to see you anymore. Move your stuff into that corner and stay there.' I don't think he got another assignment. He just came in every day and stayed in the corner. At GM, John could get away with burying people like that, and I have to admit, the young engineers thought the whole thing was pretty funny."

In his new job, De Lorean could push even harder for faster cars. The models that won the big races Saturday were selling out in the showroom on Monday. But hot rodders were taking the big Pontiac engines beyond their limits, literally strangling the machines at sustained high speeds. The Pontiac engineers' solution was to adopt a simplified version of a professional racing engine using the overhead camshaft, which eliminated parts to actuate valves. The overhead cam—OHC in hot-rod jargon—outstripped anything else on the road.

It seemed only natural to put that new engine in a lightweight, two-passenger fiber-glass body. Bill Collins was the first to suggest it, and De Lorean enthusiastically sold Estes on the idea. They code-named the project XP833 and put young Collins in charge. All work on the car then proceeded with the utmost secrecy. GM had only one two-seated sports car, Chevrolet's Corvette, and the number one division was not likely to countenance any competition. Pontiac managed to produce two running prototypes of the XP833 and then called the top execs to the proving grounds for the unveiling.

Among the guests was Zora Arkus-Duntov, Chevy's staff engineer in charge of high-performance vehicles. For the previous five years, the Russian-born engineer had nurtured the development of the Corvette in everything from engine design to body contour. No other man at GM had more vested interest in having Chevrolet maintain its two-seat monopoly. Today, Arkus-Duntov admits that he came to the showing ready to cast a jaundiced eye. "But I was very favorably impressed," he says. "They had a six-cylinder overhead-cam engine, and I thought it was quite an achievement. It was very powerful. Otherwise, there were no refinements—no great transmission or suspension. . . . The car had a very pleasant line—better than the Corvette, and that's what made me very unhappy. Later I talked to Ed Cole [the former Chevrolet chief and newly appointed GM executive vice president], and I said the car may be an empty shell, but it's better looking than Corvette. I don't want such competition."

The Corvette had special sentimental value for Cole as well. He helped the car through infancy as general manager at Chevrolet. Citing the poor payback on investment, Cole prevailed upon the other top executives on the fourteenth floor to kill the XP833. It was a crushing disappointment for De Lorean, and his first bitter lesson at GM in corporate politics.

But Knudsen and Estes taught De Lorean that there was still plenty of room to maneuver around headquarters' dictates. Even if they had to take new cars that came from the corporate cookie cutter, Pontiac could still leave its distinctive stamp on the product. The secret weapon was styling.

The responsibility for much of the outward appearance of GM cars fell to the Styling Section—a separate corporate staff housed under lock and key at the Technical Center. Starting back in 1927 as the Art and Color Section, the department had been formed by then–GM president Alfred Sloan to put a little more imagination into automotive design. For the next three decades GM styling was directed by Harley Earl, a Hollywood import who had gotten his start in the car business by customizing limos for movie stars. Earl brought a little of the tinseltown with him. The walls of his studios were often covered with pencil and watercolor sketches of futuristic vehicles. He also promoted the use of a special sulphurous-smelling modeling clay. Italian artisans who had once done decorative plastering in Detroit's skyscrapers would sculpt full-size car bodies to the specifications of styling engineers. Painted and polished, the clay took on the sheen of metal. The wildest, most impractical visions could be molded into the semblance of reality before a day was out.

Most of the styling work, however, was not in advanced body design. Primary concerns were dressing up bodies with chrome and interior appointments. Earl created a separate staff for each GM division, and kept each quarantined from the others to calm the paranoia of the general managers. But in many ways, Styling operated as a supplier to the divisions. If one general manager didn't like the suggestions of his design staff, the Styling Section was free to peddle them to the other divisions.

As general manager of Pontiac, Knudsen quickly became Styling's best customer. Designers had free rein to change the stodgy looks of his cars, and Knudsen was open to suggestions that other divisions rejected. In his first, most important styling decision, he allowed a wider space between the tires. Until then, GM had widened the bodies of cars without widening the chassis as well, giving the products an ungainly baby-buggy look. In *On A Clear Day*, De Lorean took credit for convincing Knudsen to space out the tires, but Knudsen and Bob McLean remember the development differently. Working in Advanced Engineering for the Styling Section, McLean had the responsibility of adjusting designs of the old models to fit new body types. He was the first to notice that a wider stance made the car look more stable. Buick rejected the idea as too costly. Pontiac was more receptive. "As soon as Knudsen saw the drawings he liked the idea, and when he brought Estes in, Pete banged his fist on the table and said, 'Damn it, we're going to do it.'" Pontiac's advertising agency would dub the style, "The Wide-Track Look," and one of the industry's most successful promotion campaigns was born. It didn't take long, though, before every Detroit car had a wide-track look.

While De Lorean was not the originator of the wide track, he was still closely involved with Pontiac's styling. The only sort of input most division executives had to styling was cost. They would listen to the Styling Section's suggestions, and then decide whether a particular model could afford the change. But from his first days at Pontiac, De Lorean made his own modifications in designs, and according to Bob McLean, the Styling Section didn't resent the changes. "It was clear that the man had a flair for styling," he remembers, "and if anything, most of us at Styling appreciated what he had to say."

Styling may be De Lorean's most lasting legacy to GM. While he was chief engineer and general manager of Pontiac, the division led the way with such aesthetic innovations as recessed windshield wipers, racing stripes, hidden radio antennas, Endura bumpers and squared-off headlights. Throughout he championed the cleaner body look, with less chrome ornamentation—a look that weighed less and was in turn more profitable for the company.

Back in 1962, he learned what just a little tinkering with style could do. He and Estes had pushed to bring out a "clean look" car they called the Grand Prix. Headquarters refused to let them spend any money on tooling to streamline the new car's roof. Forced to use a standard body, they just removed most of the chrome and added fancier appointments to the interior. The Grand Prix sold out its first run of 40,000.

"John may have been a good engineer," his friend Smokey Yunick says, "but he was an even better stylist. He had a natural-born talent, and I think the record shows uncanny timing. He knew just when the fender or hood should be shoved one way or another to meet the public's taste. His cars came as close to pleasing the public as any GM ever produced."

No Pontiac model better reflected De Lorean's savvy for selling cars than the GTO. Again, his memory of how this car evolved neglects the important contributions of others. He has since claimed to be the first engineer at Pontiac to come up with the idea of combining the new light version of the Tempest body with a big engine. Actually, the idea was suggested by Bill Collins, when the two men joined Pete Estes at the proving ground to get an advance look at the new Tempest. He wondered out loud if they could lengthen the wheelbase to meet NASCAR (National Association for Stock Car Auto Racing) regulations. Only then did they think about trying the car with a bigger engine. By Monday morning, De Lorean had the perfect name for the new creation—GTO: an Italian acronym, already copped by Ferrari, standing for *Gran Turismo Omologato*, a new international racing classification for high-speed cars. In the next few weeks he'd put the finishing touches on the body style and suspension.

But the GTO still had a long way to go before the GM brass would permit its entry. By 1963, the corporate staff was beginning to sour on performance cars. Drag-racing accidents had begun to mount, and although De Lorean has since claimed that his Pontiac had safer brake and suspension systems, much of the division's allure was still for the teenager who wanted to take his machine beyond the speed limit. When Pontiac's general manager Estes broached the idea of another line of performance cars to management, he heard a resounding "no." That rejection, however, was not about to stop him. He called his engineers and told them to go full speed ahead on the GTO. His way around management would be to release the car as a $300 option for the Le Mans series.

Corporate outrage at Estes's subterfuge subsided with the first sales figures. Quickly outselling the anticipated production run of 5,000, Pontiac ended the model year with over 32,000 GTOs on the road. The GTO wasn't anything like foreign sports cars and yet it could make most of them eat rubber. A new automotive breed was born that the buffs started calling muscle cars. While the GTO's power was undoubtedly a big selling point, its feline looks didn't hurt either. Two nostrils flared out of the hood, and one headlight was stacked on top of the other on either side of a darkened grille. In its second year, GTO's sales climbed to 75,000.

GM brass could no longer afford to keep the GTO in the option closet. Finally, during the fall of 1965, they allowed Pontiac to usher in the first GTO series. The division had a new general manager to oversee the youth-oriented line, and quite suitably, at forty, he was the youngest vice president in the corporation. By this time, no one familiar with John De Lorean had any worries about his youth. The only questions now concerned how fast he could make it to the presidency of the corporation.

Except for his age, everything else about De Lorean fit into the standard mold of the ambitious GM executive. Just eleven years after he had moved out of his drab working-class neighborhood, he settled into a sprawling English manor house in the woodsy suburb of Birmingham. A winding cobblestone driveway curved in front of the house and majestic pine trees swayed overhead. In local society, Elizabeth dutifully played the role expected of a corporate wife. She worked for the Lung Association, raised money for the county college and stuffed envelopes for the Republican Party. In her spare time she restored antique furniture. The day after her husband was appointed general manager, she met with the women's editor of the *Birmingham Eccentric*, who would describe Elizabeth as "this sparkling young woman who looks like a little girl." When asked about her husband's promotion, Mrs. De Lorean replied, "John is only forty and I suppose that's pretty young for this kind of position, but it's his ball to run with. I don't intend to hover. Just be standing by when needed."

Like most other GM executives, De Lorean had little time for late-night socializing. Most evenings were spent quietly with his wife and some homework. As for the weekends, one of his friends from those days explains, "Everything revolved around sports." John Quirk was a manufacturer's representative who had also achieved success at an early age. In the course of his work and play in the exclusive suburb of Bloomfield Hills, he also became close with the top echelon of the auto industry. "Detroit is very much a sports-oriented town," he says. "If you wanted to fit in, you either had to play a good game of golf or convince people that you enjoyed football. There were people with season tickets to every professional team in the city, because that's the way you bumped into the important people. The socializing then fit around those events. You had a few drinks after a workout in the gym or a round of golf, or you met everybody at the café after the baseball game."

This social pecking order suited De Lorean well. An excellent golfer, capable of shooting in the low seventies, he had no trouble impressing superiors with his athletic ability. "Quite simply," Quirk says, "he was a man's man—the sort of guy you wanted to be around. The charisma was there from the start, and also a driving ambition. You knew he'd make it to the top."

As general manager of Pontiac, De Lorean soon showed the industry his stuff, uncorking an advertising campaign that would propel the GTO into the sales stratosphere. Key to the drive was Jim Wangers, a young account executive for D'Arcy McManus, the mammoth agency that had a lock on Pontiac's business. Wangers had been intensely involved with Pontiac's development of high-performance cars ever since he joined the firm in 1958. A hot rodder himself, he went down to Detroit Dragway with a superduty Pontiac in 1960 and won the national drag championship. "De Lorean and I met shortly after I was hired by McManus and we both rose through the ranks together," Wangers remembers. "We really had nothing in common. He was in engineering and I was in advertising. But for some reason a bond immediately formed between us, and we both had trust in each other's instincts."

As he tooled around in his own hot rod, Wangers could see that the muscle cars were more than transportation or even hobbies to their drivers. The GTO was becoming part of an evolving youth culture that put an emphasis on speed and independence. With the right approach, Wangers told GM execs, the car companies could tap into this new market. De Lorean was the first to take him seriously.

"De Lorean understood marketing," Wangers explains. "That is so rare for an automotive guy. He made a study of it and I think he discovered he had a penchant for advertising. Unlike so many other guys at GM, he could adapt to new ways of thinking and see the real needs of the consumers."

With Wangers, De Lorean was ready to embark on some novel approaches to selling cars. While he was still chief engineer, a rock group called Ronnie and the Daytonas approached Pontiac asking to write an ode to the GTO. The idea fascinated De Lorean and he turned the project over to Wangers, who immediately penned the lyrics. The music had the surfing sound of the Beach Boys, and the words were just as simple, with a catchy refrain.

"Little GTO" sold a million records and helped push the car's sales over 100,000. Picking up on that promotion, Wangers put out GTO T-shirts and licensed GTO "high performance shoes." He was even permitted by De Lorean to build a special-edition GTO for the Monkees' television show.

His print ads featured kids in the song's surf motif; or else just cars poised before a takeoff. Clearly, Pontiac had struck a rich vein, and De Lorean tapped it further with the Firebird series.

The free rein De Lorean gave to Wangers typified his management style. If an executive proved himself competent, De Lorean was willing to delegate responsibility to him. Occasionally that meant going around individuals with more seniority than his protégés. "He singled out just a handful of guys to run the division," Wangers remembers. "One for marketing, sales, engineering, manufacturing, and advertising. We all met each morning at seven-thirty in his office, and then, over the next half hour we'd make all the important decisions. His attitude with us was, 'Tell me about it after it's done.' And we'd get the job done, but we also antagonized a lot of people in the process."

If De Lorean had less sensitivity for those under him, he didn't worry about his superiors, either. Once more the GM headquarters tried to put the clamps on advertising that emphasized "high performance." Too many dragsters were wiping out in Pontiacs. But De Lorean often flouted the policy, putting through ads without running them past the corporate watchdogs first. Although he urged De Lorean to press for the ads, Wangers found himself caught in the middle. Despite his close working relationship with De Lorean, he was still employed by an outside advertising agency, and his bosses were not about to jeopardize their lucrative relationship with GM so De Lorean and Wangers could appeal to the youth market.

Eventually, the dynamic duo had to heed the performance strictures. But Wangers still tried to find a subtle way to get his message out to kids while staying inside the restraints. When a

TV *Laugh-In* sketch made the line, "Here come de judge," a rage, Pontiac named its new series of GTO the Judge. But in staying tuned to his teenage market, Wangers discovered that the GTO driver had his own term of endearment for the car—the goat. From that point of departure, Wangers cooked up his all-time favorite print ad: a proud teenage owner standing in front of a soaped-up GTO with a bucket and sponge in his hand. Underneath the picture the caption read, "A boy and his Goat."

Even though the GTO sat stationary in a driveway and no further copy extolled its hog engine, corporate staff summarily dismissed the ad. "I couldn't believe it," Wangers remembers. "They told me, 'We can't let you call the car a goat. It demeans the product.'

"I immediately wrote a long, angry memo to John. In it I complained that after all the success we had had with the GTO, these old fogies still didn't understand what it took to sell the car. Of course, I meant for that memo to be confidential. John did go ahead and ask corporate staff to reconsider, but he also enclosed my memo with his memo. The next day my boss called me on the carpet. I came within a hair of losing my job, and I never had GM's confidence again. Somehow John didn't see anything wrong with what he had done. When I called to ask him why he sent on my memo he just laughed and said, 'Wangers, if you weren't making trouble I wouldn't know you were around.' "

De Lorean had no reason to fear the wrath of the corporate staff. Pontiac sales would bulge over 25 percent during his three-year tenure. He took the division beyond its muscle image with lavishly appointed luxury versions of the Grand Prix and Bonneville. Later, in all humility, De Lorean would say of the period, "We were living off the gullibility of the consumer combined with the fantastic growth of the American economy. . . ."

But the brass was not about to tamper with his record of achievement at Pontiac. The spoiled young executive soon found he could get away with antics that other general managers dared not try. "I was with John once at a Tech Center meeting," styling engineer Bob McLean recalls. "There were other big shots there too, but all of a sudden John got up and said to me, 'Let's go. This is too goddamn boring.' Together we got in his car, which was some foreign job—a Mercedes or a Porsche—and he started driving back to Pontiac. He must have hit 110 miles an hour on the freeway, when some cop pulled us over. John wasn't worried at all. 'You stay here,' he told me, 'I'll take care of this.' He got out of the car and in a few minutes he came back and somehow everything was all right. I never asked him what he did. In those days it seemed natural that John De Lorean could do whatever he wanted to do."

5
Hollywood

When news of John Z. De Lorean's second marriage splashed across the society page June 1, 1969, the *Detroit Free Press* chose to title its account, "Romantic, Private Wedding." Nevertheless, the morning paper's anonymous reporter managed to cover this "private" affair with all the detail of a moon launch.

The "lush setting," the *Free Press* revealed, was the Bel-Air Country Club—a playground for movieland's rich and famous in the Brentwood Hills of Los Angeles. Once before, the Mediterranean-style clubhouse had been the scene for the nuptials of no less than Elizabeth Taylor and Nicky Hilton. But according to the paper, the Saturday evening "De Lorean ceremony" did not take a backseat even to the likes of Liz and Nicky:

> The ceremony took place at seven in the dining room of the club, where exquisite chandeliers and candles lit the scene. Tall windows were pushed open giving a clear view of the rolling green golf course. . . . The white-robed Mitchell Boys choir . . . sang as the wedding party descended the three steps from the lobby into the room.
> The bride, daughter of Mr. and Mrs. Tom Harmon of Brent-

wood, evoked the romantic mood when she appeared, veiled in a cascade of French illusion sprinkled with shimmering aurora borealis beads and white forget-me-nots—an effect she and her sister, Mrs. Ricky Nelson, excitedly shared in creating. . . .

After the ceremony, the wedding party and their guests left the dining room with its baskets of pink and white flowers and retired to a room called "The Top of the Tee" for cocktails.

This room, decorated in rust tones with comfortable chairs and small tables . . . overlooks the famous symbol of the Bel-Air country club—a 212-yard whitewashed suspension bridge over a ravine, from the tenth tee to the tenth green.

A champagne buffet was laid out in a room off the main dining room. . . . There were also seafood appetizers . . . [served on tables covered with pink cloths] the entree was braised beef stroganoff on rice, with green beans. And, of course, for dessert there was the five-tier heart-shaped wedding cake—and ice cream.

Just to make sure nothing happened to the cake, it was moved into the dining room just before the ceremony and screened from the guests until the moment for cutting it arrived. The doves and decorations on the confection were tinted, just faintly, with pink.

The tuxedo-clad Bernie Richard's violinists, favorites of many Los Angeles and Palm Springs social affairs, played for the guests from the balcony.

De Lorean did bring a little of Detroit with him for the occasion. His best man was his old mentor and friend, Bunkie Knudsen. Among the ushers was Pete Estes, his predecessor on the rungs up GM's corporate ladder.

From the vantage point of certain moralistic matrons in De Lorean's hometown, the event was far from pristine. Only six months before, John had divorced Elizabeth, his wife of fifteen years and a tireless helpmate in his corporate and social climbing. The new Mrs. De Lorean's age hovered around nineteen—a fact that evidently caused acute embarrassment for a GM spokesman who unchivalrously added two years to Kelly's age when he first told the press of her engagement to De Lorean.

But for many other middle-aged Michigan males, De Lorean fulfilled a double fantasy. At forty-four he had landed a statuesque child bride, and at the same time, married into a legend. Only a few years older than the groom, the father-in-law, Tom Harmon, had been the idol of every red-blooded boy of De Lorean's era. During the late Thirties, "Michigan's Great Harmon" was a one-man football team for the University of Michigan. He kicked field goals, punted, played linebacker, and as a halfback ran for thirty-three touchdowns in just three years. In 1940, he was awarded the Heisman Trophy as premier college football player of the year. After starring in a film version of his life, he signed up for new heroics as a World War II fighter pilot. Crashing twice in South America and China, he emerged from jungles only after all hope was lost. At the end of the war, he returned to Hollywood and married film star Elyse Knox. His celebrity assured him a life of lucrative assignments as a broadcaster and investor. To further cement the Harmons in the pantheon of All-American and All-Hollywood families, Kelly's older sister married Ricky—son of Ozzie and Harriet—Nelson.

De Lorean first met Kelly, the story went, when her father brought him home to dinner after a game of golf. The two renewed their acquaintance when Harmon's little girl ventured to Detroit to model for the car companies in January 1969. De Lorean, friends say, became a fixture at the luxurious downtown Detroit hotel where Kelly was billeted.

The bride looked and acted her age. A college art major who dropped out to try modeling, Kelly told one society writer, "I don't plan to continue a career. My wish is to have a large, happy home filled with children and animals." The article has her going on to list "her loves in the following order: 'John, riding, snow and water skiing, music, swimming, poetry, Levi's, painting, and Rag,' a puppy she found at the Los Angeles pound two weeks before the wedding."

And yet, the middle-aged groom did not appear so ridiculous standing next to the teenager. In the previous decade, John De Lorean's aging process had taken an unusual turn. Gone was the paunchy, jowly executive with the sunken eyes. In his place was a reed-slim fellow who boasted to friends of a thirty-one-inch waist. De Lorean had not just recaptured his youth—he had recaptured an idealized version of his youth. A weak chin had been replaced by a bold, square jaw. The broad bridge of his nose had become thin and more sculpted. His jet-black hair had straightened and it hung fashionably to the top of his collar.

De Lorean did not go to such rejuvenating lengths to lure a new wife. The transformation had started shortly after he became Pontiac general manager in 1965. Kelly Harmon was only the culmination of his efforts to create a more youthful version of John De Lorean. For a while this new persona felt most comfortable in California, where the youth fetish was already in full swing and the ravages of age seemed in full retreat. By the time of his second marriage, De Lorean had already made Hollywood his second home.

According to Bunkie Knudsen, De Lorean was not the first GM general manager to be tempted by the West Coast. He explains, "You start traveling more when you become general manager, because all of a sudden you have to be responsible for things like advertising and the dealer phase of the business. In all that traveling, California has a way of jumping out at you. They start inviting you to studios to see commercials made, or the dealers start taking you on the town. There are a lot of flamboyant people on the West Coast and they really know how to turn your head. Some people can ignore the whole thing. But some others start to find any little excuse to get out there."

De Lorean could not have had a better guide to the pleasures of California life than his old friend John Quirk, once a successful manufacturers' rep in Detroit. To the surprise of his auto-industry buddies, Quirk had sold his firm and moved out to the West Coast to pursue a lifelong interest in writing. During the Sixties, six of his novels reached the best-seller lists. One of the first, a book called *The Hard Winners*, was modeled on car-company executives like Ed Cole and John De Lorean. "John was one of the few people in Detroit who understood why I [moved to California]. John was the same way. Restless with life in Detroit and searching for something."

When De Lorean first went to Le Club, an exclusive New York night spot, it was at John Quirk's behest. The Detroit auto executive had no trouble acclimating himself to the ritzy surroundings. "As the years went on," Quirk says, "John always got the best table anywhere he went."

Quirk quickly became ensconced in California's jet set and he was happy to introduce De Lorean to his new social circle. Together, they were early investors in the San Diego Chargers football team—De Lorean holding an 8 percent chunk. Hotelier Barron Hilton was among the largest shareholders and one more cocktail companion for the GM executive.

Quirk also introduced De Lorean to Burt Sugarman, a Beverly Hills native and aspiring TV producer. More than ten years younger than De Lorean and Quirk, Sugarman nevertheless fit comfortably into their crowd. A college dropout, he had gone from used-car dealer to fancy foreign-coupe importer. By twenty-eight he had made his fortune in Maseratis and Excaliburs, and he was ready for new horizons. One successful Sugarman television special and game show followed another, eventually leading to his innovative late-night rock show, *Midnight Special*. Round-faced and snub-nosed, Sugarman had a predilection for dating movie stars on the order of Ann-Margret, and flying them to weekend rendezvous. While he enjoyed playing golf and talking cars with De Lorean and Quirk, he could also show his Detroit friends more frenetic ways to spend their leisure time. They rode dirt bikes in the desert or, during the winter, took off in Sugarman's private jet for some skiing on Aspen's slopes.

De Lorean was not the only auto luminary in Sugarman's crowd. Others included Roger Penske and Robert Anderson. Penske had gained national fame first as a professional race driver and later as leader of the Penske international racing team—an endeavor that led him into a variety of auto-related businesses. A few years older than De Lorean, Anderson was also an up-by-your-bootstraps product of the Detroit system. From the Chrysler Institute he had risen to the top of the Chrysler Corporation. When passed over for the company's presidency, he defected to Rockwell International, helping to make the aerospace conglomerate one of the most powerful and profitable corporations in America.

A *Fortune* magazine profile would call Anderson "a doer, a man of action." The description fit Sugarman and Penske as well.

These were not faceless corporate drones waiting for superiors to promote them up the company ladder. These were men who were determining their present and their future, with private jets waiting for their bidding at the nearest airport.

Of course, De Lorean had his own access to GM's jets and his own band of subalterns to ferry him around any city he landed in. He once told a reporter that GM executives "travel like an oil sheikh." And yet De Lorean did not have the unbridled power inside GM that Anderson had in Rockwell. And in the mid-Sixties he had none of the name recognition or prestige of Sugarman and Penske.

Whether or not he felt peer pressure from his California golfing buddies, De Lorean started to chafe more and more against the anonymity GM imposed on its top executives. In 1967, Pontiac ads appeared with De Lorean's face as a backdrop or inset. Tom Adams, chairman of Campbell-Ewald, one of the auto industry's largest advertising agencies, remembers that De Lorean's personal imprint did not sit well with corporate management. "The corporation eventually quashed that sort of advertising. I don't think they wanted one individual to be too strong a force in any aspect of GM's business. The company's policy has always been that the system is more important than the individual. I know John could make a case for personalized advertising, and I could too. But when you're dealing with an organization that has the level of success that General Motors does, you respect their policies."

The picture De Lorean used in the ads was over five years old. He was ready to trade in both the photo and the face. "After a few years of traveling to Hollywood," his friend Quirk recalls, "John got a youth fetish. He slimmed down from 200 pounds to maybe 160." Other friends speak of an obsession with food that made him difficult to eat with.

De Lorean's exercise was no longer limited to golf. He got up early enough to run and went to the gym religiously three times a week to lift weights.

But while he could change his body, he couldn't change his face—without some help. The adolescent who was forever combing his hair and frowning at his reflection in the mirror was now a man able to afford the best plastic surgeon in the world. By late 1968, De Lorean had undergone a massive cosmetic restyling that was obvious to even passing acquaintances. Implants in his chin gave him a jutting jaw. The bags were removed from under his eyes and all the lines pulled back out of his face.

Some friends were stunned by the sudden change. "I barely recognized him at first," Quirk says. "He wasn't such a bad-looking guy before the surgery. In fact, he was a very striking guy. The whole thing gave you the sense that he was tremendously insecure."

"I remember asking him what happened to his face," Bunkie Knudsen says. "He told me he'd had some trouble with his teeth. I know he told other people the scars on his face were due to an auto accident."

De Lorean was more specific for *Fortune* writer Rush Loving, Jr., claiming he went through the windshield while test driving a car in late 1968 at the Lime Rock, Connecticut, racetrack. The accident had to be covered up, he explained, because GM executives were not supposed to engage in such dangerous pursuits. According to Loving, the man who owns Lime Rock never remembers De Lorean driving there, let alone going through a windshield.

Back in Birmingham, De Lorean's first wife, Elizabeth, was able to document the rumors of plastic surgery with bills the Swiss surgeon continued to send to their address. When she gossiped about her husband with her friends, she called him Peter Pan, and talked of his fears of growing old.

The bills in the mail, though, were her only clues to her husband's life on the West Coast. The couple had stopped living together, friends say, long before. By March of 1968 she had filed for divorce, citing "extreme cruelty."

Bitter recriminations followed. He said she could not cope with his new stature; that she failed to become more sophisticated and could not adjust to his California friends. She spoke bitterly of toiling in high society to further his career. They would not settle until the end of the year. She got the house, his new model Pontiac as well as a GM executive discount on future cars, and $375,000 paid out over fifteen years.

De Lorean did not wait for the divorce to come through before he hit the singles scene. His friend Burt Sugarman had become more of a Hollywood mover and shaker. As a result, one mutual acquaintance says, "Burt knew a lot of beautiful young girls. Through him, John and I met some very attractive starlets."

Detroit gossip columns soon had De Lorean being seen at parties with young actresses and models, including one woman who was the star of a competitor's commercials as "the Dodge Rebellion Girl."

When De Lorean was in town on business, he often stayed at the luxurious Bel-Air Hotel in Beverly Hills. At night he'd meet John Quirk, and together they'd hit such fashionable discos as the Daisy on Rodeo Drive and rub shoulders with movieland's jet-set elite. "That was pretty heady stuff for a couple of fellows from Michigan," Quirk says. "It was a lot of fun, but you had to keep a sense of humor and perspective about it and not take it too seriously. I think it's fair to say that at some point John got carried away with the program."

De Lorean's record of accomplishment at Pontiac, combined with his "swinger" image, made him a favorite for the auto-industry press corps. *Newsweek* featured him in a September 1968 article titled, "Flashy Cars—And a Flashy Executive," calling him "the auto industry's liveliest new executive model." *Motor Trend* was to be even more effusive a few months later with a piece called, "King Mover of Motor City." If De Lorean had been a Roman emperor, implies Julian G. Schmidt, there would have been no decline and fall of the empire:

> Whether lip service is paid to De Lorean under the cloistered ceiling of the GM Building's top floor is irrelevant. Even if [corporate executives] don't realize it, they love him, if for no other reason than that he represents exactly what they are not, but must be, in order to deal with the changing market. Sure, they're still the ideal image for final decision-makers . . . stable, imperturbable, stoic. But De Lorean epitomizes the ideal tool to insert into

the nitty gritty . . . lots of black hair, six feet, four inches tall, slim, athletic, always with that blue shirt, dark blue tie and incredibly tailored blue-black suit that looks more like someone first built the perfectly proportioned suit, then cast John De Lorean in it. As one of our distaff put it, ". . . one of those men at whom a girl could sit and stare all day, warmly."

Such glowing prose had some GM execs wondering whether De Lorean wasn't paying a personal press agent. But, according to one longtime Detroit auto reporter, it didn't take much for De Lorean to attract reporters. "The auto industry just didn't produce interesting executives," explains Pat Wright. Once a reporter for *Business Week*, Wright went on to help De Lorean write his autobiography. "GM's auto executives came out of a mold. When you asked them a question, they all said the same thing, and it was never negative. Most of them were conditioned by the corporate PR departments to have a great fear of reporters. They felt their job was to keep the executives away from the press. De Lorean was different. He wasn't afraid of the media. He was very willing to talk, and he always said something quotable."

Well aware that GM execs felt he pandered to the press, De Lorean often agonized over the pains and pleasures of celebrity in his public statements. In one speech, before the Detroit Athletic Club, he accepted the Man of the Year award, and then proceeded to cogitate on the importance of giving awards. The limelight, De Lorean told his audience, should be an inalienable right of every American: "It goes without saying that the quests for recognition and acceptance are basic human needs. Even the well-fed man hungers for them. Yet, our society, on the whole, parcels out its attention in extreme ways. It often seems that public recognition comes easiest to those who either accomplish far more than anyone can rightfully expect or those who choose or are unable to meet society's minimum requirements."

Sounding like some Marxist press agent, De Lorean concluded the speech with a vision of Utopia as a place "in which recognition and acceptance comes to each man, woman, and child according to his needs."

As De Lorean became more outspoken, although he was careful not to criticize General Motors, he still sounded a distinctly unorthodox note by company standards. He even started to question the traditional Republican predilection of GM executives—one which he and Elizabeth had once shared. "We in Detroit vote Republican," he told *Motor Trend*'s Schmidt. "They nevertheless seem to be our enemies, and the Democrats our friends. When the Republicans are in power, they threaten GM with the antitrust suit, but as soon as Democrats come in, they drop it." De Lorean doesn't take sides in the upcoming presidential election, but he does tell Schmidt, ". . . both Nixon and Humphrey are two of the most intelligent candidates we've had for some time, but they don't have any color."

Before this interview, De Lorean had already aligned himself with Detroit's much more colorful mayor, Jerry Cavanagh, an unsuccessful candidate for the U.S. Senate. Despite his Democratic affiliation, as a local power-broker Cavanagh was not anathema to GM brass, although none of them would support him with the fervor of De Lorean. But politics aside, the press had also labeled the mayor as a swinger—a political tendency that was after De Lorean's heart. Car executive and candidate enjoyed being celebrity barhoppers as much as political glad-handers.

To help run his Senate campaign, Cavanagh hired Bill Haddad, a former New York journalist and an old Kennedy hand. JFK had appointed Haddad to be the first associate director of the Peace Corps under Sargent Shriver. A two-fisted liberal, Haddad didn't hesitate to tell De Lorean what he thought about GM when the two met at a Cavanagh fund-raiser. "He listened kind of quietly," Haddad recalls. "I remember Jerry kicking me under the table trying to shut me up. But John ended up inviting me out to lunch at the London Chop House [the city's swankest restaurant], and listened to pretty much every criticism I had."

Very few men of De Lorean's age and position were ready to entertain such antiestablishment views, but in almost every way—politically, physically, intellectually—his internal time clock turned backwards. Despite his forty-plus years, De Lorean loudly declared his allegiance with the youth of America. He donned Nehru jackets and turtleneck sweaters—a feat comparable to running naked down the halls, in a company where even engineers grappling with carburetors wore white shirts and ties.

When Snoopy and the Red Baron were the thing, De Lorean had their posters in his office and talked of naming a car after the cartoon dog. He kept his car radio tuned to the latest popular music, telling *Newsweek*, "These rock stations, the things they say, what they discuss, that's what counts. It's the cheapest education you can get."

When other corporate executives condemned youthful protest, De Lorean argued in front of one civic group, "We should begin . . . by accepting the turmoil of recent years as a healthy sign of rebellion against the possibility of failure."

While friends like John Quirk attributed De Lorean's cross-generational posturing to a "youth fetish," the auto executive offered the media a sound economic rationale for his identification with youth. He told *Look*: "Since the dawn of mankind, youth has led the way in fashions, and the auto industry is basically a fashion industry. What youth is interested in today becomes tomorrow's products. This small-car thing really has been a youth movement, and we are responding. Today's kids are much smarter than the kids of my day."

His pronouncements on the wisdom of "kids" did not stop De Lorean's advancement through General Motors. As long as he continued to produce, his superiors were willing to tolerate his idiosyncrasies. If anything, a separate standard developed around him. "The fact that John could walk into work wearing a pair of tennis shoes and an open-neck shirt didn't mean the company was changing," one engineer says. "The rest of us knew that they'd never allow us to do the same thing."

De Lorean's attraction to youth was ultimately certified with his engagement to nineteen-year-old Kelly Harmon in February 1969. The move shook Detroit's snooty suburban society to its core, but it also revealed De Lorean's confidence that his personal life was not about to affect his future at GM. Only weeks before he announced his engagement, he was appointed general manager of Chevrolet, the corporation's largest division. News of the promotion reached him at the twelfth tee of the Thunderbird Country Club in Palm Springs. His marching orders had him putting down the clubs and returning to Detroit before he finished the game.

Of the three years De Lorean spent at Chevrolet, Smokey Yunick says, "It was probably the happiest period of John's career. Here he was, still a pretty young cat, and he had one of the biggest jobs in America, with a big salary to go with it. He might have faced problems at Chevy, but you wouldn't have known it. Everything was a kick."

All by itself, Chevrolet in 1969 was among the ten largest manufacturing companies in the world. The division alone sold almost as many cars as all of Ford. But, in *On A Clear Day You Can See General Motors*, De Lorean depicts Chevy as being a shambles by the time he took the reins: its share of the market falling, its products outdated, and its management half-buried in bureaucracy.

Robert Dewey was Chevrolet's financial coordinator for eight assembly plants at the time, and later would be the first chief financial officer for De Lorean's car company. Dewey does not remember Chevrolet being nearly as bad off as De Lorean claims in the book, but he does say, "It had become a poorly managed division. I don't think that was totally the fault of the general managers who were in before John. The division had been the cash cow for the company, so it was extremely difficult to innovate there. Nobody wanted to change the formula and risk the tremendous income Chevy was bringing into GM."

That income, Dewey explains, permitted a proliferation of management layers inside the division. Much of that excess executive manpower went fallow under the reign of De Lorean's predecessor at Chevrolet, Pete Estes. "Pete was a guy who wanted to make all the decisions. When he arrived at Chevrolet, though, he got buried in detail and nothing seemed to get done. Everyone sat around waiting for Pete to tell them what to do."

De Lorean's management style, Dewey says, was to contrast sharply with Estes's. "I think the best thing John did as a manager was to delegate responsibility to other people. That gave him time to lift up his head and look at the big picture. He was very demanding and he expected you to do the best possible job. But he had the leadership qualities to make you believe you were equal to the task. In the finance area, where I was involved, he introduced the zero-budget concept. Instead of the various departments coming to us and asking for increases over last year's budget, they had to justify their whole budget. Obviously it created a lot of work and pressure for me, but I could see how the whole process was saving a lot of money."

De Lorean tried to upgrade Chevy's product line, but he was forced to execute decisions made years before his arrival. Car development was no longer the focus of his energies as it had been at Pontiac. "Really his most important product contribution at Chevrolet," Dewey says, "was the truck program. John saw that as an area where we could dramatically increase market share and he barnstormed the idea around the company. He felt that a major stumbling block to increasing sales was the placement of the gas tank. In those days it was behind the driver's seat. He wanted to take it out of the cab and put it under the chassis. Of course there was a cost penalty in doing that, but this was one case where added cost brought back much more with increased sales of trucks."

For all his leadership qualities, De Lorean became less patient with subordinates—especially engineers. "John wouldn't mind dressing down some engineer in front of a group of fifty people," Dewey recalls. "He seemed to have reached the point where he became contemptuous of engineers, and often the demands he made on them were just unrealistic. For example, during the truck program, I remember he wanted the tank engineers to channel the fuel in a way that the laws of physics would not allow. John just didn't want to hear that."

As a student at Lawrence Tech, De Lorean had described an engineer as "trapped in a terrible tower of pure science." As a General Motors general manager, he had broken out of that tower and was ready to let others contend with the prisons of gravity and thermodynamics. Marketing, advertising—these were the areas of expertise he now espoused, and they flowed almost naturally with the currents of his career: he had gone from the engineer wrestling with transmissions to the stylist shaping fenders to the advertising man, lifting his product beyond mere substance to the realm of image.

"I really think the day of the chief engineer becoming general manager is about over," De Lorean told *Automotive Industries* in 1972. "The problem that we are looking at in the future is really going to be more in the area of marketing than anything else."

At Pontiac and Chevrolet, De Lorean directed much of his attention to the nuts-and-bolts aspects of marketing. GM, he claimed, wasn't even doing basic consumer research. In *On A Clear Day*, he charges, "the General Motors marketing effort is guided by men whose training in buyer psychology is no deeper than the Dale Carnegie course they all are required to take, and whose idea of sophisticated sales is having a few drinks with the dealers."

Despite the drinks, De Lorean discovered, dealers were seldom made to feel they were valued members of the GM team. Most general managers, like De Lorean, rose through the ranks as engineers and had little preparation for interacting with dealers.

The neighborhood car dealer remains the last throwback in the industry to William Durant, the wheeling-dealing founder of General Motors, and dealer and auto executive usually mix like oil and water. The inbred hostility that has existed between the two is ironic, because in many cases both the dealer and the executive have worked their way out of the same lower-class neighborhoods. But the dealer keeps the common touch—as he must, to stay in tune with his customers. And the sort of flamboyance that a dealer needs to sell cars and stay in business is exactly the opposite of the reserved, unassuming nature most ambitious executives maintain as they rise through the corporation. As the auto industry has grown, the "factory" and the franchise have polarized into two warring camps.

Bunkie Knudsen was among the rare general managers who feel they have to keep peace with their dealers, and De Lorean learned dealer relations at his knee. Knudsen spent considerable time crisscrossing the country making calls—with plenty of warning—on Pontiac, and later, Chevrolet dealerships. Often he boned up on names and faces before he blew in for a tour, pleasantly surprising people he had not seen in years when he asked, by name, after their wives and children.

De Lorean picked up where Knudsen left off. Unlike most other GM execs, De Lorean had tried his hand at sales in his youth, and he found a kindred spirit in the car dealer. In fact, during the course of his business life, he would number more dealers and car salesmen as close friends than auto executives. In *On A Clear Day*, he waxes eloquent on the poor treatment the dealer has gotten at GM: "I found the majority of car dealers I worked with to be hardworking, sound, and honest businessmen. In their struggles with the corporation, the dealers received the short straw more times than not. . . .

"While General Motors owes its very existence today to its dealers, the manner in which GM has manipulated and browbeaten them falls into the area of questionable ethics. . . . Chevy's dealers kept the division afloat during the mid-1960s. Our thanks for their help was to constantly put the squeeze on them for every last nickel of corporate profit. Our policies with dealers were shoddy."

Chevy dealers were pleasantly surprised to finally find a general manager on their side. For a time, in the late Sixties, George Williams's Los Angeles dealership led the nation in sales. "Most dealers thought John was great," Williams says. "He wasn't a bullshitter. He meant what he said. And he wasn't a corporate man. When we complained about the factory, he'd agree and not come up with excuses. It was like John and us against corporate."

However, De Lorean's concerns for marketing went beyond his relationship with dealers. He also took an active part in Chevrolet's advertising campaign, and considering the amount of space he devotes to that role in *On A Clear Day*, it was clearly a labor of love.

He writes that during his first months at Chevy, he became worried by the "effectiveness and memorability" of the division's television commercials. In concert with Chevy's ad agency,

Campbell-Ewald, he says he devised the high-minded "See the USA in your Chevrolet" campaign that would both sell cars and help restore the consumer's faith in his nation at a time when big business and big government were under attack. "We wanted to reaffirm our position in the minds of American consumers by building our image around the good aspects of this country and the good aspects of our cars.

"We discussed this approach with the agency, and it developed a campaign around a theme that said, 'We live in a great and beautiful country and our car with its instant availability gives you the opportunity to get out and see this beautiful country.' If there is one thing that America has, it is fantastic and diverse topography, from the Grand Canyon to Pikes Peak. . . . We put our cars in these beautiful settings alongside of clean-cut, middle American families with whom just about everybody could identify."

While De Lorean no doubt meant well with his commercials, much more interesting is the palliative effect he thought they'd have on the country; as though "fantastic and diverse topography" could somehow heal deep social schisms, and not just add a gloss as superficial as the wax shine on a Chevrolet.

De Lorean gives credit for the ad campaign to the Campbell-Ewald agency and its chairman, Tom Adams. The creative people got a "freer hand," he says, only when he stuck out his neck for them with the corporate staff. Today, Adams agrees that De Lorean was helpful and had a flair for marketing. "He was never too busy to attend any meeting that concerned advertising or merchandising. Obviously he loved those things, which is why he always found time for them. He got more involved in the preparation of advertising material than any general manager before or since, but that caused some problems for the agency with the corporate staff. John was too impatient to follow company procedures. He didn't want to wait and give due consideration to the guidelines everyone else had to live by. As he gained more power and authority, he created his own procedures. We were often caught in between his impatience and corporate policy."

While Adams could see some benefits in De Lorean's close

involvement with advertising, he could also see pure ego-gratification as well. At one point, the Chevrolet general manager had Campbell-Ewald print up thousands of posters featuring De Lorean and his adopted son, Zachary. They were sent as Christmas greetings to dealers and De Lorean's friends around the country.

Although De Lorean may have used his position at Chevy to present the world a picture of his domestic bliss, actually the demanding job was destroying his family. In many ways, friends say, Zachary's adoption had been a desperate attempt to save De Lorean's second marriage. He had tried unsuccessfully for sixteen years to have children and believed there was a problem with his own fertility. For all his reputation as a swinger, those closest to De Lorean feel he never wanted anything more than the sort of "clean-cut middle American" family he put in the Chevy ads. Children were just as important to Kelly Harmon, as she let everybody know in interviews before the wedding. But the two had drifted too far apart by the time Zachary Thomas (the first name for John's father; the middle name for Kelly's) arrived.

Looking back, it would seem that De Lorean tried hard to accommodate his young bride. An avid equestrian, Kelly shipped her horse to Bloomfield Hills, and the couple joined the local hunt club. The genteel horse-owners were soon grumbling about the new members. Kelly favored jeans over jodhpurs, and her husband, not loath to show off the results of his weight lifting, often wandered the grounds shirtless. De Lorean had never been on a horse before he met Kelly, but he cut back on his golf game to learn how to ride, and ended up cracking two ribs in a fall.

He did not drag Kelly to cocktail parties or formal dinner parties. As he explained to *Sports Illustrated* writer Brock Yates, "Since neither my wife nor I drink, we'd frankly rather take a twilight horseback ride or a late run down the ski slope than go to any party."

Kelly wanted to extend her love for children, horses, and the great outdoors into charity work, and turned to a camp for underprivileged youth in Detroit's suburbs. When Kelly suggested opening her own camp, Tom Harmon put De Lorean together with a California real estate agent who ranged the country looking for a suitable site. They settled on a cattle ranch scooped out of the foothills of the Bitterroot Mountains in the remote reaches of Idaho. De Lorean shelled out close to a million dollars for the property and some adjoining parcels in the fall of 1971. Before the year was out, he and Kelly were looking for another ranch in a mountainous area a few hours out of San Diego.

However much property the De Loreans assembled though, they still ended up with less time to share together. While he was climbing up the corporate ladder at Pontiac, De Lorean's first wife, Elizabeth, was willing to put up with his seventy-hour workweeks. Kelly was not so anxious to languish alone in their big Bloomfield Hills house while John toiled at Chevrolet.

When Arthur Hailey's *Wheels* hit the best-seller lists in 1971, Detroit gossips quickly deciphered what they took to be a roman à clef. They soon pegged De Lorean as Adam Trenton, the book's hard-charging middle-aged executive whose long hours at the office leave his much younger wife sexually frustrated at home.

De Lorean would later blame the dissolution of his second marriage on the gossips of Detroit's auto society. Kelly, he says in *On A Clear Day*, "[was] never accepted by the tight social circle of GM wives who were much older. While we rarely socialized with GM people, we were frequently thrust together at corporate functions or in the suburban clubs of Detroit, and the reaction to her, while not hostile, was cool and diffident. Kelly's California background and the cool reception she received in the automotive circles made her yearn for more time back home."

John Quirk does not remember Kelly's reception the same way. The problem, he says, was Kelly and not GM wives. Quirk, too, divorced his first wife of many years to marry a twenty-one-year-old woman. "My [second] wife had no trouble adjusting," he adds, "and was treated very warmly by the women in the community. I don't think Kelly had any interest whatsoever in being accepted in the automotive [community]. Kelly was a California girl and wanted no part of Detroit. I think she had a father complex, and the most important people in her life were her father and her brother Mark [a starting quarterback for UCLA]. . . . I remember one time John wanted her to attend some important function, but she ended up going to Los Angeles to watch her brother play ball. She just wasn't ready to leave home when she married John."

In December of 1971, De Lorean rented a bungalow at Laguna Beach, and during the next year, Kelly was to stay out there more than in Detroit. By August of 1972, she'd asked for an official separation. At first, De Lorean would not admit, even to friends, that his wife had left him. Later on in that month, *Signature* magazine prepared a profile on De Lorean, and one steamy day, Chicago photographer Arthur Shay was sent to the subject's Bloomfield Hills home to get a picture of husband and wife.

Word had already leaked out that De Lorean was about to become a member of the company's top executive staff. It was the sort of promotion, the magazine figured, that would soon make De Lorean the corporation's youngest president ever. But when Shay arrived for the picture session, he did not find an ecstatic *Wunderkind*. Instead, a sullen De Lorean answered the door, wearing only a pair of jeans.

"He must have had eight different types of cars sitting in the driveway," Shay remembers. "But I realized that no one else was around. The whole place was deserted except for his dogs. He acted very cordially, but it was clear that he wanted me to get the picture-taking over with."

Actually Shay had not come to meet only De Lorean, but Kelly as well, for a few shots of the happy couple. He explains, "I had expected to photograph him with his wife, and he seemed to be very embarrassed that she wasn't there. He didn't tell me they were separated. He just said she was away. The best I could manage was a shot of him sitting under her portrait. He was very easy with the camera, like a show-biz person, but there was no way I could make him smile that day. He was pretty down.

"After we were finished he went out in his backyard with a golf bag. He seemed eager to get back to work on his golf swing."

·6·
Falling from the Fourteenth Floor

On August 28, 1972, John Z. De Lorean ascended to the fourteenth floor of General Motors' world headquarters. Chevrolet's *enfant terrible* chief had been appointed group executive for the car and truck divisions—and by all appearances was headed only for corporate greatness. "To most GM employees," he writes in *On A Clear Day*, "rising to The Fourteenth Floor is the final scene in their Horatio Alger dream. The Mt. Olympus of business. The place where the biggest corporate decisions are made. Getting there assures that you'll be a millionaire. . . ."

Getting there, at the relatively young age of forty-eight, De Lorean argues, gave him "a better than even-odds chance of one day being [GM] president." Back in the days following De Lorean's appointment, few in Detroit would have disagreed with his assessment.

But in only seven months, the odds-on president tumbled from the fourteenth floor. Although press releases said he left of his own accord, he was given the sort of severance package that usually went to smooth the ruffled feathers of executives the company had jettisoned. Under the condition that he not defect to another auto company, he was given a letter of intent to open a Cadillac franchise in Lighthouse Point, a community just north of Miami Beach and one of the most desirable locations in the country.

His departure from General Motors shocked the industry, and, years later, the circumstances surrounding his exit still remain murky. De Lorean has always maintained that he left of his own accord. In time, he readily accepted the media's characterization of him as the man who "quit General Motors."

But all the while, retired GM executives have just as adamantly insisted—though off the record—that as a result of internal investigations De Lorean was fired. There are inconsistencies in both stories, however. Besides De Lorean, the only others who knew exactly why he did leave were the three men at the top of GM in 1973: Chairman Richard C. Gerstenberg, President Edward N. Cole, and Vice Chairman Thomas A. Murphy. Cole died in a 1977 plane crash. Gerstenberg, and his successor as chairman, Murphy, aren't talking.

But enough information has been uncovered to at least dispute De Lorean's version of his last days at General Motors. In fact, based on his own statements during litigation that occurred years later, De Lorean has revealed that his GM superiors could have found ample justification for dismissing the young vice president. His ability to emerge from the corporation with his reputation unscathed remains one of De Lorean's greatest achievements.

In light of this new information, De Lorean's jump to the fourteenth floor no longer looks like a promotion, but a kick upstairs and a few steps removed from a boot out the window. When De Lorean's three predecessors as Chevrolet general manager rose to the fourteenth floor, they became group vice presidents. He, however, was consigned to the lower tier of group executives. A subtle ignominy perhaps, but all the more curious considering that Chevrolet was not doing so badly under his leadership.

It is somewhat surprising that his sudden yank from Chevrolet was not viewed suspiciously at the time. He had served the division as general manager for only two and a half years. Sales may have plummeted in 1970 and 1971, but the drop was mostly due to a strike and then to a recession. In 1972, when the economy revived, Chevrolet was on the way to a year of record earnings. De Lorean did not come near the 30 percent of the market share he boldly predicted he would reach, but he still deserved another few years to hit his goal. Considering the importance of Chevrolet to the entire corporation, headquarters might have been expected to give De Lorean the chance. His predecessor at Chevy, Pete Estes, had taken the division on a tailspin, and even he got three and a half years before his "promotion."

So, evidently, the division's bottom line had not shortened De Lorean's Chevy tenure. Other factors were involved and they point to an April 1972 issue of the *Gallagher Report*, a weekly newsletter written for marketing, advertising, and media executives. One item reads: "DICK GERSTENBERG TAKES HARD LOOK AT CHEVROLET. New General Motors chairman unhappy with performance of Chevrolet general manager John De Lorean. Too many outside interests. De Lorean part owner of San Diego Chargers pro football team. . . . Still under cloud from internal investigation of kickbacks from Chevrolet suppliers. . . ."

The blurb infuriated De Lorean and he had his lawyer, John Noonan, hire a private investigator to find out where the newsletter got the information. His sleuth never did manage to track down the source. But the report touched on more than just idle or malicious gossip.

It was no secret in Detroit that De Lorean had many outside interests. They were far more extensive than the football team and more potentially embarrassing for the corporation. Just a few days before he made the *Gallagher Report*, De Lorean became a founding member of the board for Grand Prix of America—the brainstorm of his younger brother, Jack. The idea was to franchise racetracks for miniature Wankel-engine race cars. The public could pay a per-lap fee to race against a time clock. For the pilot racetrack, the company leased a parcel in Troy, Michigan. Coincidentally enough, their landlord was North American Rockwell, the company run by John's old transcontinental golfing buddy, Bob Anderson. More important, from GM's point of view, Rockwell's automotive division was a major supplier for Chevrolet and the rest of the car industry.

Another of De Lorean's extracurricular affairs had surfaced the year before when the Securities and Exchange Commission listed him among the directors of Patrick Petroleum Company, an oil and gas exploration firm in Jackson, Michigan. De Lorean first met the company's president, U. E. Patrick, on the auto-racing circuit and the two struck up a close working relationship (Patrick was also among the early Grand Prix investors). No one in General Motors was more vocal than De Lorean about the company's need for fuel-efficient vehicles. But his prescience about the oncoming energy shortage was not about to stop him from cashing in on the rest of the business world's shortsightedness. Although De Lorean did not let the oil investments muzzle his calls for small cars, some top GM execs still saw his role with Patrick Petroleum as the height of hypocrisy.

They were further enraged when a newspaper reported that De Lorean had sold 1,100 shares of GM stock to buy his interest in the oil company. He later explained that the stock had gone towards the purchase of his Idaho ranch. But his explanation didn't sit any better with the GM brass, who have always worried that one executive's sale of GM stock, if large enough, could touch off a bearish blitz on Wall Street.

And yet, De Lorean's outside investments alone were not enough to get him fired. Many other GM executives before and since have been heavily involved as directors or investors in other ventures. Far more serious were the allegations of what the *Gallagher Report* called "kickbacks."

Ironically, De Lorean touched on the problems of upper-management corruption in *On A Clear Day*'s most controversial chapter, "How Moral Men Make Immoral Decisions." One of the tales he tells out of school concerns an auto-dealer friend of Ed Cole's who twice got the opportunity to purchase GM real estate, and soon after sold the parcels for much higher prices (the dealer later unsuccessfully sued De Lorean and coauthor Pat Wright for libel). De Lorean does not accuse Cole of reaping any part of that dealer's profits. But elsewhere in the chapter, without naming names, he claims, "There were disturbing activities in upper management in which executives used their positions of power and knowledge to profit PERSONALLY in corporate business. These were by no means widespread and perhaps confined to only a few individuals."

De Lorean's management style often attracted speculation about his own attempts to "profit personally in corporate business." As Tom Adams explains, "John had the habit of directly contacting suppliers and bringing them into the fold even before we had the chance to go through departmental procedures. Ofttimes his selections were right and he managed to pick the people who could best do the job. But even though he was periodically right, it didn't make his arrangements very pleasant or proper when he imposed them on the rest of us."

Adams did not know if any of the contacts with suppliers were personally beneficial for De Lorean. But General Motors executives, again speaking off the record, mention one De Lorean deal in particular.

In the spring of 1971, De Lorean convened a meeting of his top marketing people at Chevrolet for a special presentation. The guests of honor were two advertising men from Hollywood, Milton Bradley Scott and Peck Prior, who claimed to have a product that would revolutionize the American car dealership. They called it the Mini-Theater. Although the device looked like a television set, it actually contained a tiny movie projector and a cartridge of Super 8-mm film capable of running over and over in a continuous loop. Loaded with films that displayed Chevrolet products, Scott explained, the Mini-Theater would illustrate for any customer all of a car's selling points including those that the salesmen couldn't begin to demonstrate or even remember.

The concept was not entirely new, and other technology like the video cassette recorder seemed more promising than Scott's repeating film cartridge—at least video cassettes could be reused, but at the end of each model year the film had to be thrown away.

Still, Scott got the contract with Chevrolet and, according to a

Los Angeles Times reporter, "found himself—almost instantly—with more than $3 million of business." The Mini-Theater was no GM giveaway for Chevrolet dealers. Each month they paid $21 for the machine and owned it after two years. They spent an additional $250 each year for a set of cartridges, and $150 for a stand. Some of Chevrolet's 6,500 dealers were not so eager to get into the theater business, but the factory helped change their mind. "There was a little arm twisting [by GM]," one California dealer told the *Times*, "but nobody got hurt—the arm wasn't dislocated."

Actually, Scott's deal with Chevrolet meant he had all of GM sewed up when the other divisions inevitably got into the Mini-Theater act. Many Chevy dealers were also distributors of other GM cars, and the corporation was not so cruel as to foist film systems on them that would be incompatible with the Chevrolet Mini-Theater. In his arrangement with Chevrolet, Scott was the consummate middleman. His company, United Visuals Corporation, supplied nothing directly to GM. Instead it subcontracted for almost all the services. The projector and cartridge system were the patented products of Technicolor, Incorporated. General Motors' advertising agencies produced the films. Someone else cut and reproduced the seven-minute reels.

For Scott, the most crucial link in the whole deal was his friendship with John De Lorean. No other connection mattered more. In fact, as both men later testified in court papers, their personal relationship was established long before Scott showed up in Detroit to demonstrate the Mini-Theater.

They first met through De Lorean's film-producer friend, Burt Sugarman. An advertising man who had once counted the TV-oriented Church of God among his clients, Scott had for some time hovered around West Coast auto circles. At one point he was a product agent, getting cars on game shows as prizes or in movies as props. For a while he ran his own Chevrolet dealership in Modesto, California. Among his most prized possessions were two Rolls-Royces—one of 1920 vintage.

Scott smoothly slipped into De Lorean's jet-set crowd. Also tall and athletic (he had been a gymnast in college), Scott could join

De Lorean and Rockwell president Bob Anderson for games of golf and tennis. One of Scott's employees from those days remembers a Christmas party Scott threw in his Beverly Hills penthouse apartment. "De Lorean showed up, and Scott didn't leave his side for the rest of the evening.

"The only people he ever talked about were De Lorean and Anderson. I felt that he always aspired to that sort of corporate power, and he was ready to do anything to be a part of their lives."

While suitably flamboyant for Hollywood, Scott could tone down his image if he accompanied De Lorean or Anderson back to their Midwestern turf. The former employee says, "What fascinated me about Milt was the way he'd change, like a chameleon, when he had to go to Detroit. He'd take off the gold, and put on a conservative suit and tie. He'd even talk differently to blend into the scene."

Scott brought some of his own famous friends into De Lorean's circle, including E. Gregory Hookstratten, Hollywood's most powerful celebrity lawyer. His clients included Elvis Presley, Tom Snyder, Cary Grant, and a number of professional athletes, sports broadcasters, coaches, and team owners. Hookstratten became one more partner for a good game of golf. Soon after he met De Lorean, Hookstratten represented him in his divorce from Kelly Harmon.

Yet another figure moved on the periphery of this glittering crowd; a man of much lesser accomplishment than the others, but of far greater importance to John De Lorean's career. Roy Sigurd Nesseth's entrée to De Lorean and Scott had been through Burt Sugarman's pharmacist father. Up to that point, Nesseth's claim to fame had been as manager of the Los Angeles dealership, Williams Chevrolet, the nation's best seller.

At six feet and six inches, Nesseth was a man of overbearing size and temperament. He could wash total strangers away with his charm—an ability that made him one of the best car salesmen in southern California. But when his powers of persuasion failed him, he could bully or explode in a frightening rage. His temper, and what one judge described as "his fast and loose" way of doing business, had Roy most often finishing his battles in court. As the years passed, all the luminaries who once surrounded De Lorean at Hollywood parties drifted away. Only Nesseth remained. De Lorean's other friends have often wondered about the tie that bound Nesseth and De Lorean together. It was first joined by Scott and his company, United Visuals Corporation.

Only in recent years have all the details concerning United Visuals emerged, as Scott has fought with De Lorean and Nesseth for the proceeds of the defunct company. In 1976 Scott sold the assets of the company to Technicolor. Nesseth has sued, claiming he possessed an option—assigned to him by De Lorean—for 49 percent of United Visuals. The suit was still unresolved when De Lorean was arrested by federal agents.

Nesseth once talked of United Visuals with one of his fellow executives at the De Lorean Motor Company. The company, he explained, provided the "seed money" for future Nesseth and De Lorean ventures. Most likely, United Visuals also provided the seeds for De Lorean's downfall at General Motors.

Both sides dispute where the idea for the Mini-Theater actually came from. Scott says it was entirely conceived by him and Prior. De Lorean argues in court depositions that Scott and Prior had only thought of using the system to show cartoon clips and National Football League highlights to lure people into the dealership. It was Nesseth, De Lorean claims, who suggested the Mini-Theater be used to actually help sell the cars with demo films, and it was Nesseth too, he says, who worked out the two-year-lease package offered to dealers.

In any case, De Lorean does not hedge about the importance of his influence in getting Scott the contract with Chevrolet in 1971. While the division's marketing people were interested in the concept, De Lorean testifies, they wanted to go to experienced contractors like the Jam Handy Corporation to implement the project. "I said, 'That's unfair. [Scott] brought the idea in here.' " De Lorean goes on to explain that Scott still had to win a competitive bid, but he adds as well, "Everybody knew that Scott was a personal friend of mine and that I interceded to protect him. . . . I think without me, there was no question he had no business at all. I helped him a tremendous amount."

Of course, while taking the credit for United Visuals' existence, De Lorean denies in his deposition that he had ever been a shareholder or involved in the company's day-to-day operations. Among the original shareholders were Scott, Prior, and lawyer Hookstratten, who also served as treasurer for the corporation. De Lorean has claimed that Scott promised Nesseth 17.5 percent of the stock. Nesseth was on the company's payroll for about a year, starting in April 1972. "We never really understood what Roy was doing at United Visuals," one co-worker remembers. "Looking back, he could have been De Lorean's man on the scene. He certainly didn't get along very well with Milt."

Although De Lorean did not directly benefit from United Visuals while he was at General Motors, he was financially involved with Scott in other deals. Some cash exchanges between the two were petty (Mint Investment, a company belonging to Myles Hymes, another United Visuals director and an associate of Scott, made payments on De Lorean's Laguna Beach home). Others were much more substantial. As a defendant in a lawsuit filed against him by Cal Prix, Inc., De Lorean testified that he moved funds in and out of a Scott bank account without Scott's knowledge because they were partners in a business.

In the March 1982 trial before a Los Angeles County Superior Court judge, De Lorean explained, "[Scott and I] owned a joint business and [$65,000 was] taken from my part of the joint business. . . . And, of course, at that time [Scott] was an officer of that company. It was a company that had a lighting concession in Las Vegas—it was a GE distributor for light bulbs in Vegas. It's a little bit complex, but the whole point was [that the $65,000] was deducted from my share of that business when it was liquidated, so it turned out to be my investment entirely; but at that point in time, the money was borrowed essentially from Scott, but [also] from my portion of the jointly owned business."

De Lorean went on to describe the company in his testimony: "We bought a lighting company in Las Vegas that had the concession for the GE light bulbs with the idea that because of all the light bulbs, it was going to be a tremendous success. It turned out it wasn't."

FALLING FROM THE FOURTEENTH FLOOR

When De Lorean was asked about his share of the lighting company, he replied, "It was a partnership," claiming further that he owned a 50 percent interest. However, he also admitted that everything connected with the company was in Scott's name.

Scott also mentions a lighting company in his declaration for the United Visuals case. According to him, the Las Vegas firm was liquidated by June 1973 and Nesseth helped him close it down. De Lorean left GM in April 1973. It's unlikely that he would have participated as a fifty-fifty partner in the lighting company for only the last two months of its existence. His involvement with Scott's Las Vegas venture must have stretched back into his tenure at General Motors. If it had been discovered by GM execs, as some now say it was, the deal could have been seen as a payoff for the United Visuals contract. Considering the fate of the lighting company, it would not have been a very good payoff.

De Lorean moved to secure far more lucrative arrangements with Scott after his resignation from GM was announced. Officially he was still under GM employ for the next year as a consultant (the company gave him a $200,000 salary to serve as president of the National Alliance of Business—a nonprofit group supporting employment for the disadvantaged).

In August 1973, Scott claims in the United Visuals lawsuit, De Lorean got a loan for $300,000 from United Visuals. The note, however, was in Scott's and not the company's name. In his declaration, Scott explains, "Mr. De Lorean required that the promissory note be made payable to my order because he did not want there to be any documents indicating that he had any connection with United Visuals Corporation because of his then employment with General Motors Corporation."

In return for the money, Scott expected a half-interest in the Florida Cadillac dealership De Lorean got as severance from GM. But Scott never got a piece of the dealership, nor did he ever get his money back. De Lorean counters that Scott had to raise over $1 million, not $300,000, for his share of the franchise. When Scott failed to come up with the funds, De Lorean says, he had to rush elsewhere to find backing. Curiously, Scott has never sued to recover the funds. In his own deposition De Lorean brazenly admits that he still had the $300,000: "Someday we'll have a lawsuit whether I was damaged by [Scott's] retreating . . . I keep the money in escrow in my Christmas fund when Scott's ready to sue."

But $300,000 is not all De Lorean got out of Scott after he left GM. In December 1973, Scott gave him an option for 49 percent of United Visuals. According to the declaration Scott filed in court, De Lorean paid nothing for the option: "Although the [option] indicates that I received consideration, nothing of any value was transferred to anyone and the recital in the document that I received consideration is completely erroneous. Mr. De Lorean dictated the substance of the letter."

In his testimony, De Lorean denies that he forced the option on Scott. His explanation has it the other way around. After he left GM, De Lorean claims, Scott "no longer had the great protector in the corporation." Scott, he says, was afraid GM would then cancel the United Visuals contract. "He pleaded with me to become involved. He wanted me to be chairman. I made a certain number of calls and talked to various people to try to help him along. . . . [Finally,] he insisted I accept this option."

However Scott felt about the option when he gave it to De Lorean, a year later he considered it dead and buried. By this time, the two had fallen out over the dealership in Florida and the $300,000 loan. In a final letter asking for his money back, Scott threatened to revoke the option as payment for the note. "Under any circumstance," he wrote, "I will consider the disposition of $300,000 plus interest as full satisfaction of any obligation or understanding relating to your involvement with United Visuals Corporation."

Scott did not hear any more about the option for over a year, until he tried to sell out to Technicolor. De Lorean at first wired Scott to tell him he wanted to exercise the option. De Lorean explains that when Scott refused, "I really wasn't in the mood to try to take legal recourse . . . I know he treated Roy very badly. Roy had done a lot of work for me in various areas, so I assigned the option to Roy." As he was to do so often in De Lorean's business career, Nesseth forged into the courtroom to fight De

FALLING FROM THE FOURTEENTH FLOOR

Lorean's battles—a cross between a hired litigious samurai and a kamikaze. De Lorean claimed the two had no "arrangement" to divvy up the take if Roy did win his lawsuit against Scott.

If, back in 1972, GM officials could have foreseen how the United Visuals affair would end up, they probably would have fired De Lorean on the spot. However, at least three different sources confirm that De Lorean's superiors knew enough about United Visuals to get him out of Chevrolet as soon as they could. While the roost on the fourteenth floor was a sort of punishment, it was also a second chance. If De Lorean had bided his time, all indiscretions would have been forgiven. He might have had his chance at the presidency, although not to succeed Ed Cole when he retired in 1974. Perhaps after that.

However, De Lorean was not willing or able to bide his time in the headquarters roost. The move up had been more of a comedown than he expected. As a division manager, he was a mover and shaker. As a junior VP on the fourteenth floor, he was a paper shuffler, reading reports and preparing for meetings. In his three decades at GM, Bob McLean remembers some division general managers who turned down the fourteenth floor. "At the top of a division, you're already a chief executive," he says. "You have all those departments and assistants under you. You have drivers picking you up in the morning and people escorting you wherever you go. Then, suddenly, you go to the fourteenth floor and it's culture shock. You just don't get any respect—whatever you do, wherever you go. Some of the executives up there don't even have their own secretaries. They share them with other executives. It's unbelievable, but even as you're on the way to running the company, the GM system first makes you feel like the lowliest functionary.

"De Lorean didn't take long to let everyone know how bored he was with the fourteenth floor. At that stage of his life, he just didn't want to sit through meetings."

In *On A Clear Day*, De Lorean offers two rather contradictory reasons for his "resignation" from General Motors. One concerns a management cabal out to get him fired. The other involves his growing disputes with the company's style and philosophy. But if De Lorean was so disenchanted with GM anyway, what did it matter whether some conspiracy formed to force him out? The group would only do him a favor.

Among his enemies, De Lorean counted Dolly Cole, wife of the president, Ed Cole, and three GM vice presidents: Oscar A. Lundin, in charge of finance; Anthony G. De Lorenzo, public relations head; and Richard L. Terrell, De Lorean's immediate superior on the fourteenth floor. Information about the anti–De Lorean clique in GM, the victim reports, came from some friends who heard Dolly Cole gossip over lunch at the Plaza in New York.

De Lorean never quite understood Dolly Cole's enmity. A beautiful woman much younger than her husband, Dolly married Ed shortly after he divorced his first wife. Her friends say she always resented the acid way De Lorean used to kid Ed, especially about her. The GM execs, De Lorean learned, "had a personal vendetta against me . . . they were using every means at their disposal to discredit me."

One of those means, De Lorean charged, was to leak a speech he had prepared for a November 1972 management conference in Greenbrier, North Carolina. While some of his statements supported Ed Cole's pursuit of the Wankel rotary engine (ultimately a fruitless and wasteful endeavor), De Lorean also delivered a warning that "poor quality threatens to destroy us." He added that "every defect, each recall, only diminishes the credibility of whatever amount of advertising we do. . . . Significantly, there has been a serious and disturbing decline in loyalty among the owners of GM products, especially in head-to-head comparisons with Ford."

Before he had a chance to deliver the speech, his remarks were reported in the *Detroit News*, by veteran reporter Robert Irvin. De Lorean denied having anything to do with the leak, and a short time later, he writes in *On A Clear Day*, another friend at lunch—this time in Detroit—ran across a private investigator who knew GM's operation and told him that the speech was leaked by a man on the GM public relations staff.

He does not mention that, at his own insistence, GM hired a private investigator to track down the leak—the same man De

Lorean had once hired to find the source of the *Gallagher Report* rumor. This time the detective's work was far more extensive, but before he had a chance to hand in his report, De Lorean was already on his way out. The investigator never got paid for his effort. Although his theory was never definitely confirmed, the investigator suspected that a GM public relations official close to De Lorean, and not opposed to him, released the speech. As for reporter Irvin, he had worked amicably with De Lorean before the Greenbrier incident, and did a few favorable profiles of him even after he left GM.

Once, back in 1971, De Lorean says, in a moment of disillusion with the auto industry, he had asked to resign and was talked out of it. But in 1972, he would ask again, going to Thomas A. Murphy, GM vice chairman, who was heir apparent to the chairmanship held by Richard Gerstenberg. De Lorean says Murphy told him, "Jeez, I don't see why you want to leave. Nine chances out of ten, when Cole leaves, you'll be the next president."

Although Murphy will not comment about De Lorean's claims in *On A Clear Day*, it's unlikely that he would have told him he'd be the next president. De Lorean was still a rank below Estes and Terrell, who were in fact the favorites for the job. It would have been without precedent to have any GM executive leapfrog so suddenly or so far into the presidency.

De Lorean says that after Murphy tried to dissuade him, he wrote a scathing report "aimed directly at a lot of corporate people and their actions." He explains further, "I figured this memo would demonstrate to management that we could no longer exist together and that it was in their best interests to let me resign on my terms." Soon after, he says, Murphy told him, "John, I may have done you a disservice in the past when I said you should stay with the corporation. It is pretty obvious you are unhappy and perhaps you should leave."

While De Lorean may have written that memo, he has also talked to friends of writing another twenty-page memo directed personally to Murphy. This one is sharply critical of the company, too, especially of what De Lorean calls GM's "lack of social responsibility." But it is also the sort of memo that De Lorean could have released as an explanation if he were summarily fired (he used to boast that he had predated it). A closing sentence reads, "I assume you will tell me to destroy this memo as you have so many others. . . ."

Whatever the real reasons for De Lorean's departure from GM, the criticisms of the corporation that he lays out in *On A Clear Day* are still of considerable value. Taken together, they are the best key to the forces that would drive him in his private career.

If one thread runs throughout his indictment, it's the tendency of the GM system to reduce dynamic personalities to dull mediocrity. De Lorean well understood why the company couldn't be swayed by the impulsive actions of one man. As he writes, "It was Durant's appetite for growth which led to his downfall." To counter the entrepreneurial boom-and-bust tendencies of one man, a committee system was designed by Alfred P. Sloan, the most influential executive in the company's history. While corporate committees set policy for the entire company, divisions were permitted a certain operational independence as well. Of this concept De Lorean says, "A delicate balance was to be maintained between the freedom of the various operations to manage their businesses, competing internally as well as outside of the company, and the controls necessary to coordinate these operations in the best interests of the corporation's growth and performance."

Sloan further divided the corporate committees along financial and operational lines, with the chairman holding the purse strings and the president directing operations. But by the late Fifties, De Lorean charges, "the delicate balance at the top of the world's largest industrial corporation was starting to tip toward the financial side of the business. . . ." Creativity, innovation, and foresight were to be neglected for "short-term profit."

Although De Lorean supports the committee idea in theory— it's the practice that disturbs him most, especially in the conformity it breeds: what he calls team loyalty. He comments constantly on the colorlessness imposed on executives in dress code and behavior: "Style and personality in the corporate mold mean simply that a GM executive is a low-profile executive. What is to be most memorable about the corporation today is the letters G and M, and not the people behind the letters."

He goes on to lament that the chief executives of other auto companies, like Lee Iacocca, are more familiar faces to the American public than GM officials. While some might see GM's humility as laudable, De Lorean finds it reprehensible, complaining that "no one individual is permitted to stand out in the corporation today. When one does, he is rebuked, ordered to disappear into the wallpaper."

Such executive anonymity, De Lorean argues, breeds public distrust. "Business in America . . . is impersonal. This is particularly true of large American multinational corporations. They are viewed by their employees and publics as faceless. They have no personality." He is just as critical of companies that stonewall the press.

In sum, he paints a picture of an ideal company quite different from General Motors—one tied directly to an individual who can provide a face and a personality that people will trust. This isn't just executive egomania, De Lorean tells us, it's good business. Of course, Henry Ford tried a personal approach. And so would John De Lorean.

All these arguments justify and reinforce De Lorean's decision to start his own company. He decries the fact that in "major businesses" there are few "people in management with very substantial holdings of the company stock." This is unfortunate, he explains, because "big individual owners of GM, like Sloan or du Pont and others, who owned hundreds of millions of dollars worth of the corporation's stock, had long tenure. Their decisions were biased as much in favor of the long-term growth and health of the company as they were in favor of the short-term profit statement." This is preferable, he believes, to today's "short-term and results-oriented" management. Of course, in his litany of big individual owners, De Lorean leaves out Durant, whose concern for pumping up the price of his GM stock almost bankrupted the company.

During a 1979 interview, De Lorean went further into the

problems of modern management, again anthropomorphizing the corporation. "I think every institution goes through a cycle. Like a human being. I think the people who built the automobile business were a rough-tough driven bunch of bastards. They used to work an unbelievable amount of hours. They were absolutely an incredibly unusual bunch of people. Really the pioneers, the developers, the builders. Once an industry reaches a certain maturity, then that guy winds up being replaced by a sort of keeper—a professional manager."

Elsewhere in the same interview De Lorean painted himself in the mold of those pioneers. "I've always been an accomplishment-oriented guy. If I had a job and I believed in it, I'd absolutely leave no stone unturned to accomplish it. That's been my motivation in life: to accomplish . . ."

Much of De Lorean's frustration on the fourteenth floor, he writes in *On A Clear Day*, were feelings that he couldn't accomplish anything in his new position. Another executive tells him, "On The Fourteenth Floor you felt like you'd lost your effectiveness because you couldn't get things done. . . . In the divisions you were a doer, and in the corporate management you were an overseer."

De Lorean paints GM president Ed Cole as a victim of the system: beaten and badgered by the financial men. One senior executive derisively refers to him as "just the chief engineer."

It is Cole, De Lorean says, who inspired his departure. He quotes Cole as saying, "If I was your age, John, I'd get the hell out of here so fast that you wouldn't believe it. The opportunities in this business are gone. Especially for a guy like you who can get things done. There are a lot of people around here who should stay up here because this is the best they can do. The system protects them. But the opportunities for you are too great."

With this word of advice from "a man who had been to the summit," De Lorean says, he made up his mind to resign. Whether or not he quoted Cole correctly, one line jumps from his admonition: "Especially for a guy like you who can get things done."

Nothing matters more to De Lorean than the image of the "doer." And yet, how much had De Lorean really accomplished in comparison to Cole himself? Right or wrong, Cole had forged ahead with difficult projects throughout his career at GM. His favorite quote was the one attributed to Hannibal, "We will either find a way or make one." Against continuous opposition from other members of management, stubby, bullnecked Ed Cole made a way: first with the Corvette, then with the Corvair, and later with his ill-fated $150 million Wankel-engine project.

De Lorean had not come close to equaling any of these corporate feats—wrongheaded as they might have been. He was an excellent performer, but in roles written by others. Aside from his unorthodox lifestyle, De Lorean flowed with the system. For all his derogatory statements about Estes as a company man, De Lorean never dared buck corporate commands the way Pete did with the GTO.

Perhaps if De Lorean had reached the company presidency, he would have had an even greater impact on the course of General Motors than Ed Cole. Yet, no matter how laudable De Lorean's record at GM, it would still have offered very little indication of his capabilities outside the company. Until April 1973, his career had been nurtured in the warm cocoon of the established auto industry. Motor City took him as a boy and gave him an excellent technical education—free of charge—first at Cass and then at Lawrence Tech. Chrysler Institute refined his training. Packard and GM rewarded him with promotions and big salaries. De Lorean had the talent and initiative to make use of the system, but he was by no means self-made to the extent of a Ford or Durant, who actually created the systems that would benefit them.

The real test for De Lorean as a "doer" was to come only after he had left the polished wood doors of the big corporation behind. He was all too aware of the challenge his independence posed. If he indeed had quit GM—as he claimed—he had to justify his abrupt exit, and more important, prove he could be just as successful outside the company.

"I walked out on an empire," he told the *Detroit Free Press*. "Now I've got to show them I knew what was happening all along."

·7·
A Very Brilliant Financial Analyst

On California's Pacific Coast Highway, just across the street from Harpoon Harry's, is a little bar and grill known as Captain Jack's. An aqueduct runs along one side of the restaurant, and a canal borders the patio in back. The little building is covered with weather-beaten wood on the outside and inside there is more weather-beaten wood in the paneling and exposed beams. Aquariums are sunk into the wall. Varnished masts serve as railings. A wooden effigy of Captain Jack with his pipe and captain's cap stands alongside the ship's wheel, right behind the Hawaiian-shirted maître d'. The restaurant's specialty is steak.

On nights when Roy Nesseth is in town, Captain Jack's can be a little noisier than usual. Living just a few blocks away, Roy is one of the restaurant's most constant customers. A large boisterous man, with a thin, broken nose and rugged Scandinavian good looks, he is the type who can seem to fill a place all by himself. His head nearly scrapes the low ceiling and his deep voice booms into every corner.

• A VERY BRILLIANT FINANCIAL ANALYST •

Waiters treat him with the deference due a big tipper and, apparently, they don't mind the slaps on the back or all the time he spends bellowing into the pay phone that hangs next to the men's room door. Some of the calls are long distance—New York, Idaho, Detroit, even overseas—and occasionally he is heard screaming at a foreign operator. As he searches for coins to feed the phone, receipts, crumpled currency, and odd scraps of paper come fluttering out of his pockets. With his huge reach, he can get change off the bar while still holding the receiver with the other hand.

At times, the other customers can't help but listen to Roy's conversations. He fills the restaurant with talk of loans, and banks, and cars, and racetracks, and cattle, and trucks. And sometimes, too, through all the clamor of the busy restaurant, people can also hear Roy talk of John De Lorean.

Roy has always been proud to work for John De Lorean and he can mention their close relationship in conversations with total strangers. Despite his unwavering allegiance to De Lorean, Nesseth has not elicited the same sort of loyalty in return from his employer. In trial testimony, De Lorean has sometimes chosen to dissociate himself from Roy or play down the influence his subordinate exercised in his affairs. But whatever De Lorean may say about Roy on any one day in any one courtroom, there is no doubt that the two have been the closest of associates over the last decade. There is no doubt either that the pay phone by the bathroom wall at Captain Jack's became the wayward nerve center of the debilitated De Lorean empire.

Until the fall of 1982, Roy would proudly display a business card from the De Lorean Motor Company. While it identified him as an employee, the caption below didn't reveal any title—only "Office of the Chairman," the chairman, of course, being John De Lorean. The ambiguous job description couldn't have fit Nesseth better. Even though Roy carried a salary as high as $180,000 a year, the car company's other top executives never knew exactly what Roy did for De Lorean or the corporation. But those who first laughed at the former car salesman's blustery behavior would come to the sober realization that, next to General

Counsel Thomas Kimmerly, Roy had more influence over the chairman than anyone else in the company.

The bond between De Lorean and Nesseth mystifies even their closest friends. It is truly an attraction of opposites. Loud and crude, Roy seems incapable of hiding his emotions. Transactions as simple as buying an airline ticket often turn into confrontations. Suave and sophisticated, De Lorean appears to have sublimated all of his feelings behind a forced smile. When he is angry, his voice gets softer. Silence is his harshest rebuke. Most often he tries to avoid arguments.

Today, car company executives suggest that De Lorean used Nesseth's temper to frighten people. Like someone ready to unleash a junkyard dog, he often bragged about how mean Roy could be.

However, during his deposition for Roy's suit against Milton Scott, De Lorean's praise for Nesseth's abilities was of a higher order. "He has an unusual combination of financial acumen," De Lorean said of Nesseth. "In fact, I've never met anybody in the world quite like him. In fact, we just closed a deal this last week [of May 1981] where he made, oh, probably a million and a half dollars for me on something that I didn't think I could have made a penny on. He's a very brilliant financial analyst. . . . He's not a financial analyst in any Arthur Andersen sense. Somebody like that isn't capable of doing this kind of thing anyhow."

De Lorean went on to testify how closely intertwined the business affairs of the two men were: "If he needs $1 million, I'll lend him $1 million. . . . He pays me back at the market-rate interest. . . . He brought me a check last week for $920,000. He handles a tremendous amount of money for me."

And yet, in courtroom testimony, De Lorean and Nesseth have always been willing to tailor their official relationship to their immediate legal needs. At times, acting as a legal flak jacket for De Lorean, Nesseth took sole possession of the De Lorean interests that went sour, accepting the blame for mismanagement or playing the part of the insubordinate partner. Little more than a year before he praised Nesseth in the United Visuals suit as "a very brilliant financial analyst," De Lorean was telling a Kansas

A VERY BRILLIANT FINANCIAL ANALYST

court that Nesseth was an untrustworthy character beyond his control. De Lorean's lawyer Kimmerly testified in the same trial that he was "well aware [that Nesseth] was a crook." In fact, in 1975 De Lorean went so far as to sue Nesseth for a $100,000 debt—probably no more than a ruse to give De Lorean title to Roy's home and keep it out of the hands of other creditors.

By taking the fall to help salvage De Lorean's good name, Roy may have risked his own reputation. But in the minds of lawyers scattered throughout the country, Roy has very little reputation left to lose. Almost his entire adult working career can be chronicled in lawsuits. Most are filed in the Los Angeles area court system, but others are stored in San Diego, Phoenix, Wichita, Detroit, and several towns in Idaho. The record adds up to a most unflattering résumé with an ever-growing number of hostile references.

The most serious charge against Roy dates back to 1954 when he was a salesman at the Ran Boys Used Car Lot in Los Angeles. Twice, Nesseth was accused of tampering with customers' contracts. According to the evidence, he did not lie about the price of the cars or the finance charge for loans. However, he did promise that the deal worked out to monthly payments that were much lower than necessary to fulfill the loan—a fact the two plaintiffs did not realize until they took a closer look at the contracts back home and worked out the numbers for themselves. Roy was convicted of grand theft and two counts of forgery and released on probation.

While that remains his only criminal conviction, over a score of judgments against Roy in civil suits have followed. Plaintiffs range from two ex-wives (one, a beautician, cited extreme cruelty in her divorce petition), to other car customers, former business partners, banks, ex-friends, travel agents, hotels, and sundry suppliers.

Litigation has become a way of life for Nesseth. According to court records, in 1976 Roy postponed a deposition for an Arizona case so he could be in California, where, on the same day, he had to give testimony in two other suits against him.

Roy's pride and joy is the Huntington Harbour split-level home he shares with his third wife and their three children. Slipped sideways in among more imposing houses in a cul-de-sac, the house is an insular little fortress. The tiny front yard is walled off and even the upper-level sun deck is fenced in. Unlike most of his neighbors across the street, Roy has no property on the canal, but realtors conservatively value the house at over $200,000.

Roy's house has been put up for sheriff's auction at least six times to satisfy his debts and, on each occasion, he has come up with the money to redeem his property—once running into the sheriff's office just fifteen minutes before the deadline. Court records show that three of the auctions were initiated by La Jolla lawyer John H. Thomas.

In southern California, Thomas has become the resident legal specialist in suing Nesseth, and his success in collecting on judgments has brought Nesseth's creditors to him from as far away as Kansas and Florida. While dogging Nesseth through all his professional incarnations from car salesman to De Lorean executive, Thomas's persistence has achieved Dickensian dimensions. The blithe response of Nesseth to the lawyer's pursuit has the touch of a modern-day Micawber. In one suit, Thomas describes the Nesseths' skill at frustrating the agents of their creditors: "I have had to expend hundreds of dollars in fruitless efforts to have them served with various processes, both by peace officers and private process servers. I have had to pay private process servers to 'stake out' the Nesseths' residence . . . but Mr. Nesseth continually evaded their efforts to serve him . . . by switching the license plates on his car, [and] by sneaking in and out of his house only at late hours of the night. . . ."

For obvious reasons, Roy does not take kindly to opposing lawyers. He has stalked out of depositions, and during cross-examination in Kansas, he bolted off his chair and rushed at the plaintiff's counsel. The first time De Lorean was ever asked about his friend by the press, he made no excuses for his behavior. "Roy's a typical automotive guy," he told one reporter, "a little too rough and a little too ready."

A VERY BRILLIANT FINANCIAL ANALYST

But back in the days when Roy Nesseth was making a name for himself among the car dealers of Los Angeles, he was not known for his short temper. Quite the opposite.

"We called him 'the stroke,'" George Williams recalls. Williams, who bears some resemblance to comedian Bob Newhart, occasionally laughs and shakes his head as he reminisces about Roy. He sits in the sort of paneled cubicle at his Chevrolet dealership that Nesseth used when he was hired as manager in 1967. "The customers just loved the guy. In no time at all Roy could work his way into their confidence. For instance, he'd ask a guy where he was from, and no matter what he answered, Roy had been there. He'd say something like, 'You remember that little church with the fence in the square?' and the guy would say, 'Yeah, sure.' Then they'd go on talking about his little hometown, and Roy had him right in his hand."

In dealer terminology, Roy was not a salesman, but a closer. Williams explains, "A salesman goes out on the floor and lines the guy up. He then quotes a price, and he says, 'My manager will make you a deal.' That's when Roy comes into the picture. Sometimes he'll show the guy a different car. I've seen people come in looking for a truck, and Roy ends up making them buy a convertible.

"When Roy went into a room with a guy, he came out with his signature on the contract. He was absolutely the best closer I've ever seen. No ifs, ands, or buts. One of the advantages he has over the rest of us is the mind he has for math. He can add figures together faster than most people can with an adding machine. That's a pretty important skill to have when some nervous guy is sitting across from you wondering what his payments will be. Roy would just go down the contract and by the time he got to the bottom, he'd figured out the payment."

Although Roy had been convicted of telling customers one thing and putting another down on paper, Williams contends that Roy never used his mathematic feats to trick anyone. In fact, he says, it was a point of honor for Nesseth to make good on any sum he added incorrectly. "Once Roy and I made a deal to buy the inventory of a Pontiac dealer going out of business. Roy added up all the cars we were buying on the top of a box and came up with an incredibly low figure. The dealer was so desperate, he was ready to take it. But when Roy looked at the box top again, he saw he'd made a mistake. He went back to the guy and insisted we make up the difference. He was very proud about his mathematical abilities and wasn't going to take anything off of anybody because he made an error. When Roy says the figures equal something, you can believe it."

His prowess with numbers, Roy told Williams, was developed in his youth, when he worked in his father's produce market. As he stood waiting to bag the groceries, he'd try and beat the cash register at adding up the bill. Born some sixty years ago on a farm in the Midwest, Roy moved to California with his family when the elder Nesseth went into vegetable wholesaling. During a hitch in the air force, he'd later tell friends, he'd lost all hearing in his right ear, and as a result, spoke louder than he had to. When Roy got in a car, he always let his companion drive, so his good ear was to the other passenger.

Roy liked to tell friends that nothing prepared him better for the rough-and-tumble world of the automobile business than the wholesale produce markets of Los Angeles. The same environment would serve as an incubator for financier Kirk Kerkorian, who also came from a family of grocers. According to Roy, he remained friends with Kerkorian after they both had left the food markets, although there's no evidence that the two did much business together.

Roy became a closer early in his car-selling career. Although his conviction for tampering with contracts probably prevented him from having his own dealership, it didn't stop Roy from working with some of the biggest dealers in southern California. Along the way, he got into the papers when he and his brother Donald—also a car salesman—managed a champion middleweight fighter named Don Jordan. When a dispute arose over who actually owned the fighter, the Nesseth boys took their adversaries to court and eventually won. The other claimants to Jordan had

A VERY BRILLIANT FINANCIAL ANALYST

Italian names and connections—Roy told the press—to organized crime. But evidently that didn't worry him. "He told the Mafia to go to hell," Williams laughs.

The fighter did not do well enough in the ring to get the Nesseths out of the car business. Like so many other times in his life, Roy came close to the big money but never close enough. While he was not able to invest, Nesseth often brought his friends together on deals where everyone seemed to make money. Williams regrets that he didn't get in on some of those schemes—especially one in Beverly Hills where a bankrupt Toyota dealership was turned into a lucrative Mercedes-Benz franchise.

But Williams did let Roy serve as matchmaker between him and another dealer to start a San Diego Toyota franchise and, in return, he loaned Nesseth $25,000 to purchase his own share of the deal. "Roy has made some good money," Williams says. "I know he made some good money with me, but he's also a hell of a spender. It's not that he spends it on any one thing. He's not a drinker. But he's got to do everything first class. He always flew first class and stayed only in the best hotels. Everybody knows him in Vegas. He's the first guy to pick up the tab. It's hard to pay for anything when he's around, and you know he'll leave the biggest tip, too. At least he will if they treat him right. I've been with Roy when he didn't like the service at some restaurant and he grabbed the tablecloth and pulled it out. Dishes, glasses, silverware—they all went flying. Things like that can happen with Roy. You just want to cover your face and pretend you don't know the guy."

Quite suddenly, in the fall of 1970, Roy had the chance to wield all the power and trappings of great wealth. One of his friends, Ross Gilbert (Roy later set him up in the Beverly Hills Mercedes dealership), introduced him to a lawyer who was trying to find a business manager for one of his clients, a wealthy widow named Hazel Upton.

Originally from Nebraska, Hazel still speaks with a Cornbelt twang. A woman with shining eyes and puckish charm, today she still manages to laugh at the incredible reverses that have shaken her life over the last decade. Of Nesseth she says, "I've been conned before. I've been conned since. But I've never been conned as bad as I was with Roy. I know it will catch up to him."

Hazel had been the manager of a small electronics shop when she met William E. Upton. He soon divorced his first wife, losing most of his assets to her before he became Hazel's second husband. Together, starting from scratch, they built an empire around the wood-siding business.

"Bill was a good man with plenty of ability," she says, "but he was also an alcoholic. That was hard on him and hard on me." As their wealth grew, she couldn't settle back into the role of the idle rich wife, but occasionally had to take the reins when her husband went on a binge. Still, there were some good times. The Uptons had homes at the Virginia Country Club in Long Beach and in one of the fanciest apartment houses in west Los Angeles. They entertained their friends and business associates in royal fashion, and nightclubbed with Hollywood celebrities. On quiet weekends they took their hundred-foot yacht south of the border and dined with Mexican president Miguel Alemán.

For a while, Hazel put Bill on the wagon, but in late 1964, on a U.S.-sponsored industrial-development mission in Ecuador, he went back to the booze. By the time he returned from Ecuador, he was wracked by cancer he failed to treat in its early stages. He died a few days after the New Year. With a trusted lawyer, Hazel sorted out his tangled affairs and in short order she was on a roll again, wheeling and dealing in the volatile lumber market. She bought a sawmill in Crescent City, California. She had another plant that was one of the nation's largest manufacturers of beveled siding and planned on yet another facility to recycle the wood chips and sawdust. She ran a lumber brokerage in Chicago and kept a large office in Beverly Hills.

An avid Los Angeles Dodgers fan, Hazel became friendly with the players (her third husband was a Dodger trainer), especially pitcher Don Drysdale. "I was always crazy about horses and Donnie was also interested in thoroughbred racing. For years he tried to talk me into buying a horse, and finally I gave in. I built a hundred-acre ranch outside of Anza called Rancho Rojo [red]

A VERY BRILLIANT FINANCIAL ANALYST

because it was all built with redwood. I had thirty-two claimers and yearlings. We also bought the 1962 Preakness winner, Greek Money, and put him out to stud. I paid $125,000 to buy him. We then had him syndicated, and we sold all the shares."

But all the high-pressure interests, Hazel says, proved "to be taxing on my health." In 1968 she suffered a heart attack. Her doctors ordered her to stay away from the office. During her convalescence over the next two years she watched helplessly as her business slowly dissipated in the hands of the incompetent executives she had hired. When the six-figure debts started to mount, her banks threatened to pull all of her financing.

Making matters even worse, her longtime lawyer and adviser died. She turned to a new counselor to find some way out of her difficulties. He gave her two dismal alternatives: either to declare bankruptcy or to turn over all her assets to a business manager who might be able to salvage something. Bankruptcy was out of the question for Hazel. Her most precious possessions were the artwork, crystal, and ceramics she had collected over the years, and she was ready to go to any lengths to keep them. Her only choice was a business manager–partner, and in late 1970 her lawyer introduced her to the man he felt was the perfect candidate.

Hazel remembers the first time she met Roy Nesseth in her lawyer's office. "I felt confident about Roy. He didn't seem like a fast or shady character. He had a nice wife and family—just like an honest workingman."

Roy assured Hazel that one way or another he could help her find a way out of bankruptcy. All she had to do was trust him. No official agreement between Roy and Hazel was made—no papers signed. "I guess that makes me look pretty foolish," Hazel says, "but I was desperate, and from the point of view of my creditors, this wasn't the straightest thing for me to do. There were liens against everything, and I was in no position to write up any arrangement to divide what I had left."

Hazel was to retire to her Palm Springs home (she had since sold the country-club house in Long Beach). Roy would make her mortgage payments and split anything he was able to clear above her debts.

• GRAND DELUSIONS •

At first, the deal seemed to be working, especially for Roy. He lived the lavish life-style Hazel had been accustomed to, using her memberships at the Balboa Bay Yacht Club and other posh playgrounds. Her Los Angeles apartment in the building known as Empire West became a popular party spot for Roy's friends. Over 1,500 square feet, with two bedrooms, the apartment was decorated with the finest antique furniture. Seventeenth- and eighteenth-century oil paintings hung on the walls. Porcelain figurines, gold statuary, and fine ceramic vases were displayed on tabletops and inside bookcases. The kitchen had a complete silver service and Royal Vienna china. Some of Roy's parties were a little louder than Empire West's management would have liked. Two of the most frequent visitors, building employees told Hazel, were John De Lorean and his father-in-law, Tom Harmon.

"Roy told me that the root of my problems had been the horses," Hazel remembers. "He said the first thing he did would be to get rid of them." Drysdale left, but Roy didn't get rid of the horses. "The next thing I know Roy is making the papers as some big horse-owner, putting my horses in races under his name."

Roy attempted to reorganize Hazel's other properties. He leased the sawmill to another firm, which promptly went bankrupt. He took some of the heavier construction equipment, refinanced it, and formed Pacific International Equipment, which also went belly up within a year. Nesseth explained to the IRS that his bookkeeper had left town, taking the company's records with him, so he could only estimate the loss. The horses were taking their toll, too. Feed bills went unpaid, and a trainer sued for his share of purses. Eventually Roy was forced to sell off most of the occupants of Nesseth Stables, Inc.

Roy's business troubles didn't surprise his old dealer buddy, George Williams. "Roy never finishes anything. He starts plenty of things, but then his attention starts to wander and he thinks about bigger stakes."

By early 1971, only months into her arrangement with Roy, Hazel could see there was trouble. The management at Empire West did not call just to complain about Roy's parties, but also to ask for rent payments. After four installments, Roy had stopped

A VERY BRILLIANT FINANCIAL ANALYST

paying her mortgage and car loans as well. Hazel insisted they meet to discuss the situation. Nesseth told her not to worry. He was very close to a big auto executive named John De Lorean, he said, and De Lorean might invest in the few holdings Hazel had left and save the day.

But Hazel would see no more money from Roy or De Lorean. For over a year he managed to string her along. "He always had a story," Hazel explains, "a typical car salesman. Something was just about to happen. Or all the problems were my lawyer's fault."

In fact, Hazel didn't need Roy's excuses to be suspicious of her lawyer. "The thing that got me was the fact he never asked me for a fee. What lawyer doesn't ask for a fee?"

Roy claimed he did pay the lawyer at least $1,000 in fees. But he also told the IRS that he paid the lawyer $4,000 more for eleven trucks and sundry equipment from Hazel's lumber business. While the price Roy paid for the trucks may seem small, the $1,000 he reported paying for all the contents of Hazel's Los Angeles apartment is even more ridiculous.

"By the middle of 1971," Hazel says, "I knew I had been taken." Since she felt powerless to take Roy to court, she decided to take the law into her own hands instead. "Let's just say I got Greek Money back. I won't say how, but I did get him back."

Hazel would sell the horse, and used her last stake from Greek Money to open a bar in Southgate. She is not as rueful today as most people hearing her story would expect her to be, but she does say, "There were times when I thought about taking a gun to myself or to Roy. Finally to remain sane, I had to pull a shade down over everything that happened and tell myself, 'You've got to start over.' "

George Williams does not think Hazel Upton is as much a victim of Roy's shenanigans as she says she is. He argues that their deal was much more complicated than she says.

However, Williams had his own falling out with Roy in 1971. "I had to let him go as manager. He just yells too much and treats the salesmen like dogs. It got to the point where I couldn't hire any help. Nobody wanted to work with him.

"Since Roy's left, we've sued each other back and forth. You always end up in court with that guy." Roy would get even angrier a few years later when Williams and his partner in San Diego allowed a creditor to buy out Roy's portion of their Toyota dealership.

"I can't say that knowing Roy was a bad experience. If he came in here today, we'd still sit down together and have a laugh. Roy taught me a lot about this business, especially about the internals of a new-car dealership.

"But the best you can do with Roy is break even. He's not a man to continue doing business with you for any period of time. In fact, when he was selling cars, he never stayed anywhere as long as the four years he spent with me. That tells you something.

"But as long as I've known him, he's never bought a car from me. He always wanted me to give up so much it wasn't worth selling the car to him. I can spend all day going around and around with him on a contract, but I can't win. He's too tough. That's his major problem, and it's something I told John De Lorean many times. Roy's just too tough."

College wit and clarinet player with his "men of note" (first row, third from left). (Courtesy of the Lawrence Institute of Technology, reproduction by Meteor Photo)

A budding engineer and playboy, De Lorean stands (third from right) with other members of the Lawrence Tech chapter of the American Society of Industrial Engineers, which he helped found. His mentor and protector, Professor Edwin Graeffe, sits fourth from the left. (Courtesy of the Lawrence Institute of Technology, reproduction by Meteor Photo)

De Lorean's childhood home on Detroit's East Side. He lived here with his mother until he first married at the age of 29. (Photo by Eric Keller)

Lawrence Tech boosters of "liberal and progressive action" support De Lorean in a losing battle for the Student Council presidency. (Courtesy of the Lawrence Institute of Technology, reproduction by Meteor Photo)

(*Above*) The old model John De Lorean, at age 40, stands behind the high-performance, overhead-camshaft engine. (Photo by Don Francisco by permission of *Hot Rod* magazine, Petersen Publications, reproduction by Meteor Photo)
(*Right*) De Lorean on the verge of separation and divorce from his second wife, Kelly Harmon, pictured above. (Photo by Arthur Shay)

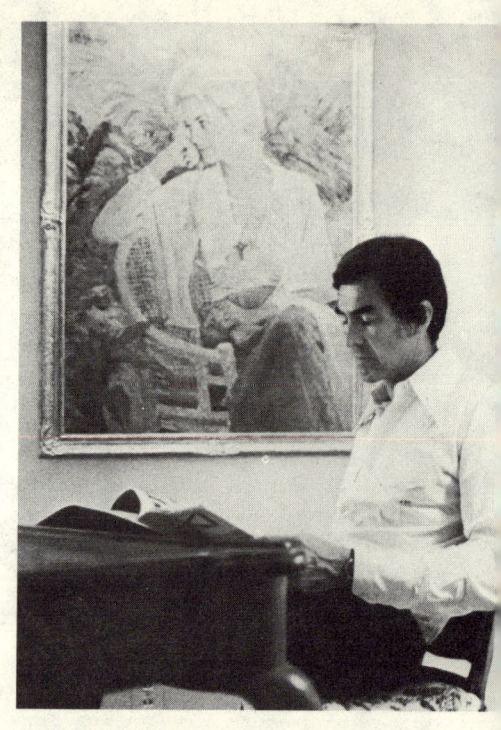

In 1979 with his third wife, Cristina Ferrare, and a prototype De Lorean car. A fashion model, she would soon become a board member of the De Lorean Motor Company. The car changed radically (especially the windows) before it finally went into production. (Photo by Tony Korody/SYGMA)

(*Right*) The new model John De Lorean at 47, after dieting, weight lifting, and face lifting. (Photo by Arthur Shay)

(*Below*) After De Lorean's arrest, hundreds of the unsold "silver beauties" sit in the warehouse yard in Bridgewater, New Jersey, just miles from his palatial Bedminster estate. (Photo by Diego Goldberg/SYGMA)

Falling from the good graces of the press: De Lorean in Los Angeles on the night of his October 19, 1982, arrest for possession with intent to distribute 100 kilograms of cocaine. (Photo by Eddie Sanderson/SYGMA)

· 8 ·
Four Bad Deals

After Roy Nesseth left Williams Chevrolet in 1971, the major source of his income would be John De Lorean. The official relationship between the two was to remain nebulous. Nesseth seldom declared himself to be an employee of De Lorean. Most often he reported income to the IRS as a self-employed consultant. But even before the De Lorean Motor Company got off the ground, Roy made a good living off the scraps of his friend's holdings—in some years earning over $100,000.

Roy started on the De Lorean dole with United Visuals, getting $32,000 from the company in 1972, and half that in 1973. Although his official employer was Milton B. Scott, Nesseth and De Lorean kept no secrets about whom Roy was really working for. During the same period he also received consulting fees from Mint Investment. A company run by United Visuals board member Myles Hymes, Mint had a major stake in a project involving the manufacture of helicopters. In his deposition in the United Visuals case, De Lorean testified that both he and Scott had an interest in Mint, and his own share was among the points of contention during his divorce from Kelly Harmon.

Roy never did get along very well with Milton Scott. Even before United Visuals, in 1971, Scott had hired Nesseth, as he later told the court, "so [Roy] could take home some money and I tried to get him involved in as many of my activities as possible. He worked in this 'troubleshooter' capacity for a couple of months and then did something that I did not care for and was discharged." But he did put Roy back on salary little more than a year after his discharge—out of pity, he says; others say at De Lorean's behest.

In his United Visuals deposition, De Lorean testified, "I know [Scott] treated Roy very badly." But even after Nesseth left United Visuals in the summer of 1973, he got another $20,000 from Scott. He was to scout out locations for the Florida dealership that De Lorean got in severance from General Motors, and eventually mind the store when business began. "[Roy] must have been down [to Lighthouse Point, Florida] twenty times," De Lorean says, "talking to Cadillac zone people."

The plans for the dealership supposedly went awry when De Lorean sold his franchise to a dealer from Indianapolis who evidently did not need Nesseth for a manager. But over the next five years, De Lorean found other ventures where he could use Roy's services. Four in particular stand out as examples of the De Lorean–Nesseth standard operating procedure. As each situation heated up with Roy seething at the center of the problems, De Lorean would retreat from personal involvement, finally contending that he was too busy to be either fully aware or concerned about his interests. Such diffidence was an ironic pose for a man who so vehemently criticized General Motors' refusal to recognize the full impact of its business on society.

The impact of De Lorean's enterprise was comparatively minuscule, but his business tactics managed to crush the livelihoods of many "little" people. Beyond highlighting a streak of unscrupulousness, these deals also raised serious questions about De Lorean's skill as a manager and entrepreneur outside the confines of General Motors—questions that cities, states, and nations didn't bother to answer before they clamored to give De Lorean millions of dollars to build his car company.

FOUR BAD DEALS

For once, the bright idea belonged to Jack Z. De Lorean.

It probably wasn't easy growing up in the shadow of his big brother—especially with a name that seemed to be no more than John's nickname. Jack didn't go to Cass Tech. He enrolled instead in the closest public high school. When Jack was drafted into the army, he didn't have John's luck to be assigned to stateside duty. Instead, the army sent him into the thick of the Korean war, an experience that left him physically and emotionally scarred. Eventually he did get an engineering degree and a job at Pontiac, but people attributed his hiring to John's influence and not his own qualifications.

And yet Jack, not John, was the one to think up Grand Prix of America. The idea was a cross between an amusement park and a competitive sport. People would get into miniature racing cars and cruise around a track, noting their speed against a large clock. They could then match their times with their friends' or just go out to beat their own best efforts. They'd pay a dollar for every lap they drove, and the track, with the help of floodlights, would be kept open all night long.

When Jack first suggested Grand Prix to his older brother, John was general manager of Chevrolet. He thought it was a brilliant idea, but he didn't want to stop with one track. America in the early Seventies was going franchise crazy—especially with fast food—and John was convinced that Grand Prix would be a natural franchise operation.

In the spring of 1972, the brothers incorporated. Jack filed as president. Documents identified John as just another board member, although he was in fact chairman of the board. He probably preferred to keep that title from his General Motors superiors. It was unquestionably John who found the first investors and raised the seed money for his younger brother's scheme. Some of the early directors were car dealers, and one of those, Norman Weise of Indianapolis, was eventually the buyer of the Lighthouse Point dealership. U. E. Patrick, the Michigan-based wildcat oil developer, was another investor John brought into the fold. Together the board raised $400,000—enough to buy a few cars and build a pilot track on land they leased from Rockwell International in Troy, Michigan.

Lawyer Thomas Payne remembers driving the few miles from his Bloomfield Hills office to see the track shortly after it opened. "People were lined up trying to get into there. You couldn't help but feel that this was an idea that could really take off."

Nevertheless, a few of the De Lorean brothers' original backers were pulling back, and in the spring of 1973, Payne joined a new team of prominent local backers capable of launching Grand Prix into the national arena. Among these were real estate developer Joseph Slavik, engineering contractor Reo Campian, and former Detroit Lions quarterback and current window manufacturer Jim Ninowski. All three were John De Lorean's neighbors in Bloomfield Hills, but they had also grown up with him and Jack on the east side of Detroit. They, too, had climbed out of the tough streets to become successful and—by the measure of their personal fortunes—were far more successful than John. Ninowski had played basketball with Jack in high school. Campian was a childhood friend of Charles (Chuck), the next eldest after John. He had kept in touch with Chuck. He knew John only on a professional basis from the few times his firm had done engineering work for Pontiac.

But John called Campian himself and asked him to invest. Reo asked his accountant's advice, but soon after, Campian says, De Lorean called again. "He said that if I was getting in, I had to get in immediately to keep this thing going."

Together, the new shareholders invested over $1.3 million in Grand Prix of America. But as the crowds around the Troy track continued to grow, Jack began to question the strategy of selling franchises. When a group from Malibu, California, approached Jack to buy a franchise he turned them down (they later went ahead and started two tracks of their own, and sold out for a considerable figure to Warner Communications). The new plan was for Grand Prix to own tracks around the country and forget about the franchises. While some board members questioned the shift, John and the majority went along with the president's decision. Real estate developer Slavik helped Jack find possible locations for tracks in other parts of the country. John approached the realtor who found his Idaho ranch to scout sites in California.

Despite all the bold plans, before 1973 was over Grand Prix had already started to run out of gas. "It seemed like a lot of money was eaten up by overhead," lawyer Tom Payne remembers, "especially in legal fees. Some expenses weren't very necessary either and, to be honest, the board members didn't pay that much attention at first. We didn't invest to be managers. Still, by the end of the year we were all wasting a lot of time holding meetings at the Grand Prix office."

John De Lorean had not been very active in the day-to-day operations of the company. On those few occasions when he did appear, he seemed sullen and distracted. Jack, a much more outgoing personality, was clearly in charge, and some board members felt that was the problem. "I think everyone liked Jack," Payne says. "He's truly a wonderful human being, but they doubted his ability to manage a business."

As finances grew thinner, recriminations started to fly. It was then, in one heated meeting when John wasn't present, that Jack tried to explain his problems. What he said would shock the other investors. "He blew the whistle on John," Payne says. "He told us that his brother was dipping his hand in the till—that John couldn't be trusted."

Years later, Payne would get some perspective on John De Lorean that would have kept him out of Grand Prix. "Shortly before he died, I was sitting by a pool with Ed Cole," he says, "and Ed Cole told me that John didn't leave by his own accord. He said, 'I told John to either resign or get fired.' " But during his first days with Grand Prix, Payne, like the other investors, found Jack's accusations hard to believe, and some questioned the younger brother's mental balance.

Jim Ninowski, who came from a big family himself, was appalled and outraged at Jack's behavior. "I grew up believing that you stick by your brother no matter what. You don't tell on him behind his back."

But the impact of the sibling squabble on Grand Prix's future would pale next to the Arab oil embargo. "The fuel crisis came just when we were geared up to start our tracks," Payne says. "The timing couldn't have been worse. In fact, it was almost comical. Here we were trying to go national with recreation based on a gas-powered vehicle to be driven at night around a track illuminated by floodlights. All our hopes for any sort of big-time success just went up in smoke."

By 1974, unable to make payments even on its Troy lease, Grand Prix appeared headed for bankruptcy. John had no trouble putting the blame for the company's travails on Jack's head. (Years later, when a related matter came to court for trial, De Lorean freely testified that Grand Prix failed because of "my brother's mismanagement." He went further to say that Jack's "behavior wasn't completely rational," explaining, "My brother spent a couple of years in a mental institution after the Korean war. . . .") The only way to salvage the operation, De Lorean told the other investors, was to bring in new management on a full-time basis.

"John said he had just the man to get the venture back on track," Payne remembers. "He told us, 'It's a guy who worked for me in California. He's a real go-getter, a street fighter—he gets things done.' And then he introduced us to Roy Nesseth.

"At our first meeting, Roy was his old charming self, and we were all favorably impressed. Besides, other than what Jack had told us, we had no reason to believe that John was not an upstanding, competent businessman."

But there was no way to save Grand Prix. An original backer, car dealer Norman Weise, pulled out. ("We were surprised when John gave him his money back," one investor says. "We figured he must have had something on John." Weise had bought De Lorean's Florida Cadillac franchise.) To make matters worse, the De Lorean brothers were at each other's throats. Campian prevailed on the middle brother, Chuck, a successful Cadillac dealer in Cleveland, to come to Detroit and help mediate. While Chuck had had to live in John's shadow, too—most people in the auto business believed his older brother had gotten him his franchise— no one denied that Chuck had proved to be a savvy businessman in his own right. Campian believed that he, more than John or Jack, could best put the whole venture back on track.

FOUR BAD DEALS

In March 1974, with Chuck as a new investor, and Jack off the board, the remaining backers reorganized what assets they had left into a new company they called GPA Systems. This entity would concentrate on selling franchises and get away from track ownership. Roy Nesseth was appointed GPA Systems' first president.

Within days of the reorganization, Roy telephoned an urgent message to the investors from a phone booth in California. In the optimistic period before the oil crisis, Grand Prix had taken an option on a potential track site in Pomona, California. Now Roy gushed that the parcel was too valuable to let slip away. The owner already had an offer of over $100,000 more than the Grand Prix option price. But they had only two days to exercise the option and make the $65,000 down payment or the deal was off. Speaking for the other investors, Payne admits, "We're embarrassed to say that we never did take a look at that property before we made the payment, but Roy couldn't say enough about it. He told us it was a 'can't lose proposition—a real touchdown.' There were several colleges in the area and he felt the students alone would keep us in business."

By this time, only five of the Detroit investors were still game enough to sink more money into the deal. But they decided to create yet a third entity, Cal Prix, that would do no more than own and operate the Pomona track. Against their better judgment, they asked John De Lorean to join them. Milt Scott, De Lorean told them, would loan him the money to exercise their option before the deadline. (De Lorean later testified that he actually took $65,000 from an account he shared with Scott, without first asking his permission.) In early April 1974, the five Detroit investors rushed to wire their share of the down payment to Roy and De Lorean so they could meet the option deadline.

When the dust cleared, Roy reported that he had secured the site, but not in the name of Cal Prix. Evidently the seller did not feel obligated to a new entity, so Roy said he was forced to put the property in the name of Grand Prix of America. Just to make sure that a Grand Prix creditor didn't swoop down and seize the investment, De Lorean took out two deeds of trust on the property worth $100,000. If any claim was made, De Lorean would have first dibs.

The scenario sounded credible to the investors. In a few months they transferred the deed to Cal Prix and thought nothing more of De Lorean's liens. Nesseth was to supervise construction of the Pomona track for the Cal Prix owners. He would then use it as a model to sell the GPA Systems franchises.

But the Cal Prix investors soon had doubts about Nesseth's business expertise and honesty. First of all, the Pomona site was not the showplace he had promised, but an almost industrial setting in the sort of rough neighborhood that would chase suburban families away. In the eyes of Jim Ninowski, "There couldn't have been a worse spot in the entire state."

The Detroit backers had further worries about the way Roy was dipping into the lean GPA Systems coffers. His contract called for a $25,000 annual salary and $7,500 in commissions. But informed estimates had his wages running as high as $64,000 a year, with almost as much in expenses. (They eventually sued Nesseth for the missing funds in a Michigan court.) To their dismay, John De Lorean didn't seem interested in Roy's shenanigans. "We'd try to reach him on the phone," Payne says, "and John would never get back to us."

Jim Ninowski was not about to take De Lorean's brush-off. On one occasion, De Lorean's secretary put him on hold for fifteen minutes, and then got back to tell him that De Lorean was tied up and couldn't speak with him that day. Ninowski got into his car and drove to De Lorean's Bloomfield Hills office. When the former quarterback reached the secretary's desk, he didn't ask for an appointment, but burst through De Lorean's door. "He wasn't too happy to see me," Ninowski recalls, "and in a few words, I let him know what I thought of him. At one point I said that Roy Nesseth was raping him and the company. I told him that if he continued to associate with Roy and ignored what he was doing, then John De Lorean was as bad as Roy Nesseth. All he said was 'Thanks, I'll look into it.' "

The final straw for the Cal Prix investors came when it was time to finance the purchase of new cars for the Pomona track.

FOUR BAD DEALS

Each put up a $26,000 letter of credit. Nesseth sent them a telegram confirming that De Lorean had done the same. In fact, De Lorean did no such thing. "That was it," Ninowski says. "We wanted nothing more to do with him."

But it wasn't that easy to shake De Lorean. As the new track's construction neared completion, Cal Prix's attorneys conducted a title search on the Pomona property and found that De Lorean still had liens on the deed. De Lorean told Payne that his lawyer had merely forgotten to remove the liens and he'd see the matter was attended to. But as weeks went by, he claimed he could no longer find the documents to make the change.

When Payne suggested a method for canceling the deeds of trust, suddenly De Lorean replied with the demand that he receive $100,000 first, claiming he deserved repayment for several out-of-pocket expenses.

In Payne's eyes this was extortion, and he let De Lorean know as much in an angry letter. De Lorean told him not to get concerned. He felt there was still some amicable way they could handle this. "I can remember John saying, 'If I'm not entitled to the money then I don't want it.' "

De Lorean asked only that Payne meet with his lawyer, Thomas Kimmerly. De Lorean promised that if his lawyer was satisfied with Payne's explanation, he'd turn over the deeds of trust.

Payne met with Kimmerly and painstakingly took him through every step of De Lorean's investment in Cal Prix and Grand Prix. Kimmerly listened impassively and then explained that he was not empowered to make a decision one way or another. Despite De Lorean's promise, he did not have the deeds of trust. However, Nesseth was coming to town and might have brought the deeds along. He asked Payne to return the next day and meet with Roy.

When Payne came back to Kimmerly's office for the appointment he did not find the charming Roy of yesteryear. This was a sour, belligerent Nesseth who told him that De Lorean had $100,000 coming. Either he got the cash or he kept the deeds. Payne asked to see the expenses to back up De Lorean's claim. "Roy then said, 'I'll testify that you guys gave me the money to buy the property and I kept it. I'll say that John had to come up with the whole $65,000 for the down payment himself. You don't have any proof that you paid for it. All your checks were to me and John. There's nothing you can do about that.' "

Astounded by Nesseth's brazen threat, Payne looked to Kimmerly, but the lawyer sat impassively. "I'm sure there are some people who would have jumped over the table and wrung Roy's neck," Payne says. "I knew enough about the law to contain myself. Whatever may have possessed them, they were forcing us to go to court, and it was a black-and-white case that they were bound to lose."

Cal Prix filed suit against De Lorean in 1976, but the matter was not to reach trial until March of 1982. Payne traveled to a Los Angeles courtroom to give testimony. Shortly before he left Michigan, the judge called to tell him that De Lorean had offered to remove the deeds of trust for a $40,000 payment. "I told the judge that we didn't find that an acceptable settlement. We owed him absolutely nothing for those deeds and [nothing] was the most we were going to pay."

De Lorean spent the first morning of the trial under tense and what proved to be embarrassing cross-examination. While claiming to have forgotten most of the details concerning Grand Prix, De Lorean did adamantly maintain that he had secured a lien on the deeds to guarantee repayment for certain expenses he had bankrolled. But Payne's lawyer would then show the judge that those expenses came *after* De Lorean secured the lien—not before. Over the lunch break, De Lorean and his lawyer decided not to go any further. He agreed to release the deeds to Cal Prix along with any stock he had left in the company.

Since the settlement, the Cal Prix group has put their track up for sale. At best, they hope to recoup some of their losses. But almost everyone involved with Grand Prix agrees that the man hurt most by the venture's failure was Jack De Lorean.

One of the earliest officers of Grand Prix remembers hearing from Jack shortly after the whole business went bankrupt. "Jack gave me a call to say he was going to resurrect Grand Prix—with God's help. It was very strange. Of course there was no way, with or without God, that he'd ever bring back that company. But Grand Prix was probably the one great dream of his life. I guess he couldn't accept the fact that it was dead."

"I'm the best mechanic in the world," says Walter C. Avrea, who is not a man given to idle boasts. At fifty-nine, with no more than a high school education, he has proved himself to be a genius of the internal combustion engine. A handful of automotive inventions that he patented himself have made him a man of considerable wealth. One such device—his coolant recovery system—is so basic and so significant that it establishes him as the most successful independent automotive inventor of the last fifty years. It was exactly the sort of invention that should have let the succeeding years slip by for "Pete" Avrea in peace and luxury. But then he met John De Lorean and Roy Nesseth. Within months he'd be in the fight of his life to wrest back control of his valuable patents.

Nothing ever came easy to Avrea. A tall, lanky, balding man, he still speaks with the west-Texas drawl of his childhood. As he grew up he had to scrape for a living. He followed his family as they moved around the South and Southwest. His first real job came as an apprentice mechanic for Caterpillar land-movers. During the war he served as a mechanic gunner in the air force, and afterward returned to fixing Cats in the copper mines.

His luckiest break came in Texas, when he met his wife, Shirley. A pretty, brown-haired woman, originally from Cleveland, she would refine some of the roughness out of Pete, and also give him the ambition to reach for greater things than most of his working buddies expected out of life.

They moved to Pico Rivera, California, where Avrea got a job fixing trucks for Navajo Freight Lines. In a year, at the age of twenty-five, Pete was the shop superintendent—a job that had its occasional frustrations. "I was never satisfied with just replacing a part," Pete remembers. "I always wanted to find out what caused the failure." Avrea gave his ideas to truck manufacturers like Peterbilt and Cummins.

"I told him he was crazy," Shirley says. "They were getting his ideas for nothing. At least once, Pete had to try to get a patent." The couple took a second lien out on their $8,000 tract house. With two children to feed, Shirley was forced to go back to work while Pete fiddled industriously with prototypes in their one-car garage.

His first patent would come with deceptive ease. His idea was to equip trucks with a warning light that would signal the driver before he lost his air brakes, resulting in major damage. In 1955, the U.S. Patent Office accepted his application for the Reserve Brake Indicator (over the years he'd discover how rare that initial acceptance was), but then Avrea had to find someone to produce and market the invention. He chose an aggressive young manufacturer, who also turned out to be an addicted gambler. When authorities discovered that he had embezzled over $1 million from his company, he committed suicide. Avrea's invention died along with him.

He persevered and patented a new parking brake for trucks that he called the Anchor Lok. It took three years and untold numbers of trips to Washington before Avrea could patent the device. When he did, in 1960, he finally struck pay dirt. From then on he joined the tiny band of inventors who can actually live off their patents.

In 1965, as he tinkered with his wife's Buick, he hit on an idea for an auto part that would dwarf any other mechanical device he had ever thought of. Car makers had always had difficulties keeping engines cool. In recent years, power-hungry accessories like air conditioners only put more strain on cooling systems. The water-filled radiator was really the last big mechanical breakthrough in engine cooling, but that system was far from perfect. As the coolant circulated through the engine, it didn't uniformly quench all the hot surfaces of the engine's chambers, and the rubber hoses funneling the water from the radiator to the engine often corroded after only a few months of use. As a result, engines overheated and radiators boiled over.

Bubbles, Avrea discovered, were at the heart of the cooling

problem. Too much air was getting into the system, creating bubbles that didn't allow cooling liquid to reach metal surfaces. Oxygen was also the culprit in hose corrosion. Pete's solution was to seal off the entire cooling system. Instead of permitting the cap to release pressure when steam built up in a hot radiator, Avrea put a little plastic reservoir bottle next to the radiator to catch the overflow, and he hermetically sealed the cap to prevent any air from getting into the system. The results were dramatic. He did not just reduce corrosion and heat but, without the bubbles, the coolant circulated with less vibration, even further diminishing wear and tear on engine parts.

Avrea first filed for his patent in 1967. It took five years before it was finally granted, but then it was reissued shortly thereafter—a medal of honor from the U.S. Patent Office recognizing and further protecting the pathbreaking nature of the invention.

Pete didn't need anyone to tell him what he had wrought with his Coolant Recovery System, and he wasn't about to entrust it to some strange and untrustworthy manufacturer. The plastic parts for a coolant kit were so simple that almost anyone could go into business to manufacture them. In Tempe, Arizona, his older brother, Bill, had gotten fed up with his job, and offered to form a corporation to start molding the parts for his invention. In 1968, Bill incorporated Saf-Gard Products. For sales manager, and eventually president, he turned to Norm Bernier, a former air force colonel who had been a longtime auto buff. Pete moved to Tempe and set up his workshop in their factory.

Almost immediately orders came in. Some were from national chains of auto-parts stores; others from the car makers in Detroit—especially Ford and American Motors—that were ready to install Pete's invention as original equipment. Then, a huge order came from Chevrolet in 1971 and 1972, when John De Lorean was still general manager. The division was stuck with the Vega, one of the most poorly designed cars in decades. Within months after the car's introduction, Chevy had been deluged with consumer complaints about the aluminum engine overheating. Production was choreographed so Avrea's product could be added on the assembly line. Some kits were even flown in overnight to the Lordstown, Ohio, factory.

Within a year, Bill Avrea moved out of his two-thousand-square-foot plant and leased five times the space. But despite the orders, Pete and his brother quickly discovered that mass-producing relatively inexpensive products was no way to turn a fast profit. Saf-Gard president Bernier had estimated that just counting used cars, the potential worldwide market for the system was one billion. But it was hard enough to turn out thousands, and the company's production levels were just about paying the bills.

Meanwhile, other manufacturers had stepped in to infringe on Avrea's patent—some so bold as to advertise their forgeries as coolant recovery systems. Besides taking money from the inventor, they were also putting out shoddy merchandise that seriously detracted from the patent's reputation. The worst offender was a company called Service Parts that distributed its imitation through the National Auto Parts Association. Even some loyal customers in Detroit became so discouraged when their orders went unfilled that they started producing the kits themselves. Pete had loaned his brother money to help pay for the caps, but now it seemed that their major supplier was also ready to assemble and sell the system as well.

The Avreas started legal action, but they did not have the resources to send out a squad of attorneys after all the infringers. By the spring of 1974, counterfeit kits had driven Pete's brother into bankruptcy. He looked instead to sublicense his patent to a large manufacturer. But Norm Bernier gave Pete another idea. He talked of a Detroit auto executive who had just left General Motors—a legend in his own time. All they needed, Bernier told Pete, was to have a man with De Lorean's connections in the auto industry, and Saf-Gard Products would take off into the stratosphere.

In later years, De Lorean would claim that he had never heard of Avrea or his inventions until Avrea came persistently knocking at his door. After the inventor's relentless entreaties, De Lorean says, he finally took a look at his cooling system.

But evidence later entered in court showed that the first contact with De Lorean was a letter sent by Norm Bernier in the last week of April 1974. De Lorean received the letter on a Tuesday and immediately called the president's home, leaving a message with his answering service. He was indeed very interested in Avrea's product. By Friday, May 3, De Lorean was in Pete's workshop.

"Until Norm told me about him, I had never heard of John De Lorean," Avrea says today. "I wasn't the type who followed the auto industry closely."

But upon meeting De Lorean, Avrea felt he had found the perfect person to handle his inventions. "One of the first things John said was, 'You know what you're offering me, Pete? You're offering me a twenty-year monopoly on an auto cooling system. No one in the history of this industry has ever had control of something this important.'"

When they walked through Pete's workshop De Lorean continued to pour on the accolades. Avrea's suppliers had had difficulty providing him with an airtight metal radiator cap, so he had invented a plastic one composed of only four pieces—compared to the sixteen in conventional caps. Just the cap, De Lorean told Pete, could make them both a fortune.

Yet De Lorean's compliments did not impress Pete as much as one negative comment. They were both looking at a prototype of another Avrea invention that had a patent pending. "He told me that the simulator wouldn't work, and he was absolutely right. I didn't want to give away all my secrets in the demonstration model. Right then and there I could see that he really did understand what I was talking about. I went home and told my wife that De Lorean was the smartest man I had ever met."

Before De Lorean left Phoenix, he had Pete write a letter of intent in his Scottsdale hotel room. They would work out the details, but De Lorean agreed to establish a company that would produce and market the coolant recovery system as well as sue the patent's infringers.

Their courtship continued at breakneck speed after De Lorean left, although two ominous incidents would occur over the next few weeks that should have put Avrea on his guard. The first concerned De Lorean's choice as president of his new company. He told Avrea that there was a fellow named Roy Nesseth who had done wonderful work for him in California. Nesseth would fly to Phoenix and meet with Avrea and his lawyers to nail down the details of their agreement.

Pete arranged to meet Roy at a Roadway Inn near the Tempe plant for breakfast at 9:00 A.M. and brought along two lawyers to advise him. Nesseth had not chosen to stay at the motel, but instead had booked into Mountain Shadows, a fancy Scottsdale resort over thirty minutes away. He finally showed up for breakfast two hours late.

Pete, who admits he has a "short fuse," was outraged. "I said, 'Mr. Nesseth, I've had two lawyers waiting here with me. Do you know what that's costing me?'

"Roy just laughed and said, 'I got a gal spread-eagled back at Mountain Shadows. Do you know what that's costing *me?*' "

Pete was not amused. He went to the nearest pay phone and called De Lorean and filled him in on Roy's explanation for his tardiness. "I told De Lorean that if this was the man who would take charge of the company, then there was no way I'd make a deal with him."

De Lorean apologized profusely and told Roy to take the next plane out of Phoenix. He assured Avrea that he would find someone else for the job, and negotiations continued. But before the end of May, the sky seemed to open up with the sort of manna from Detroit that made everyone forget about Nesseth. General Motors sent Saf-Gard Products an urgent request for 167,000 coolant recovery kits—a purchase worth $750,000.

Avrea now insists that De Lorean knew about the imminent Chevrolet windfall before he flew down to Phoenix to meet with Pete and sign a letter of intent. De Lorean has replied that the timing of the GM order was merely a coincidence.

Neither the GM order, nor the scene with Nesseth made Avrea unusually suspicious. Early in June, he went to Detroit to sign an agreement with Saf-Gard *Systems*, the new company De Lorean created to distribute his invention. The contract assured Avrea of a royalty equal to 5 percent of all sales or a minimum of $5,000 a month. He was guaranteed access to Systems' books, and information about any licensing of the patent to another company. Avrea went even further and assigned his other patents—including the plastic radiator cap—to Systems under the same arrangement as the coolant recovery kits. De Lorean, however, did not sign a thing. Those honors were done by his choice as Saf-Gard Systems first president—a young Detroiter with previous experience in the auto industry.

Before the new team could get rolling, Systems had to sign an agreement with the invention's old manufacturer, Bill Avrea's Saf-Gard Products, and negotiations dragged on into the fall. De Lorean would manage to secure the company's assets for only a promise of royalties a year down the line. In fact, his new company would continue to use Products' checking account, checks, and stationery throughout its short history.

De Lorean later claimed that he put $100,000 into Saf-Gard Systems to get it off the ground. But the company was evidently capitalized with no more than the $750,000 purchase order from GM.

Avrea would not have much use for De Lorean's choice as Systems' president. The man seemed bent on commuting to Phoenix from Detroit rather than setting up permanent residence. He showed no commitment, either, to learn the business, and at one point signed a contract to supply the plastic parts of the kit at a price lower than the production cost.

Pete was even more concerned by Systems' strategy for dealing with patent infringers. De Lorean seemed more inclined to settle than sue. De Lorean later explained that Avrea was too anxious to go to court. Calling him "eccentric," he said, "His inventions were like his children. He wanted to tie up too much money going after the companies he felt were infringing on the patent. We had no room left to operate."

De Lorean would also complain about the minimum royalty he had to pay Pete. However, no one had forced him into the contract. Years later, he'd admit, "I woke up and found out I made a very bad deal. When I met Pete he [was] such a big open-face, firm-handshake type, I fell in love. That was stupid."

In April 1975, De Lorean sent a telegram to Avrea declaring that it was "not possible to raise funds or operate Systems." Instead, he had decided to license out the invention to other manufacturers for $200,000. Pete, of course, refused to accept that option. De Lorean's telegram, his lawyer told him, could be read as defaulting on their agreement, and Avrea could get his patents back to do the licensing himself. Actually, Pete had considered breaking with De Lorean even before the telegram arrived. Contrary to the agreement, he hadn't received a financial report in months. Also, he had strong suspicions that De Lorean had already licensed his patent to another company behind his back—another stipulated reason to cancel their contract.

He replied to De Lorean by sending his own telegram that their agreement was canceled. But De Lorean was not ready to say goodbye. He pleaded with Pete to reconsider, promising to borrow some more money to keep the company afloat. Avrea insisted that he also find another president, and De Lorean agreed.

But over the summer the situation deteriorated. In August, De Lorean called Avrea to tell him he had settled with General Motors. Although Chevrolet had been one of Saf-Gard's best customers, there was evidence that GM was building additional kits on its own. As a result, De Lorean had his former employer over a barrel. It was a situation he should have relished and exploited to Saf-Gard's full benefit, but when he emerged from negotiations with GM, he had won only $130,000 for past violations. He further permitted the company to make kits on its own in the future.

Pete thought the settlement was ridiculously low, and he let De Lorean know it. There was no way, he said, that he'd sign off on that deal. De Lorean convinced him to come up to Detroit and discuss the matter further. When they last met, Avrea recalls, "I really let him have it. I pounded the table and told him what a lousy businessman he was, and every time I hit the table, he dropped a little lower in his chair. Finally he said, 'Pete, you're right.'

• FOUR BAD DEALS •

"I still went ahead and signed that fool settlement. First of all, he promised me that he'd finally fire that president [who was commuting from Detroit], and then he assured me that GM [had] privately guaranteed him the right to make 50 percent of all the kits they [would need]. He told me that he still had friends over at GM who owed him some favors. He claimed that he was the one who got Chevy's general manager his job. I don't know whether any of that's true, but I do know that GM never let us make any additional kits they used."

After he left De Lorean's office that day, Pete would never see another dollar from De Lorean or Saf-Gard Systems. While De Lorean had fired the first president and replaced him with a former top executive of the Bendix Corporation, there would be little impact on the company. The new president visited Phoenix even less often than his predecessor. He finally admitted that he was only a consultant and had more pressing interests elsewhere.

All at once Pete's worst fears for his inventions were realized. He stopped receiving his monthly royalty checks. He learned from Systems employees that De Lorean had settled with a major infringer for a royalty of only ten cents a kit. Even worse, the molds from his plastic radiator cap were missing. When they were eventually returned they were damaged. Previously, Avrea had approached the Celanese Corporation, a plastics conglomerate, to consider producing the cap. But, behind his back, De Lorean went even further with the company and secured a $200,000 development loan. No one ever found out what happened to that money. The two Celanese executives responsible for the loan later left the company.

In December 1975, Avrea sent De Lorean another termination notice. At that time, De Lorean would later testify in a deposition, he decided to wash his hands of the entire venture: "As soon as I saw it was a pain in the ass and a lot of people were trying to nickel-shit [me] to death, I said I don't want anything to do with it. . . . [There are] all kinds of files and records that will show the harassment and hassle and baloney. It was just too much crap."

At the end of the month, De Lorean claimed he had turned all his stock in Saf-Gard Systems over to Roy Nesseth for one dollar. Roy became president and sole stockholder. In papers they would soon file in court, Avrea and his lawyers called the move a "sham," intended only "to insulate De Lorean from liability or publicity when the true extent of the company's financial difficulties become public."

Both Nesseth and De Lorean claimed Saf-Gard Systems owed as much as $900,000 to creditors. But Avrea knew of at least $1.5 million that had gone into the company, and he wanted some accounting of what had become of those funds. In January, as was his contractual right, he sent his accountant over to the factory to look at the books, but all records had been removed. Nevertheless, some evidence of the firm's fiscal ill health remained: the phone had been disconnected, rent was long overdue, and creditors' notices were piling up in the mail basket. There wasn't even money left for plastic stock, bringing kit production to a virtual standstill.

Despite the fiscal constraints the company faced, Nesseth did not cut down on his lavish life-style. He went to the fanciest restaurants in Phoenix and kept his girlfriend in a Scottsdale resort. "We were getting bills from that hotel for $1800 a week," one of Systems' top executives remembers. "There was no real effort to record or justify expenses like that."

At one point, when Nesseth couldn't get a local manufacturer to make the plastic reservoir bottles, he shipped the molds to California. "He never did get anything out of that," the executive remembers. "Roy would often take drastic action and accomplish nothing."

Nesseth made it clear to his Systems employees that the company was not long for the world. "He told us he had come to straighten out the mess for John De Lorean and then he'd have to go elsewhere. I remember him telling me, 'I wear the black hat.' " Fulfilling that role, Nesseth brought in a locksmith to lock Avrea out of the factory and even his own workshop.

The ultimate Nesseth black-hat move would come when one creditor finally forced Saf-Gard Systems to sell the coolant recovery kits in stock to satisfy their debt. A company came to the auction and bid for the entire lot of 6,000 kits, but could only truck away half of its purchase that afternoon. When they returned the next morning, Nesseth refused to let them in to pick up the remainder. That night, at 9:00, Roy's men tried to sneak off with the kits. Someone tipped off the creditor and the Tempe police were called in to stop the truck.

Avrea had much more trouble catching Nesseth and De Lorean red-handed. He filed suit in February 1976. It would take two and a half years before the case finally came to a preliminary hearing. Both Nesseth and De Lorean practiced continuous and ingenious delays. They were accomplished subpoena-dodgers, and process servers had to chase them across the country before they could catch them. De Lorean kept telling the judge that he was no longer involved in Saf-Gard Systems' business and should not have to travel to Phoenix to testify. The judge, eventual Supreme Court justice Sandra Day O'Connor, did not accept his excuse and threatened to issue a bench warrant.

Avrea remembers De Lorean's first deposition as particularly rancorous. It was given in his lawyer's office. At one point, during a testy cross-examination, Avrea says that De Lorean threatened to knock his lawyer's head off. "I told John that before he did that, he'd have to deal with me. My lawyer then was a small man who was also ill. I'm not small and I'm not afraid of anybody. That made De Lorean calm down, but before the day was over he said to me, 'I'll tie you up in court until your patents run out.'"

For a while, it looked as though De Lorean could make good on his threat. Of all his stalling tactics, the most brilliant was simply not to pay his crew of rather gullible Phoenix lawyers. The delays mounted as each legal team withdrew and their successors asked for time to bone up on the case. In just one year, De Lorean and Nesseth went through three sets of counsel.

Finally, the suit was set for a hearing the day after Labor Day 1978. Two months before, Shirley had gotten a call from De Lorean. He began by sounding cordial, she says, "but then he started telling me that Pete better settle before this went to court. He told me that if Pete didn't settle, Nesseth would go to the company that was producing another of Pete's inventions and get them to stop payments. Then he said, 'And you know, Roy Nesseth can be a very mean man.' I then said, 'Mr. De Lorean, are you threatening us?' That got him very upset. He said he wasn't doing anything of the kind.''

A few days later the Avreas would get another strange, but anonymous call. The phone rang in Pete's shop at 11:00 in the morning. "It was a guy with some kind of foreign accent," Pete remembers. "He said, 'You're a dead man. You are dead before September fourth. Don't make any plans for Labor Day weekend.' Then he hung up. He called again two days later.''

Pete Avrea was there for the hearing after Labor Day, but he never did go to trial. Ill with diabetes and valley fever, Avrea had no more stomach for the case. "I lost four years on the life of my patents, and I had to put De Lorean totally out of my own life.''

He would pay De Lorean $494,000 to get his patents back. Half the money came out of an escrow fund, the rest De Lorean would collect from the cheap settlements he had made with infringers.

Shirley Avrea says, "You can't imagine how much it hurt to give De Lorean that money, knowing that he never deserved it and should have paid us. Even today I get tremendously resentful and angry just at the sound of his name.''

But in many ways, the Avreas have gotten the last laugh. When he finally gained control of his patents, Pete pursued his case against one infringer through the courts. A judge eventually decided that he deserved $11 for every kit sold behind his back. De Lorean had settled with far worse infringers for ten cents a kit. If the judge's penalty had been computed for General Motors' infringement alone, the company would have owed Saf-Gard Systems over $30 million.

In his deposition to Avrea's lawyers, De Lorean declared that the automotive industry has "never made a substantial award to anybody on any patent." But six weeks after he settled with De Lorean, Avrea got a $1 million settlement from Ford. And when he won his favorable judgment against the infringer, the car companies and parts suppliers practically fell all over themselves to offer him very substantial awards. And Avrea has yet to cash in on the real jackpot. He still expects the biggest settlements or judgments from some large Japanese automakers.

"If John had been anywhere near a cagey businessman," Pete says, "he could have had this and more. I figure, conservatively, he would have made $60 million from Saf-Gard Systems. All it took was a little patience. His problem was that he wanted to go for the quick buck. But look what he gave up in return."

One day during the summer of 1959, Clark Higley stood in south Idaho mud up to his ankles and looked out at a flat rocky field covered with sagebrush. It was the most beautiful sight he had ever seen. This 173-acre piece of scrub, near the town of Rupert, had been Higley's prize in a state homestead lottery, and was valued at $20,000. But to Clark's wife, Colleen, even that price seemed too high. To get there, the couple had driven for miles through a fierce rainstorm, going over roads that were little more than muddy ruts. Now Colleen contemplated leaving Idaho Falls behind to settle on a scrubby patch of ground in the middle of nowhere. "I stayed in the car," Colleen says, "and bawled my head off."

For a few months, Clark lived alone on his land in a sheep-camp wagon. He pulled out most of the sagebrush by hand, and then he got started building a barn, and finally the house. An aerial photo taken later in that year shows two plain rectangular structures—looking much like the house pieces in a Monopoly game—surrounded by flat tilled fields, cut only by a dirt road. Less than ten years later, an aerial picture of the spread would look like it came from a different part of the planet. There'd be a new home and barn in this shot, and a tool shed. Grass grows around the house and a few lawn chairs are scattered in the yard. A boat on a trailer sits alongside the trucks.

Over the years, he bought more land around his property as it became available, eventually building up over 500 irrigated acres. His big crop was potatoes. "The idea was to work a piece of land and then take the money from the crops and buy the piece of land next to it. I never wanted to lease someone else's land."

His two sons became farmers too, and together the three men kept expanding their boundaries. Clark made enough money to buy two gift boutiques for Colleen to run in Burley and Rupert. They built another house for themselves in Heyburn on the Snake River. But Higley's fortune was amassed with the backbreaking labor of farming. In 1975, at the age of forty-eight, he wanted to wake up in the mornings to another challenge. "Every farmer," he says, "wants to be a rancher. When you're breeding cattle, there's more prestige. When you're farming, you're a dirt digger."

With a local real estate agent, Clark started scouting the state for a cattle ranch. He didn't look long before he found the Pine Creek Ranch in Salmon, almost two hundred miles north of Rupert. Higley is a man with a chiseled, hawklike visage, and his pale blue eyes mist over as he describes the Pine Creek Ranch he saw in 1975. "It was a gorgeous place," he says. "That's why we got in so much trouble trying to own it."

He also saw the ranch as a way to keep the family together. It was big enough for his two sons and their families too, and if the boys came along, Clark felt he could manage Pine Creek without hiring much outside help.

Colleen was not so anxious to leave her stores in southern Idaho and get stranded in Salmon, an area, Colleen says, that made Rupert look cosmopolitan. "In Salmon," she says, "you're one hundred and fifty miles away from anything."

The ranch lay in a narrow valley scalloped out between the Bitterroot Mountains on the Montana border to the east, and the smaller Lemhi range to the west. The Lemhi River winds through the valley, swelling and shrinking alongside the two-lane state highway that is the region's main road. Explorers Lewis and Clark stumbled along the same trail, almost meeting their match in the dense forests and treacherous mountain passes of mid-Idaho. Today, even stretches alongside a snowed-in highway don't appear to have been made any tamer by the intervening centuries.

The Pine Creek Ranch extended for miles on either side of the road, the largest spread in the Lemhi Valley. It was the sort of place people called a showcase. First hewed out by a reclusive Dane, who drained most of the bog himself, it was sold in 1956

FOUR BAD DEALS

to a friendly cowboy named Emmett Reese. Originally from New York, Mrs. Reese, heiress to a steel and mining fortune, had been given up as an old maid when she finally fell in love with Emmett, one of the hands at a Western dude ranch she was visiting. After their marriage, they moved to Salmon. Mrs. Reese instantly became the town's leading philanthropist, building the local hospital and financing scholarships to help local children go away to college. Meanwhile, Emmett used his wife's wealth to breed one of the best registered Hereford cattle stocks in the state. Money was often no object and, at times, Reese paid the local townspeople to do chores just to have a little company around.

Over the years, the Reeses created a storybook image of the perfect Idaho ranch, and local folks often brought visitors by for a look on a Sunday afternoon. With a big green roof, the Reeses' house sat on its own little half-acre of grass surrounded by a white wooden fence. On the other side of a huge circular drive were two smaller whitewashed homes, a bunkhouse, brightly painted red barns, tack houses, sheds, and haylofts.

By 1971, Emmett had become senile and could not manage the ranch by himself, and Mrs. Reese was forced to sell off the property, keeping only a little corner for a retirement home. When fall came around, her lawyers completed the sale for $1 million to John De Lorean. It had been a purchase partly inspired by Kelly Harmon, but it was also an investment that made sense as a tax shelter. De Lorean quickly tried to make Pine Creek the GM of Salmon ranches. He added to the Reeses' 1,600 acres, buying 1,000 acres on the other side of the road and 400 more ten miles south. He then hired a professional manager to run the ranch.

For the first few months of ownership, De Lorean played the role of country squire. He paid a few visits with his young wife and they spent weekends riding horses around their massive new range. One picture from that time shows a thin, long-haired De Lorean, standing next to his manager and a prize steer. He wears sneakers, a faded blue denim jacket and pants, looking more like a tourist than a rancher. After his divorce from Kelly, De Lorean's enthusiasm for cattle breeding began to fade.

"I think I saw John five times in five years," the ranch manager, recalls. Still, he did not stint in keeping up Pine Creek's image. He was reputed to have a $600,000 credit line at the local bank and he added his own touches, like California-style wooden corrals, to Emmett Reese's model ranch. De Lorean thought about syndicating his herd, but the plans fell through. "In those years the whole livestock business was in chaos," the manager says. "The ranch just didn't pay its way and the loss was too big for De Lorean to use. He put the place up for sale, but nothing happened."

By 1975, De Lorean had decided to sell off most of the registered herd. To help out he sent the ranch manager a man from California. "He told me this fellow Roy Nesseth knew about livestock. When Nesseth blew into town, I could see immediately that he knew nothing about it. His only experience had been with racehorses, but he seemed to be in charge of John's property."

Roy claimed that De Lorean had given him a share of the ranch and that he stood to gain much more if he managed to sell it. "Roy didn't really mix that well with the people in Salmon," the manager says. "He seemed like the high-powered salesman type. Quick with the numbers. Whether or not they were accurate was beside the point."

Nesseth apparently had more interests in Idaho than just the Pine Creek Ranch. Along with his brother Don, he was opening a Chevrolet dealership in Lewiston. The ranch manager remembers, "Roy wanted me to put the ranch money in a Lewiston bank under his name to show GM he had enough assets to support the franchise. Of course, I would do no such thing without John's approval. But he told me to go ahead. I wrote the check for the transfer. I believe that John got the money back as soon as Chevrolet okayed the franchise."

Before he left De Lorean's employ, the ranch manager helped De Lorean refinance Pine Creek with a $1 million mortgage from the Seattle office of the Metropolitan Life Insurance Company at 10 percent interest. Mortgages of that size weren't often collateralized with the property alone, but the insurance company's agents were mightily impressed by the fledgling rancher.

Clark Higley and his real estate agent were unfortunate enough to come knocking at Pine Creek's door in November 1975—just a few months after the mortgage was in place. Suddenly, as a beneficiary of Metropolitan Life's largesse, De Lorean was not as interested in selling the ranch as before.

But Higley soon discovered that neither De Lorean nor his manager would do the negotiating. All business affairs regarding Pine Creek were in Roy Nesseth's hands and, at first, that suited the Higleys fine.

"Roy can be a real charmer," Colleen says. "He keeps telling you how much he loves your family and asks about your grandkids and your folks. We had him over to dinner a few times and he couldn't have been nicer."

Clark had enough money to swing an outright purchase of the ranch, but Roy talked him out of it. "He was very persuasive. He told me there was no way they could redo the Metropolitan mortgage for me, and that it was too valuable to let drop. Instead, he told me I could make the payments in a lease arrangement."

Higley's real estate agent and lawyer tried to talk him out of that course of action, but Roy seemed to have the better arguments. First of all, he told Clark, if they had a lease, then the realtor wouldn't have to be paid his commission and there'd be more in the deal for everyone. Nesseth also convinced him that the taxes put on a straight purchase would hurt both buyer and seller.

"Roy was just a mesmerizer," Clark says today. "We would sit down and go through all the details and Roy remembered every figure we ever discussed. That impressed me. I thought he had a tremendous mind. He had a way of taking your idea and somehow twisting it to work in his favor."

In March of 1976, they finally settled on a deal. Higley turned over his house on the river and his potato farm (worth over $800,000 together), and $300,000 cash, and agreed to make lease payments of $189,000 a year. In return he got a lease, an option to buy the property, an assignment of the 500 head of cattle and a security agreement on ranch equipment.

Actually, considering what he gave up, Higley received almost nothing. His lawyer would later charge that "none of the . . . written agreements set forth the true intent, purposes, and agreement of the parties." Nesseth, they said, "so structured the instruments to confuse, misstate, abort, and avoid [Higley's] legitimate intent."

Shortly after he moved onto the farm, Clark went over to visit Mrs. Reese. Her husband had just died and she didn't have much longer to live herself, but she warned Higley to watch out for De Lorean. "She told me her dealings with De Lorean over the ranch had been real tough," Higley says. "She believed that if it hadn't been for her New York lawyers, she would have really been taken."

By the first summer on the ranch, Clark would realize how tough a De Lorean deal could be. When he went to sell the cattle, he discovered that Nesseth still had a mortgage out on the herd. Higley thought that he had bought the cattle free and clear for $300,000.

Enraged, Higley made a frantic call to John De Lorean in New York to let him know that Nesseth had a lien on the cattle. De Lorean agreed to stop off in Boise on his way to the West Coast and meet with Clark. "He couldn't have been more friendly or sympathetic," Higley recalls. "He said, 'I don't know what kind of mess Roy's gotten you into, but I'll straighten it out.' "

De Lorean promised to pay off the Idaho bank and get the mortgage removed, but until he did, Higley was stuck with a herd of cattle and no cash to pay the mounting costs of keeping up a big ranch. "Now I realize that in that first summer, I should have gotten a recision and backed out of the whole deal," Clark says. "In the eyes of the law, I would have had a perfect right. But I grew up believing that you should finish anything you start, and my lawyer was of no use. He and Roy were going out to lunch together and playing golf, and he told me this Nesseth isn't a bad fellow at all."

But as the second year of the lease ended, Clark had no money left to pay the next installment, and his credit had run out with his bank. Nesseth offered to secure a loan through his connections, if Higley swapped back the cattle. Clark transferred title to the herd, but Roy never followed through with the loan.

Today, as Colleen Higley listens to her husband rehash the sequence of events, she shakes her head and says, "What a mess we got ourselves into."

After two years of hard work, Higley had almost nothing to show for his investment in the Pine Creek Ranch. He had lost his potato farm and $300,000, no longer had the cattle, and never had title to the equipment (De Lorean and Nesseth still claim they never sold the equipment). To make matters worse, Metropolitan Life did not receive any of the three lease payments that Higley gave Nesseth to keep up the mortgage.

In March 1979, Metropolitan Life Insurance started foreclosure proceedings and soon after, when Clark told Roy he wouldn't be getting any more lease payments, Nesseth and De Lorean tried to evict the Higleys.

Clark got another lawyer and fought back in court. Unable to sell off the Pine Creek herd, he used the ranch to graze a friend's 1,000 head of cattle. The room and board he charged for the herd helped him eke out a living. Colleen had already sold the boutiques to make ends meet as well.

When summer rolled around, it looked like a Mexican standoff. While the Higleys held onto the ranch, De Lorean could neither sell it nor pay off the Metropolitan mortgage. But suddenly, a possible compromise cropped up, in the person of Utah rancher John Stephenson. Familiar with Pine Creek's reputation during the Emmett Reese era, Stephenson leaped at the chance to swap his ranch for the Salmon Range when he heard it was on the block. He was not about to help De Lorean force Higley off Pine Creek, but eventually he and Clark agreed to work together to get control of the ranch. By this time, Clark was willing to settle for no more than the 400-acre spread ten miles down the road in Tendoy.

To help smooth the way, Higley turned to a Boise auto dealer friendly with both De Lorean and Nesseth. The dealer had offered to mediate, and if necessary, provide some backing to arrive at an arrangement that would make everyone happy. "We called up John in New York," Clark says, "and I asked him what he wanted to put an end to all this. And he answered, 'All I want is $350,000, and for someone to take over the mortgage.'

"Well, that was fine with us, and I said, 'John, you've got a deal.' He then said he just had to make a quick check with his banker and be right back to us. He called back fifteen minutes later to say that the Tendoy ranch was still in Kelly Harmon's name and that he couldn't go through with the deal.

"Of course John was up to his tricks again. We all knew that ranch wasn't in Kelly Harmon's name. He probably called Nesseth, and Roy told him to hold out for more money."

For the next few months Clark felt he was in court more often than he was on the ranch. "We must have gone to trial sixteen times," he says. There were some legal victories for the Higleys. They sued De Lorean for ten months of cattle care and feeding, winning a judgment of $100,000. "We had one deposition session with Roy that lasted from nine A.M. to four in the afternoon. While our lawyer cross-examined him, he'd get up, cursing and screaming, and would leave the room. He must have done that four times."

But the Higleys could not stave off the foreclosure. Metropolitan seized the property and evicted them in the spring of 1980. The memory of the day he left Pine Creek behind is still bitter for Clark. "We had three families and no place to go."

The Higleys couldn't collect on their judgment until September, and then, by the time the lawyers and the banks were through, only $48,000 was left. For Clark and Colleen, it would be even harder when they returned to Rupert and got a look at their old farm. Roy had changed the name to the Mini-Cassia Ranch, but he had done little else. The fields hadn't been watered. Weeds grew waist-deep around the house. Leaning on Clark's reputation in Rupert, Nesseth established credit with local merchants. He even took a piece of a short-lived farm-equipment dealership nearby. By the time Clark had left Pine Creek, the lawsuits against Nesseth had piled up in the Rupert courthouse.

Clark thinks back to all he once had and says, "It was all reaped out of the ground. No fancy investment. Just backbreaking work. And I thought that was all it would take with Pine Creek. Our friends used to say, 'How could you have been so dumb?' "

Some other people had even worse things to say about Clark. Higley, like most of his neighbors in Idaho, is a Mormon. The more religious types said he had lusted after the ranch too much, or that his problems stemmed from trying to cheat the real estate agent out of his commission to begin with. Others wondered whether Higley had been very honest in his dealings with De Lorean and Nesseth.

John Stephenson stands in the muddy circular drive of what was once the Pine Creek Ranch and says, "I'm sure Clark Higley is an honest man. I know exactly what happened to him. I did business with Nesseth and De Lorean, and I got beat too."

After Metropolitan foreclosed, Stephenson still tried to pick up the ranch. Since De Lorean had a year to redeem his property, no one bothered to bid at the sheriff's auction and De Lorean was still free to peddle the ranch. Roy followed Stephenson back to Utah. "He was like a flea on a dog. He used to say, 'We don't need any attorneys. You know what you want. I know what I want. So we can make a deal.' "

But soon negotiations got heated. "Roy got to throwing a fit one day in the lawyer's office," Stephenson remembers. "He was cussing so badly with ladies around that my son Gordon just had to get up and take him aside. He said, 'Roy, either you act like a decent man and quiet down or else get out of here.' Gordon's not the biggest man, but people tend to know you don't mess with Gordon. Roy shut up pretty quickly."

Stephenson got trapped in Pine Creek when he agreed to put his ranch holdings into an escrow account. He could get them back if the deal were to go sour, but they couldn't be used again to garner tax benefits in a land swap for another spread. At last Stephenson signed over his ranch to De Lorean, paying off the $1.9 million mortgage. Roy got $500,000 more out of him as well. "Even with all that," Stephenson says, "they pulled one last stunt. When the contract got written up, we first saw the months of penalty on the mortgage that I'd be responsible for. That one little change added another $50,000."

A week later, during his deposition on the United Visuals case, De Lorean would crow about the Pine Creek land transaction when he addressed Roy's "very brilliant" financial abilities: "He made, oh, probably a million and a half dollars for me on something that I didn't think I could have made a penny on."

Almost a year passed between the time Higley moved off and Stephenson put his own name over the ranch. During the interim, Nesseth's manager let the place run down. The houses went unpainted. Fences fell down. Fields went dry. Stephenson hasn't yet had the money or time to make all the repairs and do all the painting necessary. One gray winter morning, while he squints off at the clouds breaking over the mountains, he voices doubts about whether he can keep up his own hefty interest payments to the bank.

"Once," Stephenson says, "Roy came down to my place in Utah and claimed he ran out of cash and didn't have any personal checks or anything else to get back home with. So I loaned him $300. I never mentioned it again, but every time I saw him, Roy would tell me he hadn't forgotten about my $300. Finally, six months later, he gave me a check for $350, and it bounced. I still have that check."

In the spring of 1976, John De Lorean was not very happy with Roy Nesseth. GPA Systems had gone bankrupt. Saf-Gard was on the verge of failure with Avrea in court, and process servers were chasing De Lorean all over the place. Meanwhile, back at the ranch in Idaho, Roy had put Higley's $300,000 into his brother's dealership and Metropolitan was pestering De Lorean for a mortgage payment. According to George Williams, De Lorean wondered whether it was a good idea ever to have taken Roy off the auto showroom floor.

"John and I were talking on the phone," Williams recalls, "and he said, 'George, all that Roy does is cause me grief. You don't know how much trouble he's gotten me into.'

"And then he told me that the best thing for Roy was to put him back in a dealership. He said he had found the perfect store for Roy in Wichita and that he was going to give it to him—just to get him away from all the trouble he caused."

De Lorean had found the dealership in 1976 while negotiating to buy glass roof tops for sports cars from a manufacturer in Wichita—another of his myriad business ventures. De Lorean had also come to Wichita to scout out a site to build his own sports car, but it was the glassmaker who told him about a local Cadillac dealer struggling to stay in business. Cadillac dealerships are considered the gold mines of the auto industry and De Lorean quickly sought out the bank financing the franchise. Quite contrary to the stereotype of the conservative banker, Kenneth E. Johnson, chairman of the board of the Kansas State Bank and Trust Company, had a special affinity for freewheeling entrepreneurs. He proudly kept a picture of aviation pioneer Bill Lear on his wall, and pointed out to visitors a reference in Lear's biography that mentions Johnson and his memories of a time "when he talked his own institution into loaning Lear four weeks of payroll" so he could sell a few planes and pay off a short-term note.

Johnson was to be as impressed by De Lorean as he was by Lear. When De Lorean inquired about the faltering Cadillac dealership, Johnson jumped to accommodate the VIP inquiry.

In fact, Dahlinger Pontiac-Cadillac was in no more trouble than most dealerships after the devastating impact of the oil embargo. And Gerald W. Dahlinger was no flaky wheeler-dealer, but a responsible young businessman with roots in the community.

If Gerry Dahlinger had any flaw it was overaffection for the auto business. The son of a barber, Dahlinger worked his way through college, pulling time mostly at the local refineries. Of those days, he says, "I never had enough quarters to put back to back."

One summer he helped out a relative who owned a Pontiac dealership. It was a job Gerry could see himself doing one day, and when he got out of school, he tried leasing cars for another dealer. One of his clients had gotten involved in a fast-food franchise, and he convinced Dahlinger to move to Florida and take a stake in the company on the ground floor. The name of the company was Pizza Hut, and Gerry ended up owning the Florida franchise. When he sold out in 1972, he had turned a $1,500 investment into a $500,000 nest egg.

Gerry was ready to come back to Wichita with his bankroll, and he had no doubt about what he would do with it. "My dream had always been to put together a solid deal," he says, using the auto vernacular for dealership. "If you stay in business ten years, you become an institution, and when you reach that stage, you have the world by the short hairs."

He started with a Buick dealership sixty miles out of town, and then bought a failing Pontiac store in Wichita from its aging owner. He quickly showed GM his skills as a salesman, cutting the losses the prior owners had suffered. Just thirty-eight years old, with a gift for gab and an easy smile, Dahlinger appeared headed for a bright future.

Shortly after he took over his second dealership, Gerry had the "sneaking suspicion" that he might be able to "dual" the store with a Cadillac franchise. When he got that, in August 1975, it was the first time in five years that GM had allowed a dealer to dual their prestige line. To celebrate, Gerry had a party in the ballroom of the Hilton.

"I sold twenty-seven Cadillacs before they delivered my first one," he says, "but I was undercapitalized from the word go." Near exhaustion from commuting between dealerships, he sold his Buick store and tried to concentrate on cutting his losses in Wichita. The bank had tried to get him a partner, but after difficult negotiations with Gerry the partner backed out.

Still, Gerry continued to make progress against his losses, almost tripling his sales volume in three years. "I had everything I owned in that dealership. And [Kansas State Bank chairman of the board] Johnson assured me we were going to tough it out. Then one day in late April 1976 he called me to say, 'I've got a buyer. The buyer's representative, a guy named Roy Nesseth, is coming to tour the place.' "

Nesseth flew into Wichita full of smiles, handshakes, and assurances all around that he and De Lorean could pull Dahlinger's dealership into the big time. Johnson turned supervision of the account over to his bank president, J. V. Lentell. Later in court testimony, Lentell remembered that the first thing Nesseth talked about was "Mr. De Lorean's tenure with General Motors and that one of the benefits of his being interested was the fact that through his friends in General Motors, they could get probably an unlimited amount of Cadillacs which this dealership probably needed more than anything . . . in order to make it go."

Roy took a quick look and was ready to make a deal. Tom Kimmerly flew in to help him work out the details. Dahlinger stood back in a state of shock, watching his precious dealership get bartered. It was clearly being sold out from under him, but in an unusual fashion. Johnson asked Gerry to sign powers of attorney to Kimmerly and transfer his stock. At first he protested, but then, he says, Johnson told him, " 'We'll put this deal together or we'll lock the doors at five o'clock.' In effect, Johnson had called my loan, and there was no way I'd raise the money to pay it off in four hours."

Helpless, Dahlinger watched as De Lorean's men took control of the dealership for no more than the debt and a refinanced loan of $200,000. Dahlinger was to get a one-year employment contract for $80,000. But the dealership was still to bear his name, and no official documents would show any trace of De Lorean. Bank president Lentell still secured guarantees from De Lorean, but he asked Kimmerly why De Lorean didn't want his name on the stock. He testified that "Kimmerly answered me by saying that 'I handle it this way because Mr. De Lorean and I have our own side deal. We could not permit his name to appear on any records because in addition to his friends, he also had enemies in GM and that would blow the whole deal and his name will never appear in this dealership.' "

If that answer was suitable for the bankers, it didn't make any sense to Dahlinger. Within days, he asked Pontiac's zone manager to drop by his house and filled him in on the transaction. Gerry promised to keep him informed, but asked that Pontiac not move yet and jeopardize his $80,000 employment contract. Besides, Nesseth had promised that once the dealership was "straightened out," Gerry would have a chance to buy it back.

Roy stayed in Wichita after the papers were signed and asked Gerry to look for a house. "We went to one of the nicest places in town—a home designed by Frank Lloyd Wright, but Roy didn't like it."

Roy would be most interested by an abandoned factory. "He made me stop the car," Gerry remembers, "and we got out and walked inside. He was real excited to see there was still some big machinery inside. He had all kinds of ideas of how to get that machinery away from the poor guy who went bankrupt. He then said, 'We have to find out who has true title and interest.' Whatever that means. He was clearly an expert on bankruptcies."

Otherwise, Roy was not much impressed by Wichita. "He let me know it was too small a town for him," Gerry says. "Johnson had put him up in the bank's hotel, the Royale, and I met Roy the next day for breakfast. He ordered a fried egg and when the waitress brought it, he told her it was overcooked, and he just tossed it off the plate and onto the floor. That's when I realized what kind of a guy we were dealing with."

Gerry spent the next two weeks on vacation. He returned to find that Nesseth had taken over his office and was alternately using and terrifying his salesmen. Sometimes he'd walk over to one and just push a $100 bill in his hand. Other times, he cursed a blue streak, tearing telephones out of the wall and throwing them across the floor. Any cash that appeared went right into Roy's pocket. No one seemed to be keeping records.

"I was like a blue suede shoe with a bad personality," Gerry says. "I wasn't allowed to do anything. I was just supposed to show up and act like I was still the dealer."

At night, Dahlinger would wander through the dealership alone. Like a ghost in a horror film, he had come back in his old form, but without the corporeal substance to affect anything. And yet, eerily, his name was still on the door, and as far as everyone but the bank was concerned, he still owned the place.

No one could stop Gerry from reading, and during his late-night haunts Gerry couldn't help but see that the remnants of the dealership were being systematically looted. First of all, there was Roy's lavish life-style. Dahlinger Pontiac-Cadillac was picking up his American Express and hotel tabs, which hovered between $5,000 and $6,000 a month. Hundreds of dollars went to clothing stores. One check for $566 was written to the Fairmont Hotel in Dallas, where Roy told Gerry he was going to meet a friend for the weekend.

Roy did not scrimp in his salary either, sometimes paying himself $5,000 a week, although not directly. The dealership would write the checks to the bank instead and the bank would issue cashier checks to Roy (the better to go unreported to the IRS). Meanwhile, Kimmerly was periodically pulling in $1,000 fees, and De Lorean was on an annual retainer of $150,000.

There were some large checks Dahlinger did not understand at all. One, for $10,000, was written to Clark Higley; another, for $5,000, to the Bank of Idaho for the Mini-Cassia Ranch. Roy had the dealership pay $60,000 for two phantom Peterbilt trucks that never appeared in Wichita.

But the greatest recipient of the dealership's largesse was Saf-Guard Systems. In just one month Dahlinger Pontiac-Cadillac sent $79,000 to Saf-Guard, and the Phoenix company sent $61,000 back. Along with the checks, Gerry found frantic notes to Roy from the respective accountants asking for funds to be forwarded as soon as possible. One August note from the Saf-Guard bookkeeper mentions two enclosed blank checks and says: "I should have at least $15,000 for our needs at Tempe. . . . We will have very little coming in in September as August sales were small."

From some of his notes, the Wichita accountant seems to have found Roy's antics amusing. He writes in the margin of his calendar: "R.N. gave me two checks he had written, total $1,500, to [a clothing store]; said to classify as salesmen's clothes incentives; really [the clothes] were his!!"

But the interstate transfer of funds between the two companies to keep their checking accounts afloat—legal authorities call it kiting—was definitely illegal and no laughing matter. And one other piece of the accountant's marginalia anxiously notes that someone had told the bank in Phoenix about the checks going back and forth between Saf-Gard and Dahlinger.

Gerry spent several nights making meticulous Xeroxes of the papers that lay strewn about on what was once his desk. "When I told Johnson about the things I was finding," Dahlinger says, "he would answer back, 'Bullshit,' and tell me to butt out."

Although he had no power, Gerry was still the figurehead president, potentially liable for Nesseth's actions. "I was walking the tightrope, trying to get my money, but not letting them get away with too much. I'm just sorry I stuck around as long as I did."

Even letters written to the bank did not seem to sink in. At last, ten months after Nesseth took over, Gerry became convinced that no one would put the brakes on Roy and he walked out. Before he left, however, he let the GM zone manager know that the charade was over. Soon after, General Motors moved in to take away the franchise.

The debt for the dealership had soared to $800,000, and the bankers faced the specter of a total loss. They won a reprieve from GM and found a mutually acceptable dealer to buy the property and franchise from De Lorean, but first they had to consolidate the debt. In a deal worked out with Kimmerly, the bank issued yet another loan and De Lorean got the opportunity to buy the land under the dealership, which he then leased back to the new owner. The remainder of the loan was to be repaid with the sales of the Dahlinger used cars still on the lot. The sum was personally guaranteed by De Lorean.

But as the Kansas State Court would later find, "Nesseth proceeded to sell all or a portion of the used cars . . . but with one or two minor exceptions, failed to deposit the proceeds in the [Kansas State Bank]." De Lorean was held liable for the loan. Both Kimmerly and De Lorean tried to distance themselves from Nesseth. Kimmerly testified that "he was well aware [that Roy] was a crook."

De Lorean claimed that Roy had gone out of his control. His

note, he argued, was solely to "help" the bank in its time of need. The judge called this argument "quite unbelievable" and ordered De Lorean to pay $237,124 plus interest—a sum that had reached $400,000 by the time De Lorean's last appeal was rejected in the spring of 1982.

Roy wouldn't escape Kansas law either. A doctor who couldn't get the title to his Cadillac after he fulfilled all his lease payments sued Nesseth successfully in Wichita for over $130,000, and then pursued the defendant into California, where he finally collected his judgment—with attorney John Thomas's help—in 1982.

As for Dahlinger, he left the state soon after he left his dealership, afraid that his name had been irreparably muddied in Wichita by the whole affair. "I had to sell my house, my car, the whole thing," he remembers ruefully. "All I had left was furniture and some personal belongings." He tried to get another start in the Florida fast-food business, but that didn't work out. His pilot store was, coincidentally, across the street from a Pizza Hut. "Six years later," he says, "and I'm still busted."

But in all his dealings with De Lorean, nothing hurts Dahlinger more than the loss of his antique car. A Mercedes-Benz 300SL, it was one of only a few thousand in existence. Gerry had seen it advertised in an Oklahoma City newspaper and picked it up for $6,000. "The guy could have charged me $35,000."

It is a car that has developed almost a cult status. "The one thing that makes the 300SL so special," Gerry says, "is that it has gull-wing doors. It was the first production-model car ever to do that, and the last to do it in any sizable numbers."

When De Lorean heard Gerry owned such a car, he asked if he could borrow it for a month. He wanted to shoot a commercial with the gull-wing Mercedes to advertise the car he was thinking of making. In December of 1976, Gerry had the car shipped to Bloomfield Hills. He flew over as well, just to make sure it arrived in good condition.

It was the last time he ever saw the car.

· 9 ·

100 West Long Lake

On January 4, 1974, Bob McLean became the first employee of the John Z. De Lorean Corporation. For thirty-five years McLean had worked at General Motors, mostly in the design studios and finally as an expert in auto safety. A big man, with a round face and sparkling blue eyes, he laughs as he remembers how De Lorean persuaded him to join his fledgling firm. "John just had a way of working you into his dreams. He talked of us doing great things together—especially about his plan to start his own car company. But he had a few projects that he wanted me to attend to first, so we could get a little seed money."

McLean's initial assignment was to find quarters for the new concern. Previously De Lorean had borrowed office space from Bunkie Knudsen, and McLean merely walked across the street from that location to lease 1,800 square feet at 100 West Long Lake Road, a two-story structure built within the previous year. Propped on stilts, with a gray-slate façade and smoked-glass windows, 100 West Long Lake looked more like a slice of a much larger building. It stood at the hub of professional activity in Bloomfield Hills, America's wealthiest community. Around the corner were the two posh Tudor-style restaurants—the Fox and

Hounds and the Kingsley Inn—that were lunchtime favorites for the local elite. The Bloomfield Hills Country Club was just up the street.

"I remember De Lorean brought in some expensive carpeting," says 100 West Long Lake's landlord, Jerry Rowin. "But the thing that struck me the most was that he wanted to put up a picture outside his office. Of course, I had no objection to that. It was some kind of contemporary oil painting and it broke up the line in the hall."

The most significant ramification of De Lorean's move to the building would come one morning in the bathroom on his floor. There, for the first time, he struck up a conversation with the lawyer in the office next door, Thomas Kimmerly. In appearance and manner, the two were as diametrically opposed as possible. Tall and distinctive, with a naturally stentorian voice, De Lorean had no trouble standing out in a crowd, and more than likely wore his favorite office attire: a work shirt and jeans. On the other hand, short and soft-spoken, Kimmerly tended to blend into the subdued stains of legal-suite paneling. He undoubtedly wore his usual conservative suit.

Despite their physical disparity, both shared a hunger for greater financial conquests than either one had previously known. Gradually, from their introduction in the bathroom, Kimmerly and De Lorean would embark on the most important professional association of their respective careers. As years passed, neither one would be embarrassed to talk about that first meeting, or to wonder about what course their lives might have taken, if they hadn't stopped to talk after they left the urinals.

Kimmerly, one of 100 West Long Lake's first tenants, had moved his three-partner law firm from downtown Detroit to be closer to his retired clients. He also wanted to be closer to his own home, as he too approached, in his mid-fifties, gradual retirement from a busy practice. A CPA as well as a lawyer, he had very quietly become the tax counselor of choice to several wealthy industrialists, and occasionally counsel to corporations as well. Mild-mannered to a fault, he had always taken great care to stay out of the limelight. His closest brush with publicity came with an oil-exploration venture he had put together with his client and friend Ray Dahlinger (no relation to Wichita car dealer Gerald Dahlinger), a controversial Detroit businessman who has claimed to be the illegitimate son of Henry Ford. The oil deal eventually fell through, and several prominent Detroit personalities, including one television newscaster, were burned for five-figure losses. It was the last time Kimmerly emerged from advisory shadows.

That is, until he met John De Lorean. In De Lorean, he'd find the reason to throw his standard caution to the wind. Kimmerly was later to characterize De Lorean for the *American Lawyer* as "a client of enormous energy and absolute dedication. . . . He's head and shoulders above everyone else I've encountered in [the automobile] industry." He started by offering De Lorean tax counsel, after De Lorean's longtime accountant died. But in a few years, he froze out De Lorean's attorney, John Noonan, who had previously been the auto executive's closest adviser. As De Lorean's personal affairs became more entangled, Kimmerly waded in even deeper, assuming positions on the boards of Saf-Gard Systems, Pine Creek Ranch, and Dahlinger Pontiac-Cadillac just as they appeared to be headed for bankruptcy. In time, the man who only a few years before had contemplated retirement faced the most demanding and potentially risky endeavor of his life as John De Lorean's personal counsel. Throughout, his devotion to De Lorean would be unwavering.

As a calm, steadying gray eminence, Kimmerly countered the more volatile influence of Roy Nesseth. But many deals that emanated from 100 West Long Lake involved neither man—especially in the first few years after De Lorean left General Motors.

When De Lorean moved into 100 West Long Lake, he was still officially working as president of the National Alliance of Business. Although the job was unsalaried, General Motors was donating $200,000 to pay De Lorean. GM chairman Richard Gerstenberg, who then filled the ceremonial NAB chair, had been the one to appoint De Lorean to the one-year presidency. Some in auto-industry circles saw the move as an attempt to get De Lorean off the street and away from competitors. It was also a way, some thought, to finally hog-tie De Lorean with his moralistic rhetoric. Despite his pronouncements about social responsibility, his superiors often sardonically noted that De Lorean never found as much time for charity work as did his insensitive colleagues.

But according to Fred Wentzel, NAB vice president, De Lorean responded enthusiastically to his nonprofit post. Serving mostly as a cheerleader, he traveled the country encouraging local business groups to hire the disadvantaged worker. "Comparing him to other NAB presidents on a scale of one to ten," Wentzel says, "I'd give him a seven. John definitely seemed committed to the concept and he spoke with commitment. We have since invited him back to participate in other activities, and he hasn't responded. But to be truthful most past presidents don't respond either, because they're scattered across the country." (In fact, De Lorean's own hiring record at De Lorean Motor Company would be considered dismal by NAB standards. At any one time in the company's history there were fewer than three blacks at low-level positions, and no minorities or women in executive positions.)

Although he kept a townhouse in Washington to be near NAB headquarters, De Lorean continued to commute back to Detroit and pursue business ventures on his own. In June 1974, when his presidency of NAB was up, he told a magazine, "Now I have to get back into the cold, hard world and earn a living." But six months earlier he had incorporated the John Z. De Lorean Corporation with Michigan's Department of Commerce, listing himself as a "product-design and business consultant."

He had already found that life did indeed go on after GM—if anything the financial world was even warmer and more receptive than before. As a free agent, he rapidly expanded his business interests, especially in New York. He no longer bopped into town just to visit the swinging discos, but also to be seen at the VIP tables of the 21 Club. In his last year at General Motors, he had accepted George Steinbrenner's offer to buy a piece of the New York Yankees ("I sat down and drew up a list of men I know to be doers," Steinbrenner told one reporter when asked about how he chose investors). His investment in the team was relatively small—$50,000—but it gave him the chance to rub shoulders with the likes of lawyer Thomas W. Evans, oil czar Nelson Bunker Hunt, and theatrical producer James Nederlander. Free of GM's strictures, he was able to do business with them as well.

He showed his first corporate allegiance in New York to Chris-Craft, joining the company's board. Previously, he had been a close personal friend of the company's chief executive, Herbert Jay Siegel. Among De Lorean's other Manhattan business patrons was William D. Fugazy, a travel and transportation broker whose firm had a number of lucrative contracts with the auto companies. Fugazy provided De Lorean entrée to some of New York's most powerful executives.

A mutual fascination often sprang up between older business titans and the much younger GM outcast. "No matter how important John claimed to be," one of his friends says, "he was always mystified by the people who managed to make vast sums of money. He liked nothing more than to talk about how some big deal was pulled off."

For a while, J. Peter Grace, Jr. was willing to share his big-deal magic with the aspiring mogul. In twenty-five years as chief executive of W.R. Grace & Company, Grace had turned his father's shipping and trading concern into a diversified conglomerate with holdings ranging from fertilizer to fast-food restaurants. Fugazy introduced Grace to De Lorean and their relationship took off from there. Both were inveterate golfers. Both could discuss their cattle-ranch tax shelters. According to Bob McLean, "Peter Grace was instantly enamored of John and often asked him along on business trips. He tried to hire him, but John wasn't ready for that. I think John was tremendously intimidated by him. Grace had a reputation as a terribly demanding man. He wanted facts and figures on everything—projections for the next ten years. And he could be ruthless. If the numbers didn't look right, he'd sell a division in an hour. John told me, 'A guy like that would just chew me up.'

"So John asked instead that he do some consulting work for Grace, and evidently the old man then flipped through his huge array of subsidiaries and found the division he thought would be the right fit. It was called Shasta, and it made recreational vehicles.

With that, they decided that John would design a fuel-efficient motor home. John said he told Grace, 'In four years you'll be the biggest factor in the recreational-vehicle business.' "

Grace gave De Lorean a consulting contract that paid him $25,000 a month for 50 percent of his time and also compensation for two full-time employees. "I think that consulting fee tended to hurt John more than help him," McLean says. "From then on he'd quote that as his monthly retainer, and he scared a lot of people away."

A week after the contract with Grace was signed, De Lorean called McLean into his office. "John told me not to bother with the stipulations of the contract. John always felt contracts were interesting pieces of paper and no more. He said I should go ahead and bill all the people in the office to Grace."

Many of the other people in the office were working on another project, funded by the Allstate Insurance Company. De Lorean had long been the most vocal advocate of the airbag safety device in the auto industry. Allstate chief executive Archie R. Boe held much the same distinction in his own industry and actively sought out De Lorean to both lobby and consult on the airbag. McLean was GM's expert in the safety field and Allstate was willing to back the airbag research he did for De Lorean with a $250,000 investment.

Boe was also taken by De Lorean's talk of producing his own car. With the advent of the oil crisis, Allstate worried about the fuel-efficient tin boxes that were cruising America's highways, and their propensity for fatal accidents. If De Lorean were to design a fuel-efficient commuter car that had safety features, Boe told him, Allstate would be willing to underwrite the project. For a payment of $600,000, De Lorean contracted to produce two safety prototypes: one for crash testing and another that Allstate could take on tour around the country. Soon after, in June 1974, he boldly predicted to *Ward's Auto World* that he'd start manufacturing the minicar in fifteen months: "Plans are to start out in the area of 40,000 or 50,000 units and let it go wherever it goes."

"We never did deliver those cars," McLean says. "In fact, nothing even went beyond the paper stage and I was sure that there'd be a lawsuit over it. But somehow the whole thing got smoothed over." Today, an Allstate spokesman says the company and Mr. Boe have no regrets over their contract with De Lorean.

Nothing would come of the project for Grace, either, although more work had been expended on the motor home than the Allstate commuter car. A De Lorean assistant had once been a crack marketing man for General Motors, and he conducted extensive research on what consumers looked for in motor homes. In what the industry calls clinics, he took people through existing recreational vehicles, closely noting their comments and reactions. "We had a very clear idea of what people wanted," McLean says, "down to the kitchens and bathrooms. We built a styling prototype, which basically shows what the interior of the vehicle will look like.

"We stored the prototype with an industrial designer and one night it caught on fire. It was insured for $100,000, and although some of us felt it was the property of Grace, John put the insurance money in his pocket.

"In all, Peter Grace must have spent $1 million on the project, but he just lost patience with John and sold the recreational-vehicle division. John couldn't get anyone else interested, and I think he ended up feeling betrayed by Grace."

De Lorean would engage in even more fruitless discussions with another elder statesman of American business, Armand Hammer. Chief executive of Occidental Petroleum, Hammer had long been capitalism's ambassador to the Soviet sphere of influence. Evidently, he approached De Lorean early in 1974 about distributing the Lada—the Russian version of a Fiat subcompact. "Hammer's office," McLean remembers, "was in Los Angeles, not too far away from the Grace recreational-vehicle division. Once when we were in town, John had me drop him off. He went alone to see Hammer, and came back exhilarated. He was just in awe of the man."

In June of 1975, newspapers carried stories that De Lorean was ready to direct sales of Ladas for the Soviet government trading company. But at a time when the American auto industry was still reeling from the fuel crisis, Congress showed no inclination to let thousands of Russian cars into the United States.

The cheap labor costs of Eastern Europe and the desire of the governments there to break into American markets continued to appeal to De Lorean, and he didn't let the idea drop. At one point he offered to oversee a Rumanian effort to manufacture a Renault subcompact. Even after he started his own company, he considered marketing a Polish-built utility vehicle. While he may have denied his own Eastern European roots, De Lorean would not give up on the region's products.

One of his car-company executives believes his motives were not entirely altruistic: "John used to talk to the newspapers about how cars from Russia would bring international peace, but he'd tell us about the markup he could get on one of those little shitboxes. They don't cost you any more than $2,000 apiece, and you can probably get away with selling them here for $4,000."

Beyond just monetary return, De Lorean was also impressed by the reverence communist countries were ready to show Western executives. As Armand Hammer had proven, a businessman in that incongruous setting could end up wielding political as well as economic power. Using the imperial "we," De Lorean told one magazine, "One thing we plan to do, and that's one reason I went to Rumania recently, is to try to establish a relationship with one of the developing nations, and I would like eventually to win their confidence. I'd like to assume a role as [Rumania's] industrial adviser."

Whatever services De Lorean might have offered a foreign country, some of his employees back home were wondering what he could do for them. Bob McLean lost track of John's proliferating business interests and retreated into a separate division of the De Lorean Corporation that did contract research for the government on auto safety (by 1980 it split away from De Lorean entirely). "We were probably the only division that made some money for John over a long period of time," McLean says. "Not a lot, but at least we were profitable." He had long before put aside his hopes of being a part of De Lorean's new car: "John had a way of telling you what a great member of the team you were and then putting you on a shelf. Besides, I could see that it wasn't in his nature to concentrate on any one thing. He got so quickly bored with whatever was at hand, he had to have a thousand other things going."

In fact, McLean couldn't even tell all the players without a scorecard. "Suddenly there were people around like Nesseth. You knew they had something to do with John's extraneous deals, but John would never talk much about Nesseth. At most he'd say, 'Roy helps me out.' "

Another mysterious figure at 100 West Long Lake was a hulking man named C. W. Smith. Once a Chicago Bears linebacker, he had gone on to make a fortune with an engineering firm in Detroit. Although he had some severe reverses, he still had the contacts that interested De Lorean. Some of his deals involved overseas ventures, but few in the office knew what he did. Evidently, one of Smith's most productive deals for De Lorean involved a refinery, which De Lorean convinced truck-rental magnate James Ryder to buy. After De Lorean had spoken at one of his management meetings on the fuel crisis, Ryder signed him up as a consultant. Ryder says he figured De Lorean to be a "strong, competent businessman" and that the two considered manufacturing a truck (De Lorean went so far as to incorporate a Ryder–De Lorean subsidiary). However, Ryder adds, "I decided I didn't want to get into manufacturing." De Lorean did get him into the oil business when he purchased a Louisiana refinery that C. W. Smith had located. Ryder later sold it to John's fellow Yankees board member, Nelson Bunker Hunt. De Lorean told friends that he and Smith got a commission from Ryder when he picked up the facility and also when he let it go.

In late-morning phone calls and long lunches in dimly lit restaurants, Detroit's dealmakers courted John De Lorean. Many of these people didn't expect De Lorean to personally invest in their schemes. They were willing to pay him just to be a part—a name on the letterhead or annual report. Inventors and manufacturers trooped into his office showing him new designs or products that only needed his stamp of approval to make a fortune. There could be gains of millions and he didn't even have to lay out a nickel.

At most they wanted him to sign those "interesting pieces of paper," like contracts and letters of credit. By 1976, De Lorean's personal financial statement showed him to be worth over $10 million with a varied portfolio of stocks, ranches, business ventures, oil wells, and pieces of real estate developments. Banks seldom asked to see anything more.

"De Lorean's name was magic," Mike Brasch explains. As head of a successful advertising agency, Brasch had the chance both to work for De Lorean on some projects and to be a partner on others. "The man was like a legend—the sort of person you wanted on your side. First of all, he could galvanize a crowd. He had that sort of FDR charisma that reached almost everyone in a room, no matter how many people were in the room. At GM he had the reputation of giving the best presentation of any executive in the whole corporation. One on one, he was overwhelming. He could turn on the personality and the charm like a light switch, and when he talked to you, it was as though all of his attention was focused on you. He just enveloped you with affection. Soon he'd be telling you how you're an important part of the team or say, 'I hear you're doing a great job,' and you'd just sit there thinking that you'd finally found someone capable of recognizing your talents."

But once he got involved with De Lorean, Brasch found him a difficult partner and an impossible customer. "John has a nasty habit of not paying his bills. I did a few promotions for some of his business ventures and he owed me $2,100. Sometime later, in connection with another deal we were doing together, I was about to turn over a six-figure check, when I remembered the bill and asked that he pay me back first. He told me he was shocked that I hadn't been paid. This was the first he'd heard of it, and he assured me that the $2,100 would be in the mail that day.

"Of course, I gave him his check, but he never sent me my money. Soon after, I went into the hospital for some rather painful surgery. As I lay in bed I couldn't get the whole thing out of my mind. It wasn't the money anymore. It was the principle. For twenty-four hours I kept asking myself how I could have been so gullible as to let him off the hook. When my wife came to pick me up from the hospital, I told her to drive straight to De Lorean's office at 100 West Long Lake. I must have looked like death warmed over, but I barged into his office and told him I wanted my money or I wouldn't leave. Once again, he starts with the crap, saying, 'You mean you weren't paid?' and acting all upset. He was going to write me a check right on the spot. But then he started to look all over for his checkbook and he couldn't find it. He was going to call his house and make sure the check was delivered to me that day. Believe it or not, I fell for his line again, and left the office. Guess what? No one delivered the check that day."

Once De Lorean and a mutual friend asked Brasch in to discuss a consignment of Mitsubishi CB radios he had purchased with a sizable bank loan. It was the height of the CB craze and retailers were clamoring for all the radios they could get their hands on. But De Lorean didn't know how best to approach retailers. Brasch put him in touch with importer Larry Yanitz. "I sold a few thousand with a big retailer," Yanitz says, "and once John saw how I did it, he told me he didn't need my services anymore."

But soon after, while Yanitz was on a Florida vacation, he says De Lorean made several frantic calls asking him to help sell off the radios. "I made a deal with an Oklahoma outfit that was going to pay $30 a radio. I would have gotten $5 a radio in commission, which would have added up to $26,000."

But De Lorean wasn't happy with the price. He refused to let the radios out of the warehouse until Yanitz came up with a better offer. In the meantime, the government was not stalling in its regulations of CBs. While the merchandise sat in a warehouse, the FCC issued new rules permitting the number of channels per radio to increase from twenty-three to forty. Overnight, De Lorean's stock became practically worthless. He would end up getting only a few dollars per radio. Yanitz later tried, unsuccessfully, to bring suit against De Lorean for his lost commission, but the two men had no written agreement and the suit was dismissed.

De Lorean still had to repay the bank for the letter of credit issued against the radios. To come up with the money to cover the loan, he sold his share in the San Diego Chargers to Barron Hilton. He would later tell a Detroit newspaper that, "I sold out of [the San Diego Chargers] because I really got very upset when they were fined for that drug thing." As it turned out, soon after De Lorean relinquished his share, the National Football League received a massive new television contract that practically doubled the value of his stock.

De Lorean stood to bungle even more lucrative deals with another former GM executive, Raymond F. Prussing. Once an overseas salesman for General Motors' Detroit Diesel Allison division, Prussing had the international connections on which export fortunes are made. In 1975 he became vice president of the John Z. De Lorean Corporation and, through an influential Arab sheikh, got De Lorean involved with several projects for Saudi Arabia. One was a study for creating a bus system. The other involved shipping auto parts and providing maintenance for Saudi vehicles. Both deals would fall through when the sheikh discovered the sort of markup De Lorean was taking on the parts.

Their best chance at the proverbial killing came in 1976 when Prussing and De Lorean secured the rights to a diesel engine manufactured by the Japanese auto giant, Isuzu. The De Lorean Diesel Corporation had the license to sell the engine only for nonautomotive purposes, but just the product's agricultural uses still offered them a huge and potentially lucrative market. Although his name was on the letterhead, and he claimed in his financial statements that his interest in the diesel company was worth $500,000, De Lorean had not personally put up the money to buy the license. Most of the backing came instead from an Oldsmobile dealer in Lansing, Michigan.

Within a year, Prussing needed more cash to keep the company afloat, but despite repeated assurances, De Lorean came up with no further investment. "Prussing wouldn't take any crap from John," McLean remembers. "We got into the office at 100 West Long Lake one day and found that Ray had moved to Livonia [a distant suburb]." In a take-it-or-leave-it proposition, the Oldsmobile dealer gave De Lorean $50,000 for his share in what was now known as Isuzu Diesel North America, Inc. De Lorean took it. Prussing and the dealer would later sell their license back to Isuzu for several million dollars.

When the split between Prussing and De Lorean hit the papers, Prussing told reporters that De Lorean had gotten out of the project so he could devote more time to building his own car company: "For John, this new car is the greatest thing in the world. He's so intense on this project it was asking too much of him to expect him in both companies. He had to make a choice on which way he was going to go. Don't go reading anything into this."

Prussing didn't have to worry. The press hadn't been reading anything negative into De Lorean's career, even though it took him just three years to be associated with the sort of repeated business disasters that would have destroyed the reputation of another man.

One Detroit-area financier who tried to put together a number of deals for De Lorean says ruefully, "Anything John touches he ruins. He just doesn't fund a thing. All he does is take money out. No one can ever make it big if they don't know when to spend. John fell on his ass as an entrepreneur because he refused to put money on the line."

Grand Prix of America; Saf-Gard Systems; Dahlinger Pontiac-Cadillac; De Lorean-Ryder Corporation; the Pine Creek Ranch; the De Lorean Diesel Corporation: all added up to a relentless litany of failure. By the mid-Seventies every major enterprise De Lorean had undertaken was bankrupt, defunct, or defective. This astounding record of entrepreneurial ineptitude was tainted even further by the host of broken contracts and lawsuits that raised serious questions about his honesty and integrity.

And yet, even though several of the courtroom feuds were of a rancorous and controversial nature, none of John De Lorean's misguided business exploits made the news. Journalists continued to write stories about him, but his latest pursuits were tossed off in a few lines at the end of the piece. De Lorean must have learned that if he didn't say too much, the reporter wouldn't bother to check any further. According to De Lorean's 1976 profile in *Current Biography*, Grand Prix of America was a "string of miniature racetracks." In fact, by that time the company had been bankrupt for two years and, even when extant, never had more than one track. In the same article, he is given further credit for having "transformed his . . . cattle ranches into year-round camps for underprivileged children," which would have certainly been big news to Clark Higley as he and his children struggled to stave off eviction.

Clearly, in the mid-Seventies, reporters were not asking searching questions about John De Lorean. They were still looking for the dirt on General Motors, and the ex-executive was more than willing to give it to them. He had distilled his most cogent criticisms, and they came out in pithy lines and telling anecdotes—more bitterly cynical as time went on. In fact, only months after he left GM, De Lorean was already discussing a book project with *Business Week* reporter Pat Wright. By the autumn of 1974 they had a contract with Playboy Books for *On A Clear Day You Can See General Motors*. Wright compiled the book mostly using transcripts from lengthy interviews with De Lorean. His other information came from notes, files, and memos De Lorean had kept over the years.

In Wright's mind the book was not primarily about John De Lorean. He says, "I got into this project for one reason: to open up American industry to close examination. General Motors was the prototype of the well-run American business, but anyone who covered the company as a reporter kept asking himself, 'How does anything ever get done there?' De Lorean told us that, in fact, it doesn't get done."

Wright, along with several other veteran automotive writers, found De Lorean's criticisms of the GM system to be valid. His research, he says, was to verify De Lorean's charges. He did not feel, however, that De Lorean himself was worth the same scrutiny. "I was interested in General Motors' story. I didn't see my mission as doing a biography—authorized or otherwise—of John De Lorean."

But aside from Wright's work, De Lorean's comments about GM in newspapers and magazines dwelled as much on his own record of accomplishment there as they did on his criticism of the company. And those accomplishments, great as they were, grew even greater in De Lorean's reminiscences.

De Lorean, the only subject who permitted himself to be identified in Gail Sheehy's *Passages*, was enshrined in the book as one of the few "strivers and superachievers" with the courage to turn his back on the ultimate prize. De Lorean, she writes, "got religion" and realized that "big business does not want people with a 'broad vision.' . . ." Before his departure, she asserts, he was on the brink of the presidency, but "breathing down the neck of his dream, De Lorean knew at last that it would not be deliverance."

The fabrication of the De Lorean legend started almost immediately on his departure—with his salary. In just the following few months anyone reading the mass media could have seen his final salary figures jump dramatically—almost as though he had been given a retroactive raise. In the first announcements of his April 1973 departure, *Time* and *The New York Times* put his salary and bonuses at $300,000. Two months later an auto magazine quoted De Lorean's annual pay at "$400,000-plus." In September, *Fortune* reported that compensation for De Lorean had been as high as $550,000. One month later, De Lorean told a *New York Times* reporter, "Even at $650,000 a year, if the job is not satisfying, you do something else."

As years passed, he was portrayed as changing the fortunes of Pontiac single-handedly. Some articles failed to mention either Estes or Knudsen. De Lorean also became the sole progenitor of the GTO and the Wide-Track Look. In a freelance story for the *Times*, reporter Robert Irvin wrote, "He brags about his performance at [Pontiac and Chevrolet], although other persons at GM and elsewhere in the auto industry have suggested that he sometimes takes more of the credit than he deserves."

Reporters, however, did not share the skepticism of those "other persons." Some of them didn't even bother to check boasts as easily verifiable as patents. According to *Current Biography*, De Lorean "owns more than two hundred patents, including those for the recessed windshield wipers and the overhead-cam engine." In fact, De Lorean has been listed by the U.S. Patent Office as holding a total of fifty-two patents—nothing to sneer at, but nowhere near two hundred. Thirty-one of the patents were for GM, but none for the wipers or the overhead cam.

Journalists can't take the entire blame for being sucked into the De Lorean myth. Investors proved just as gullible. There was much about this post-GM De Lorean model—in both his personality and life-style—that could blind even the most cynical eye. As his byzantine little empire reeled about him, he could still find time to talk to a reporter and seem as self-assured as ever. Indeed, his memories of pulling the irons out of the fire at GM may have helped bolster his confidence.

Besides, he certainly lived like a successful man. His cars were lined up in the driveways of his homes. When he flew, it was only first-class. When he ate at fancy restaurants, he was always at the best table. Besides his ranch in Idaho, he had another spread nestled in the mountains just two hours northeast of San Diego. He called it Cuesta de la Cammalia, after the camellia flowers that grew there. The entrance was through a gate and up a winding road lined with wooden fences. The actual home and the two guesthouses did not quite live up to the plantation entrance. Instead they were unprepossessing ranch-style places—the kind you might expect to see in a middle-class suburb. But sitting alongside the pool, De Lorean could listen to the bees buzz and smell the rich, syrupy smell of the camellia flowers growing in terraced gardens nearby and point out to the avocado trees on the green hillsides in the distance, or to the lush groves of grapefruit and oranges that rose behind him, and say that all these 500 acres were his. Later, he would take visitors out on little motorbikes, to roar up and down the steep dirt roads that circled his property, or ride down to the country club at the bottom of the mountain, where, of course, he was a member in good standing. After such a tour, it would have been hard for anyone to classify the lord of this manor a failure.

And as befits a man of success in America, there was a beautiful wife back at the hearth. Joe Slavik, one of the Grand Prix investors, remembers going out to Cuesta de la Cammalia with De Lorean. "I was there to look at the ranch. When we went inside the house, John called out first, 'Cristina, are you presentable?' She came out in a T-shirt and shorts. I'd never seen anyone so beautiful. She didn't just say hello and go away again. She was very gracious and practically waited on us. I really got to like her."

De Lorean married Cristina Ferrare just a few weeks after he left General Motors. They met in the office of their mutual divorce lawyer, E. Gregory Hookstratten, and tied the knot five months later. The timing is important here because it deflates De Lorean's reputation as a womanizer. When his divorce from Kelly Harmon became imminent, gossip columnists had him out with Hollywood beauties on the order of Ursula Andress, Candice Bergen, and Tina Sinatra. According to a *Detroit Free Press* profile, De Lorean and Roger Penske were "systematically dating and discarding the best-looking girls from New York, Miami, and L.A. The two had a gentleman's agreement that De Lorean would get all the girls over five foot eight, Penske all those under." All playboy bravado aside, De Lorean's third swinging singlehood was as short-lived as his second. In December 1972, he reached a divorce settlement with Kelly Harmon. He started dating Cristina Ferrare the next month.

A tall brunette with large almond-shaped eyes, she was two years younger than Kelly Harmon. If anything, De Lorean was proud of their age disparity. When Cristina joined him for one speaking engagement, he started out his remarks by telling the predominantly male audience, "I'm glad, as I see you are, that my wife, Cristina, could be here with me today. Of course, she had to skip out of school. That's okay, honey, I'll write a note on Monday."

But unlike Kelly Harmon, Cristina Ferrare was no fragile naïve schoolgirl. Sophisticated beyond her years, she had begun modeling at the age of fourteen, and eventually rose to the top of her profession, looking out from the covers of fashion magazines and cosmetic ads. Her father, who had been a butcher in Cleveland, followed her to Hollywood when she tried to break into the silver screen. Although she got only a handful of movie roles, her modeling career still supported her family in luxury. While a teenager, she carried on a torrid romance with California computer-kingpin

Fletcher Jones, more than twenty years her senior. He died in a plane crash during their affair. She would be married briefly afterward.

Having earned a six-figure salary on her own, Cristina had a few lessons to teach her older spouse about the finer things in life. "John used to complain about Cristina's expensive tastes," one of the De Lorean Motor Company executives remembers. "Evidently she was used to extravagantly expensive things, and he'd say, 'Her shopping will break me before the car company will.'"

But for all her sophistication, Cristina also had an earthy sense of humor that occasionally shocked some of the more staid auto-industry types that surrounded her husband. Often during board meetings she sent him notes marked "urgent" with salacious suggestions inside. "I remember once being out with John and Cristina in New Orleans," one of the car-company executives says. "We were there for the NADA [National Auto Dealers Association] convention, and the top officers of the company had gotten together with their wives for dinner. While we were eating, Cristina launched into a story about how John took her skiing shortly after they had met and she ended up breaking her leg and getting a cast up to her thigh. She then gave us a graphic description of how they tried to make love around the cast. She thought it was all very funny. My wife and I almost dropped our forks."

For a while after they married, Cristina still tried to break into acting on the West Coast. She coveted a lead role in the TV series *Charlie's Angels*, which coincidentally enough followed the adventures of three beautiful women crime-fighters squired about by a smooth-talking older man. Cristina did not get the part, and reconciled herself to the life of a high-priced model back on the East Coast. With their mutual business interests gravitating to New York, she eventually convinced her husband to move out of his Bloomfield Hills home and buy a co-op on Fifth Avenue.

Although she kept up her career, Cristina also added a measure of stability and domesticity to her husband's life. John had gained custody of the child he had adopted with Kelly, and Cristina raised Zachary from the age of eighteen months as though he were her own son. Soon after their marriage, *Detroit Free Press* reporter Paul Hendrickson visited the De Lorean household and left the world an enduring picture of the harmonious, prosperous family: "At home, on three-and-a-half rolling acres in Bloomfield Hills, set off by white fences and a fleet of cars in the driveway [John De Lorean seems] a warm, happy man, surrounded by three romping dogs, a wife who playfully cuffs and pokes at him and is yet incredibly mature, a baby who mugs for pictures better than Carol Channing. When there is soft snow falling and symphonic music coming from another room, it can all kill you softly. You could care less how many Picassos are on the wall."

· 10 ·
Silver Beauty

"John started out with an image of the car in his head," Bill Collins says. "He'd say it was a hazy view of the car sitting in a field somewhere with the gull-wing doors open."

Bill Collins was the man John De Lorean chose to bring his hazy image to life. Just six months after De Lorean left General Motors, Collins followed. For the next five years he'd learn both the exhilaration and disappointment of making another man's dream come true.

Although, reportedly, De Lorean had promised GM to stay out of the car business for a few years in exchange for his Florida dealership and deferred bonus payments, his ultimate career objectives were almost immediately clear to anyone who knew him. "It was always the sports car," Bob McLean says. "From the moment John De Lorean left GM, he was determined to build his own sports car."

De Lorean had always been something of a sports-car fanatic, happier tooling around in a Maserati than in a Cadillac. But his reasons for wanting to manufacture sports cars on his own were more practical than aesthetic. "He had to start out with a limited-production car that had a big price tag," McLean explains. There was no way De Lorean could immediately produce the hundreds of thousands of moderately priced cars that are the meat of the Big Three's output. Tens of thousands were far more manageable for the novice manufacturer and, if expensive enough, could also be more profitable.

Ironically, De Lorean fashioned his independent automaking ways after a General Motors example. Since 1953, Corvette had been an almost self-contained little ma-and-pa store inside the giant supermarket of the Chevrolet division. Officially, the two-seat sports car was part of the Chevy line, but its appeal was not for the middle-class family, like the rest of the division's products. It was the only American product that legitimately met the performance standards of a sports car, and it attracted the same wealthy young men who shelled out big bucks for the foreign coupes.

When De Lorean took over as Chevrolet's general manager, he was shocked to see how profitable the sports car was, especially considering how little the company was putting into the product. The car had undergone minimal styling and engineering changes since its inception, and was still assembled in an antiquated St. Louis factory of World War I vintage.

To some extent, the Corvette did suffer from lack of innovation. In typical GM fashion, headquarters had been reluctant to approve any wholesale changes in the car as long as it continued to make money. In the late Sixties, Corvette's preeminent engineer, Zora Arkus-Duntov, tried to buck the status quo. For two decades he had monitored the car's slow development and, believing the time had come for an abrupt change of course, he designed a new version that shifted the engine closer to the center of the car. The advantages of placing a car's power plant just behind the driver were manifold. The driver would have a better field of vision. The car would have a lower—and hence safer—center of gravity, and no need for convoluted exhaust and steering systems.

But when Arkus-Duntov made his radical redesign sketches, some Corvette purists, including De Lorean, found the change too much to take. "At one point while I was working on the design," the engineer remembers, "De Lorean came to look at the clay styling model and he didn't like some of the vents I was putting into the body, so he'd say, 'What is this? It looks like a hole to piss in.' "

Arkus-Duntov believes De Lorean helped kill his first attempt at pushing the car through. But he prevailed on his old friend and mentor Ed Cole to save the project. Cole was mired in his own $100 million mission to convert General Motors to Wankel rotary engines, and he saw the Corvette as a prime candidate to lead the way. Arkus-Duntov had his midship sports-car project revived, but he reluctantly went back to the drawing board to accommodate the Wankel. Again, De Lorean was antagonistic. "I told him at one product meeting that with the Wankel the car just doesn't have the power it should. But then, De Lorean started yelling at me, trying to embarrass me in front of everyone there. He said, 'You're supposed to be such a genius, so why don't you invent something to make the engine more powerful?'

"That made me very mad. I ran out of the room and got in my car and drove back to the Technical Center. But by the time I got there, I figured out how to get more performance from the Wankel engine. My idea would make De Lorean turn around 180 degrees on the midship Corvette. He became my biggest supporter next to Cole."

But Cole and De Lorean were not enough to convince the rest of GM's top brass, and one more innovative project bit the dust. It did not, however, lose De Lorean's wholehearted support. Shortly after he left General Motors, he managed to buy the designs for the mid-engine Corvette—much to the surprise of their author. GM rarely releases blueprints, even concerning projects it never intends to finish. "One day, late in 1973, I went over to see De Lorean when he was occupying Knudsen's office. Then he first told me he wanted to produce the midship Corvette on his own, and he asked me if I wanted to be chief engineer. I declined. I decided to stay with Chevrolet until I retired in one more year. And I knew that after that, my contract wouldn't let me work full-time for a possible GM competitor." A few months later, De Lorean invited Arkus-Duntov to his home for dinner and made one more stab, but the engineer was not to be lured away.

De Lorean continued to court the Wankel as well. At one point he had an option to buy 30,000 Wankels a year from one company, and when that firm went under, he tried to make the same agreement with Mazda, Japan's foremost Wankel evangelists. But while the rotary engine was cheap to build and easy to maintain, it had an inordinate thirst for petroleum. Arkus-Duntov estimates that his midship Corvette might have gotten six miles to the gallon—unacceptable fuel efficiency with the oil crisis then at hand.

Bob McLean was to shift De Lorean's attention away from his prospective car's engine and closer to the skin. At first, De Lorean had envisioned using the standard sports-car shell of fiber-glass. While lighter, cheaper to produce, and more aesthetically pleasing than steel, fiber-glass also required safety measures that made a car a little heavier and more complicated than engineers would have liked. With a tendency to disintegrate on impact, a fiber-glass body required a steel skeleton and backbone underneath to protect the passenger and keep the shell in place. McLean would tell De Lorean of a friend who had found an amazing alternative to fiber-glass—a new plastic material that was stronger than steel and almost half the weight. The process was called Elastic Reservoir Molding, and it was as simple to confect as the chemical equivalent of a grilled-cheese sandwich. Epoxy resin—quite standard stuff found in glues and coatings—was placed between two sheets of open-celled foam. A fiber-glass mat or cloth would then go on both sides of the sandwich and all would be pressed together. The glue squashed right through the foam, creating a new superhard substance between the outer sheets.

There were other resin-and-foam-combination plastics on the market, but they required expensive and time-consuming methods for molding. Like a good pair of pants, the ERM seemed to need no more than a quick press.

"De Lorean hopped on a plane to go and take a look at it," McLean recalls, "and he came back very enthusiastic. The next thing I knew, he and his patent lawyer were traveling all over trying to license the rights to ERM."

De Lorean found that a few overlapping patents linked Shell, Dow, and Freeman Chemical Corporation. Much smaller than either Dow or Shell, the Wisconsin-based Freeman had the lock on the all-important fabricating process, and De Lorean turned to them first. Once he had secured from Freeman exclusive rights to ERM in all ground transportation, Shell and Dow fell into line. While he paid a total of $100,000 to gain the license, his contract put further payments into the future and guaranteed that certain amounts would be spent each year on research.

De Lorean saw ERM as the linchpin of a new innovative vehicle. First and foremost, its minimal weight would require a smaller engine to tug it around and result in better fuel efficiency than in any other sports car. Its strength meant that the fuel savings could be had without sacrificing safety. Also ERM would be easier and cheaper to fabricate than steel. A few plastic molds could take the place of all the tools, equipment, and extra manpower necessary to machine metal. De Lorean sold both the safety and fuel-efficiency aspects of ERM to Grace and Allstate, making ERM development an integral part of those never-to-be-finished projects.

While De Lorean may have abandoned the Allstate safety prototype, he didn't lose faith in the market potential for a safe car. Passenger protection, he felt, would significantly contribute to a sports car's appeal. The ERM process went a long way in providing structural strength, and he also wanted to make airbags standard equipment, along with bumpers that could withstand impacts of ten miles an hour without any damage (the industry standard was three miles). The major car companies had always downplayed safety features, fearful of associating danger with auto driving in any way. But De Lorean saw safety—especially in the Nader era of consumer consciousness—as an important selling point.

ERM did have one major drawback. It couldn't be painted. But De Lorean would turn that factor into one of the car's most striking features. Forced to cover the plastic with a thin metal coat, he decided to go with the most durable material available—stainless steel. Back in 1936, in a demonstration, stainless-steel manufacturer Allegheny-Ludlum had fitted a Ford with a stainless-steel body, and the car still looked like new. Stainless steel was armor that would never rust, and also never need paint. As a result, the car would come in only one color, but that made it easier for repair shops to stock De Lorean fenders. "You can have the car in any color," De Lorean joked, modifying Henry Ford's observations on the Model T. "As long as it's stainless."

Stainless was also to heighten the futuristic look of the car when it combined with the gull-wing doors. Nothing about the De Lorean car made a greater impression than its entry hatch. The gull-wings were first used by Mercedes-Benz after World War II to cut down on the wind resistance in their racing cars. But the German company put the doors in only one production series, the 1956 Mercedes 300SL. Despite their distinctive appearance, they proved too much of a headache to engineer and maintain. Mercedes did not waste another production run to work out the wrinkles, and the car became the Vermeer of auto collectors.

De Lorean would not be the first entrepreneur to think of reviving the gull-wing. Nor was he the first to see the financial advantages of producing a two-seat sports car with an accent on safety features. In August 1974, Malcolm Bricklin, a thirty-five-year-old entrepreneur from Philadelphia who had made a fortune, first in convenience hardware and then as a Subaru importer, began producing his own two-seat gull-winged safety car in two New Brunswick, Canada, plants. Much of his seed money came from the federal and local Canadian governments in a bid to bring down the province's chronic unemployment. Little more than a year and 3,000 recall-ridden cars later, the company crashed to a halt.

It was exactly the sort of stillbirth that could have smothered De Lorean's own efforts at conception. And it was only the latest in a junkyard full of attempts to break into the American market during the preceding fifty years, including Kaiser-Frazer and the Tucker. Walter Chrysler, back in 1924, had been the last to make a go of it. But De Lorean had an answer for anyone who raised the Bricklin specter with him. As he explained to *Motor Trend*, "I don't think that since Walter Chrysler . . . you've really had anybody who's been professional about it, from the standpoint of having a background in the business. . . . Walter Chrysler was general manager of Buick when he decided to go off and start his own motor company. He really knew the business, and he hired some of the finest technical people of that day. . . . I think that we have, and are assembling, an extremely competent and professional organization of people who have been quite successful in their own end of the business. . . ."

Whatever De Lorean thought about the stodginess of the American automobile industry, he realized that nothing would add more credibility to his own company than seasoned executives from Detroit's Big Three. While part of his hiring strategy was directed at impressing investors, he also looked for the sort of "doers" who could force projects through to fruition—at least in the context of a big corporation.

De Lorean recruited the first key member of his team in October 1974 when he hired Bill Collins away from General Motors. One of Pontiac's engineering stars, Collins had followed in many of De Lorean's footsteps as head of the division's Advanced Engineering and later as assistant chief engineer. They worked together on the GTO, Tempest, and most important, Pontiac's ill-fated two-seat sports car. When GM's corporate staff decided to downsize their entire line of cars, they pooled the best engineering talent from all the divisions and put Collins in charge. To some GM old-timers, Collins, though more subdued, was the latest model of John De Lorean. A tall, angular man, with a prominent forehead and, in those days, a carefully trimmed moustache, Collins also stood out from the rest of the pack. Renowned for the meticulous care he showed every project, he was pegged as another young engineer with a very bright future.

But Collins was to have less stomach for corporate politics than De Lorean, and shortly after De Lorean left the company, he let an engineering headhunter know that his scalp was available for other endeavors. Quite unexpectedly he got a call from one of the people he had listed as a reference on his résumé. "As usual, John was calling from an airport somewhere," Collins remembers. "He wanted me to be president of Grand Prix of America. I told him I had no interest in that sort of a job. That was entertainment; not engineering. But he kept after me about helping him build his own car."

Already, De Lorean's marketing man had worked up a presentation featuring a De Lorean safety vehicle. "I remember," Collins says, "that it had gull-wing doors, advanced safety features and an engine somewhere in the back."

At first Collins tried to talk De Lorean out of the gull-wing, but eventually he agreed that the door did add something to the car's sex appeal and also had practical benefits. "If a two-door car is low to the ground, the door has to be very wide to get comfortably inside it. That makes it difficult getting out of a car in tight parking spaces. With the gull-wing, you could park within fourteen inches of a wall and still get out of the car."

Collins had important design work to do even before he knew what the car was going to look like. The basic concept of any vehicle must start with the driver's seat, or more specifically, the anatomical seat of the driver: what designers delicately call the Depressed "A" Point. De Lorean and Collins, both hovering around six foot three, obviously had a taller driver in mind and, since they wanted to end up with a sports car, they envisioned the Depressed "A" Point riding as low to the ground as possible. With that information, the roof, steering wheel, dashboard and gearshift were positioned. Eventually all the interior appointments were arrayed in a little sit-down cage known as a seating buck.

To arrive at the outward appearance of the car, Collins, along with De Lorean and Ray Prussing, journeyed to the Mecca of sports-car styling—Turin, Italy. Much as Milan is to clothing fashions, Turin is to the latest in car-body fashions. The hand-tooled prototypes are rolled out each November in the Torino Auto Show. Collins and De Lorean passed by the biggest names at the show, like Sergio Pininfarina and Giuseppe Bertone, and took the closest look at a relatively new arrival on the scene, Giorgetto Giugiaro. "Far and away, Giugiaro was the look we wanted," Collins says. "It was the cleanest and most contemporary."

Some might have even called Giugiaro fancifully futuristic. Although his most widely known designs were to be the Volkswagen Rabbit and Scirocco, in those days Giugiaro was concentrating on low, wide metallic wedges that he incorporated into model lines for Maserati and Alfa-Romeo. Back in 1970 he had completed a prototype for Porsche, called the 914/6 Tapiro, and it became his model for the De Lorean car. It too had gull-wing doors, but he would not use hidden headlights with the De Lorean as he did for Porsche; he came up instead with a wide but thin snout that could take exposed headlights and a heavy-duty bumper.

In February 1975, Giugiaro flew to Detroit to finalize contracts with De Lorean and get the specifications from Collins's seating buck. By summer he had finished his full-size wood and plastic mock-up. Collins would be amazed that Giugiaro's services added up to a total of only $65,000, payable when the car went into production.

For most of 1975, Collins was to conduct research and development on the sports car through the charity of Allstate, W.R. Grace, a seat-belt company in Canada, and the French auto giant, Renault (which had De Lorean conduct clinics on Le Car, its new entry into the American subcompact market). Collins would be listed as a participant in several of these projects even though he worked mostly on the sports car.

By the end of the year, the car was far enough along for De Lorean to go out on the hustings and start attracting backers. In October 1975, the De Lorean Motor Company filed with the state of Michigan for incorporation. As Bill Collins became the guiding genius of the De Lorean car, Tom Kimmerly became the guiding genius of the corporation. Starting a new car company was nothing new for the lawyer. He had been peripherally involved with two prior unsuccessful attempts: Tucker and Kaiser-Frazer. But De Lorean didn't see that experience as a dangerous omen. He relied on Kimmerly's counsel to structure a complex web of wholly owned subsidiaries and the transactions that transpired between them. Earlier Kimmerly had formed the Composite Technology Corporation, which had the sole task of getting ERM ready in time for the car's production. Shortly afterwards Kimmerly added yet another layer to the top of De Lorean's cake— and another layer of insulation from public scrutiny—by creating Cristina, a Nevada corporation, which held all the stock in the John Z. De Lorean Corporation, which in turn held De Lorean's share of the stock in the motor company. While the two latter firms had to comply with the unusually stringent reporting requirements of Michigan, Cristina needed to file little more than a list of the officers to satisfy Nevada law.

For the company's first funding vehicle, Kimmerly devised the De Lorean Sports Car Partnership. Limited partnerships were seldom-used sources of financing for fledgling companies, but they offered several advantages to both investors and investment. If the funding was directed at research and development, the IRS offered generous tax shelters for the partners. That was enough to keep the investors very silent and let management maintain control. The Sports Car Partnership offered thirty-five units at $100,000 apiece. In return, the partners got the chance down the line to convert their units into a healthy slice of De Lorean Motor Company stock. With the $3.5 million the partnership put up, De Lorean expected to finish the development of a prototype and a dealer network that would eventually sell the cars when they came off the assembly line.

Kimmerly got the prestigious New York law firm of Webster, Sheffield to give the limited-partnership offering a legal stamp of approval. But that would not be enough to sell the idea to skeptical investors. De Lorean quickly found that his wealthy friends were not so fast to jump on his car company bandwagon. It was one thing to say nice things about him at dinner parties, but another to actually put $100,000 on the line. In the case of old buddies Roger Penske and Bob Anderson, neither wanted to do anything to jeopardize his valuable connections with Detroit's established auto industry, and General Motors in particular.

De Lorean was forced to hit the road and appeal to strangers. But along the way, in Houston's prestigious Petroleum Club, he stumbled across someone who offered to make the fund-raising ordeal more painless. After he had finished pitching a group of oil executives, De Lorean was approached by a former Ford executive who had moved down to the Sunbelt and gone into the venture capital business. He had a partner named Tom J. Fatjo, Jr., a young man in his early thirties who was already a Wall Street sensation. Just a few years before he had bought out a Houston construction company and, fueled by public stock issues, built the nation's largest private garbage-collection company, Browning-Ferris Industries. Now he was ready to pass his wondrous Wall Street formula on to other growth companies.

De Lorean and Fatjo hit it off as soon as they were introduced. The Texan soon followed De Lorean back to Detroit and 100 West Long Lake where they struck up a deal. De Lorean promised to pay Fatjo's firm a $250,000 annual retainer and 10 percent of all the stock they sold in a future offering. De Lorean had yet to hire a comptroller, and Fatjo helped him work up a credible business plan he could show to investors.

Feeding on each other's optimism, De Lorean and Fatjo looked ahead to a future Wall Street issue. Preliminary talks started with the Texan's underwriter of choice, E.F. Hutton. All but forgotten was the limited partnership. Units sold at a snail's pace. Hardly one third were gone by the end of the summer.

What transpired next between the dynamic duo is a matter of dispute. Fatjo was to end up in court with De Lorean, like so many of the others who did business with the auto executive. Unhappy with the partnership's progress, De Lorean refused to pay Fatjo's fees, claiming that they were only meant as commission for any units Fatjo helped place. In September, De Lorean testified in his deposition, Fatjo became "convinced that we were not going to make the grade . . . and completely lost interest."

Fatjo countered that he was owed payment just for working up De Lorean's business plan. He claimed he never promised to sell units, only make a few contacts. (For a while Fatjo and his partners were officers in the partnership, which allowed them to sell units directly. One unit he did work on was bought by a New York Cadillac dealer who also wangled the exclusive franchise for two of the city's boroughs—an arrangement De Lorean salespeople later regretted.)

According to Fatjo's testimony, when they decided to part, De Lorean admitted he owed him $150,000 for services. Later, Fatjo said, he settled for one and a half units of the partnership instead. De Lorean was to have sent him a check for his services and he was to return it in exchange for a share of the Sports Car Partnership. Fatjo returned the check, but he never got his units, and later sued in Dallas court (De Lorean eventually settled).

In several interviews, De Lorean freely admitted that he was ill-prepared for the world of high finance and the vagaries of fundraising. "When you work for General Motors," he told *Business Week*, "and you want to build a new foundry in Tonawanda, New York, and you need $600 million, you fill out a form and send it away. You might get a phone call or two, or you might not. Then within a few months this document comes back with 100 signatures on it which says go spend the $600 million. Unfortunately, that was all I knew about raising money."

In real life, he found, corralling investors was a much more laborious process, and something he preferred to leave to others. Fortunately for the car company, Vice President C. R. Brown was more than willing to slog through the carpeted trenches of hotel conference rooms. During his sometimes stormy tenure with the De Lorean Motor Company, Brown continually pulled the irons out of the fire, and he, probably more than anyone else, kept the limited partnership alive.

The De Lorean Motor Company was not Brown's first start-up. Back in 1971 he took command of the North American operations for the Japanese automaker Mazda, and within two years brought the company from no standing in the market to fourth place among all importers. He is not shy about commenting on the magnitude of this feat, and claims that it may have eclipsed anything De Lorean had accomplished at General Motors. "My position at Mazda was far more taxing and significant than that of any general manager at General Motors," Brown explains. Japanese executives would visit regularly in California to query him on the state of Mazda in America, and he had to be prepared to answer questions dealing with all aspects of the business—financial, administrative, legal.

The first time he met De Lorean, Brown says, he found him, "congenial, articulate, and enthusiastic," but, he adds pointedly, "I wasn't awestruck by the man. John didn't know as much as I did about putting together a company. It was the idea that impressed me."

SILVER BEAUTY

De Lorean, he says, approached him twice when he ran Mazda's American operations: first, to offer consultation on fuel economy, and later to ask Brown to hire Jim Wangers—onetime father of the GTO ad campaign. Brown did not assent to either request.

But when De Lorean came back a third time, in August 1975, Brown had already left Mazda in the wake of controversy, helped dispose of a bankrupt electronics company, and was thinking about opening his own Chrysler dealership in Garden Grove, California. Brown flew to Detroit and met De Lorean in the 100 West Long Lake office. "The idea of starting a new car company from the ground up did not terrify me," he says. "I felt I had come pretty close to that with Mazda. I've always felt that if you have competent management and enough capitalization, it's possible to break into the American market with an entirely new product."

De Lorean was not yet able to offer Brown a salary. He started first as a consultant. His pay was to be accumulated until the company could afford to reimburse him. Brown took the flyer, working on and off for De Lorean throughout the first half of the year. "One month I didn't think John was going to make it," he says, "and I went ahead and opened up the Chrysler dealership in Garden Grove."

Born of evangelistic stock, Brown could turn a business goal into something on the order of a religious mission. His fervor was not one of exhilaration, but deep and troubling responsibility, and it seemed to weigh in the lines of his broad, fleshy face, and the deliberate pattern of his speech. His gravity was perfectly suited to selling shares in an investment that more skeptical souls might find flighty.

Brown took De Lorean's rudimentary presentation and tried to give it some polish. He hired a former promotions man from his Mazda days to put together an audio-visual slide show, and put together a program that had himself as the emcee and De Lorean as the finale.

Hamilton Gregg, a New York broker in 1976, was one of those in the audience during a De Lorean team performance. "Somebody had told me about De Lorean and suggested I go hear him talk about his plans for a car company," he remembers. "His little meeting was at one of the hotels—somewhere like the Waldorf—and to my surprise I found it to be quite impressive. They had slides with enlarged drawings of the car and a film about their patented plastic process. Bill Collins explained the car's engineering principles, and then Brown spoke about building the dealer network. I most remember some very convincing statistics on the potential for a sports car in the American market. De Lorean made a big deal about how GM was making so much profit on the Corvette without really trying. Seventy million, he said, which was peanuts for them, but a good thing for a smaller producer."

Of course, De Lorean did not talk to his audiences about the entrepreneurial experiences he had had after he left General Motors. He concentrated instead on his achievements while he was with the company. Ironically, for all the fault he found with GM, his experience there was his greatest mark of distinction. Gregg, for one, saw his vaunted corporate record as De Lorean's greatest attribute. "In my mind, John's background at General Motors was exactly what set him apart from failures like Bricklin. Until he left, he was expected to be president one day—at least that's the story I heard. I did some independent checking of my own. I called up a few dealers I knew, and they said he was the real thing. If anything, they felt he took their side against the company. They told me he had also been a demon on service and used to stress that service could build driver loyalty. Evidently most general managers only stressed sales.

"Obviously, the Sports Car Partnership was a risky venture, but I found a few very wealthy people who were interested. These were people in the 70 to 80 percent tax bracket anyway, so they didn't stand to lose much. One of them was once head of a very major U.S. corporation. He was a guy with tons of money, and he told me this wasn't his first investment in a new car company. Evidently, way back when, he had helped finance a man named Olds who started a car company that eventually became Oldsmobile."

With Gregg's help, the units sold a little faster. Ten went to dealers, who got franchises in the bargain, including John's younger brother, Chuck. The biggest share, four and three quarters, was held by a group of executives at the brokerage house of Merrill Lynch Pierce Fenner & Smith. Although the firm considered making the offering, the officers finally decided it was wiser for them to invest as private individuals, and they formed their own partnership, M.L. Associates, to buy the De Lorean units. The rest of the shares were scattered among the usual mix of investors: wealthy widows, Texas oilmen, and a couple of corporate executives. In a relative rush, the remaining two thirds of the Sports Car Partnership sold between September and November 1976.

One of the last partners was a California car dealer invited in by Brown. De Lorean and Brown had assembled several Southwestern dealers for the presentation in a Las Vegas hotel. "Besides the dealers," Brown says, "there were two other men whom I didn't know. After the meeting, my friend, who had been all ready to purchase a unit, came up and pointed out one of the men and asked, 'Is that Roy Nesseth?' I had never met Nesseth so I couldn't answer, but my friend said, 'If Nesseth is involved with De Lorean then I don't want anything to do with this. Nesseth has a deplorable reputation.'

"Immediately I pulled John aside to ask about Nesseth. John was very smooth. He went over to the dealer and told him not to worry. He said Nesseth was just an old friend who had stopped by to see the presentation. At one point he said, 'I give you my assurance Roy has nothing to do with the car company.'"

Almost as soon as the limited-partnership funds were raised, they were spent. Collins finished the first running prototype in October and immediately got started on the second. Throughout the following year, 1977, there'd be a constant scramble for money to keep the company afloat while executives traveled around the world, seeking a site for the car's eventual assembly, and asking governments to provide tens of millions for the privilege.

One young employee of this nervous era remembers both the excitement and the anxiety at 100 West Long Lake. "At times, it seemed as though we were some colossally important corporation that just happened to be run by a few people. The phone would ring from city and state governments all over America trying to get our ear. Eventually we just couldn't take any more calls from the Chambers of Commerce. We were talking about raising $90 million and breaking new ground with research partnerships. And on top of that Collins was working on this futuristic car that would be the best and the safest thing on the road. Everything at De Lorean was the biggest and the best and the newest.

"But we were also stuck in this cramped little office wondering whether or not we could make next week's payroll."

The precarious budget balancing was handled by another De Lorean recruit from General Motors, Robert M. Dewey. For twenty-six years, Dewey had been keeping financial tabs on various aspects of Chevrolet operations. As De Lorean's chief financial officer, he'd prove invaluable in preparing the very speculative business plans for the car company. He'd also become, in short order, one of the De Lorean plant-site ambassadors. "For all the troubles of those first years," Dewey says, "it was still a hell of an experience, and a hell of an ego trip. I knew what we were doing was a monumental task, but I thought that if anybody could do it, John De Lorean could."

In the midst of all the turmoil, De Lorean himself was not often around. By 1977, he and Cristina had set up their household in a duplex apartment overlooking Fifth Avenue and Central Park. A tiny office at the Chris-Craft headquarters down the street became his principal place of business. On his brief visits to Detroit, he stayed at a condominium owned by Roger Penske (although that arrangement and their friendship fell apart in a dispute over lease payments).

When De Lorean did appear at 100 West Long Lake, the junior staff member says, the troops clamored for his attention. Different camps were beginning to form. In one was Kimmerly; in another Collins and Dewey; and then the third: the motley, and to him, mysterious band of dealmakers including Nesseth and C. W. Smith. "Everyone," he says, "was jealous of John's attention and affection."

The immediate goal was to find some money to replace the diminishing partnership dollars. Wall Street experts had advised De Lorean and Kimmerly that they were unlikely to push through a public stock offering. But Brown suggested they try a more limited issue, directed solely at car dealers. In exchange for $25,000 they'd get a block of stock as well as a franchise to sell the car. His plan was a radical departure from auto-industry history. Although each dealer would in fact have a tiny piece of the entire pie, he had an interest beyond the number of cars on his floor to see the De Lorean Motor Company do well. Perhaps of even greater symbolic importance, he was not just a pawn of this car maker, but a part of it.

Kimmerly would shoulder the burden of preparing the stock registration, and he quickly found that any stock issue, even a limited one, is at best a time-consuming obstacle course. Besides passing muster before the Securities and Exchange Commission in Washington, the offering also needed the approval of state agencies. The process was to drag on throughout the year. Six states—California, Louisiana, New Mexico, South Dakota, Texas, and Wisconsin—refused to approve the stock without modifications.

The skeptical state commissioners wondered whether the dealers were really getting their money's worth from the investment. If De Lorean sold every share to the maximum number of 400 dealers, the issue could bring $10 million. But after having contributed over two thirds of the cash equity, the dealers would be left with only 13 percent of the stock. John De Lorean, in the corporate identity of the John Z. De Lorean Corporation, would control 65.6 percent.

On the books, De Lorean was shown as paying absolutely nothing for his share of the stock, although he claimed a $3.5 million value on all the developmental work for the prototype and ERM before the incorporation of the car company (developmental work actually subsidized by Grace and Allstate). But even if De Lorean's contribution was computed at $3.5 million, he would have still ended up paying only thirty-five cents a share for his stock. The dealers, meanwhile, were asked to pay $5 a share.

California demanded that De Lorean first donate some of his stock back into the company, which he did, and eventually Texas made him sign an agreement not to sell out his equity for a number of years.

The U.S. Securities and Exchange Commission was to be no easier on the De Lorean offering than the states. Each month new hoops were held up for the company to jump through.

In the rush to get off the mark, De Lorean executives almost committed a fatal error. When the SEC examiner asked how many dealers would be necessary to have a viable company, Brown came up with the round number of 150. Unknowingly, he had erected the hurdle, and the company would soon be forced to jump over it. Finally in August 1977, the SEC approved the offering, but it was set to expire on October 31. In only four months, De Lorean Motor Company had to sign up 150 dealers or go into extinction before a car rolled off the assembly line.

To make matters worse, the company ran out of money just in time for the big stock push. Help came from an unexpected source, whom SEC registrations first identified as John W. Carson. He was more widely known as *The Tonight Show* host, Johnny Carson. In return for $500,000, this investor received 250,000 shares of stock and "the right on terms and compensation to be negotiated, to be a public spokesman for the Company in connection with the sale of the Company product." In other words, if the pay was high enough, he wanted the right to make commercials for the car—a right De Lorean would have gladly surrendered to Carson (although that sort of advertising never did come to pass).

The social connection with the entertainer came through Cristina. But Carson was not the one involved in protracted negotiations over the stock purchase. Those arrangements were made by his business manager and lawyer, "the Bombastic Henry Bushkin" Carson jokes about in his monologues. Bushkin would later be named Carson's designee on the motor-company board and actively get involved in De Lorean's personal affairs as well.

Compared to the Johnny Carson deal, the stock sale to the dealers was to be a much more tedious and disappointing affair. The company couldn't cash a check until the minimum number of dealers had invested. Other SEC restrictions kept muzzles on Brown and his staff. There could be no talk of pizzazz—only the cautious objectives and risks laid out in the prospectus. Their one big attraction was Collins's first prototype. Although the engineer still had some work to do on it, Brown appropriated it for the roadshow.

"I conducted all of the dealer meetings," Brown says. "We'd call anywhere from ten to seventy-five dealers at a time. Each state had different requirements about who could make a presentation. In some you had to be an officer or a registered broker just to talk about the deal. I tried to stick as close as I could to the prospectus."

Brown remembers De Lorean attending about one out of five of the presentations, but adds that De Lorean wouldn't help much because he "invariably exaggerated," putting them in jeopardy with the SEC, and also alienating some of the conservative dealers. "They're not stupid. In fact, they're very astute businessmen," he says, "and yet, John could make the wildest claims. He'd talk about how many barrels of fuel we saved by not painting cars. None of us had any idea how he got those figures. In those days he also kept telling people he'd have a twenty-five-year warranty on the body. At that point, we had no idea what our warranty program was going to be, but we could be sure it wouldn't be twenty-five years.

"He went on about the most irrelevant things. When it looked like we'd build the car in an air-force base in Puerto Rico, one of his favorite pitches was how we'd fly the cars into the country. He'd say, 'Can you imagine the impact of all those silver beauties with the gull-wings open lined up on the runway?'"

Brown would be most astounded by De Lorean's claims that he had sunk $4 million of his own money into the company. "First of all I knew that wasn't true. But, secondly, there was no way the dealer could see any evidence of John's $4 million investment in the prospectus. All those statements could do was confuse them."

After presentations, Brown had four field representatives who followed up with the audience. William A. Morgan, who worked with Brown at Mazda, was one of the first representatives he hired. Morgan's memories of De Lorean's performance are a bit more positive. "I thought John was great with a group and really held their attention. I think he was even better socializing with them afterwards. He had a very amiable way about him that made people think he was the type of person who would listen to them."

Morgan soon learned the intensity of feelings for De Lorean among GM dealers. "There was no gray area," he says. "They either thought he walked on water or they hated his guts. A lot didn't like his life-style, or what they thought his life-style was. But I found that, as a group, Pontiac dealers had the most respect for him."

Whatever dealers thought of De Lorean, Morgan still had an uphill battle selling them stock. "Dealers aren't the most flamboyant investors in the world," he explains. "They go for safe investments like real estate, not something nebulous like stock. We really had to concentrate on the hard business aspects of getting a franchise—how the car would increase their traffic in the showroom, and how they stood to make some good money on the markup."

By early September, eight weeks before the deadline, Brown had signed up 110 dealers. "I thought we were doing very well. I had just four guys with me. One of them signed forty-eight dealers. But during that month we had a very big meeting scheduled for Chicago that John attended. I could see he was very nervous that we weren't going to make the deadline. He told me, 'I don't care what this takes. I don't give a shit if we have to pay someone, but I want this to get done.'

"I told him it was getting done, but then he told me that he wanted Roy Nesseth to come in. 'Roy has guys who can get it done.' I told him that unless they were experienced, they wouldn't help. John said I could teach them what they're supposed to know."

Soon after, Roy appeared with ten other men and they set up shop near Brown's dealership with a bank of phones. While so-called boiler-room tactics are fine for selling stationery, they are specifically prohibited by the SEC. De Lorean executives later learned that the men had been promised at least $1,500 for every stock offer they sold—another violation of SEC regulations, which permit commissions only for registered brokers.

SILVER BEAUTY

"I wasted two weeks going over the dealer program and SEC rules with them. They were supposed to wait for dealer meetings," Brown says, "and then do follow-up after the dealers heard a proper presentation. But they didn't wait. They went out and tried on their own."

A couple flew into Bill Morgan's East Coast territory. While he gave them a few dealers to check back with, he soon found that they were making other calls as well. "At one point, they called every dealer on Long Island, Philadelphia, and some of the top people in New England. Later when I got back to some of those dealers, they were still mad. They'd make a point of telling me that they'd already been hit by 'De Lorean's boiler room.'"

Both Brown and Morgan maintain that Roy's crew picked up no more than a handful of dealers, which didn't matter much anyway, since they came in at eight dealers over the minimum.

But De Lorean was to hold a different opinion of Roy's efforts. In later years, when a reporter asked about his relationship with Nesseth, De Lorean quickly replied, "Back in 1977, Roy saved DMC [De Lorean Motor Company]. It's as simple as that. I never forget the people who help me."

De Lorean went on, without any reservation, to describe Roy's boiler-room methods. "Roy dropped everything. He immediately set up operations, bringing in people to help and totally disregarding everything else in his life."

His reward for Roy was to be a salaried position with the company, starting at $75,000. "That whole story about Roy saving the company," Morgan says, "was just a way John had of rubbing C.R.'s nose in the dirt."

No matter who saved the company, it was not saved by much. The stock offering yielded another $3.4 million—not enough to finance further development. Major hopes for big funding rested with whatever city, state, or nation would most want a De Lorean assembly plant.

Then, out of the blue, an alternative in the private sector suddenly emerged—right in the midst of the rush to meet the SEC deadline. One of De Lorean's friends in Detroit had approached financier and Diners Club founder Alfred Bloomingdale about investing in the De Lorean Motor Company, but he found that Bloomingdale had a better idea. Along with senior partners of Lehman Brothers and other Wall Street power-brokers, Bloomingdale had secured options on a sizable chunk of stock in the foundering American Motors Corporation. AMC chairman Roy Chapin was about to be forced into retirement, and the company's president was slated to take his place. An opening then remained for AMC's chief operating officer. The mere announcement of De Lorean's appointment as president, Bloomingdale figured, would have made the AMC stock soar, and mean even more exponential gains for his options.

De Lorean eagerly entered into frenzied negotiations. For two weeks a top AMC officer visited 100 West Long Lake to brief the putative president on the company's shaky finances. "They were ready to let De Lorean build his sports car—do anything he wanted," explains the go-between, who prefers to remain nameless. "The major interest of the Bloomingdale group was the stock. John would have gotten some of that action too—maybe several million from the whole deal. But John had never negotiated this sort of a deal before with someone on the level of a Bloomingdale. With people like that, their word is their bond. Once you agree verbally on a contract, whether it's signed or not, you live up to it. But John always tried to squeeze that extra bit, and this time he squeezed the wrong guys. The morning when the board was ready to vote on his financial package, John got in touch with one of the Lehman Brothers partners and told him he wanted the deal doubled. That was the end of negotiations with John De Lorean.

"Bloomingdale called me at home that night, and he didn't sound very upset. I remember he said, 'I'm delighted we had a chance to find out what he's like before we hired him.'

"A little later John called me. 'Hell,' he said, 'I was just trying them on for size. Why don't you call Bloomingdale and tell him I was just kidding?'

"I told him I was sorry, but it was too late. These people don't listen to apologies."

·11·
Forty-five Days

On the last Friday morning of July 1978, the Manhattan conference room of the law firm Stroock & Stroock & Lavan was packed with lawyers and government officials. After a year of hard-fought negotiations, the De Lorean Motor Company finally seemed resigned to build its factory on an abandoned air-force base sixty-five miles northwest of San Juan, Puerto Rico. Assembled for the occasion were representatives of the island's governor and business development agencies, their legal counsel from Stroock & Stroock & Lavan, United States officials from the Federal Farmers Home Administration and the Federal Economic Development Administration. Only one person was missing—an officer of the De Lorean Motor Company. A lawyer representing De Lorean had shown up, and seemed genuinely shocked to find himself alone on the other side of the table. As the rest of the room started to fume, he grabbed the nearest phone and frantically tried to find out what was happening. He would not hear another word for the rest of the day.

A few blocks away in New York's Hilton Hotel, Bob Dewey sat anxiously in his room and listened to his phone ring. For two days he had alternately stalled and cajoled Puerto Rico's disparate forces. He knew full well that across the Atlantic another team of De Lorean officials were frantically moving to close a deal with the British government that would put the assembly plant in Belfast, Northern Ireland. It was the ultimate squeeze play conducted over international phone lines, although one party doing the squeeze—Puerto Rico—would not know anyone else was in the game until it was finished.

The De Lorean people had hoped the British deal would be signed earlier in the week but, by Thursday, both sides were still thrashing out the details. Friday morning, as Dewey dressed in his hotel room, he was all but ready to walk down the street and sign an agreement with Puerto Rico. But De Lorean, calling from his Chris-Craft office, caught him before he could leave. "They were close to signing with the British," Dewey says, "and John told me to stay in my room."

They would talk again at noon, and agree to meet at a nearby hamburger joint for a quick bite. The British were offering more than the $90 million De Lorean executives estimated they'd need to reach production. Never had De Lorean's dream of manufacturing his own car seemed so close, but when he joined Dewey at the luncheonette, he did not look like a happy man. "John was extremely nervous, and it seemed to me that he was more worried that the deal was going to go through. I think he realized he had what he asked for. He would finally be forced to show the world what he could do. The shopping days were over."

Before Collins had finished designing a car, De Lorean started to look for a plant to build it in. While there was some doubt about the market for new luxury sports cars, there was no doubt about the market for auto-assembly plants. Governments all over the world clamored for new industry—for the jobs created on the site, and the employment spillover to the myriad smaller firms that spring up around a large factory. Even industry giants, like Ford and General Motors, who often complained about government regulation, were more than happy to have the government intervene in financing new facilities, and during the Seventies they began pitting governments against each other to see which could come up with the sweetest package of incentives to lure an expanding conglomerate. Bricklin proved that the public sector could be just as receptive to speculative new ventures as well.

From the start, De Lorean set his sights beyond the borders of the United States. Among his first contacts was an entrepreneurial Jesuit priest with connections to Spain's king, Juan Carlos. De Lorean's onetime diesel partner, Ray Prussing, put him in touch with the priest, and their initial conversations were over a plan to market Spanish castings to American industry. In the course of several trips to Spain in 1975 and 1976, De Lorean was shown an old, abandoned Ford plant. "Right off the bat, John had an offer from the Spanish government that was over $100 million," says one man involved as an intermediary in the deal. "But the Spanish government wanted a lot more control than John was willing to give up, and they also wanted to push a few partners on him who had some sort of family ties."

De Lorean's search didn't neglect territory closer to home. When he worked with Tom Fatjo, he seriously considered another old Ford plant in Fort Worth. He looked at potential sites in Wichita and one in Marysville, Ohio, where Honda eventually built its first U.S. plant. There were several meetings on a site in Allentown with Pennsylvania's governor, Milton Schapp, and midnight telephone calls, De Lorean told one magazine, from Alabama's governor, George Wallace.

However, the most serious and realistic offer came from Puerto Rico. No other political entity had previously offered either the financing or the tax abatements that were available to the Commonwealth. The investment banking firm of First Boston Corporation made the initial contact with the Puerto Rico Economic Development Administration. Throughout the negotiations, aides from the governor's office were closely involved.

De Lorean figured that he needed over $90 million to bring his car on the market, and the Puerto Ricans were ready to come up with two thirds of that, primarily through a mix of loans guaranteed by federal and local authorities. Forty million dollars' worth were to be backed by the Federal Farmers Home Administration (since some of the site was on agricultural property) and the Economic Development Administration. Puerto Rican agencies and banks provided $20 million more in low-interest loans, half of which would be converted into stock. The Commonwealth was ready to throw in an additional $3 million if certain employment levels were met, and a 90 percent tax abatement for fifteen years.

On April 4, 1977, De Lorean signed an agreement with Puerto Rico. The island promised to keep its offer open until May, and in return De Lorean gave assurances that he wouldn't look elsewhere. But the car company still had a long road to travel before it could even qualify for the deal. U.S. bureaucrats insisted that De Lorean first raise the $30 million of privately backed capital he predicted he'd need to complete the project. On top of that, they wanted to see orders for 40,000 cars.

The car company executives had hoped to raise $10 million from their dealer offering (as it turned out, an overly optimistic assessment), and if, indeed, 400 dealers participated, each could easily average ten orders. But raising $20 million on top of that was a different and much taller order.

Again, Kimmerly thought about a limited partnership, but he needed more help to bring off one of this unprecedented size. On the advice of another De Lorean lawyer, Eric Javits (son of New York senator Jacob Javits), he turned to the investment banking firm of Oppenheimer & Company, one of New York's most innovative venture capital firms. Several of the senior Oppenheimer executives got involved as both planners and participants in the mammoth undertaking. The eventual package for the De Lorean Research Limited Partnership priced over 130 units at $150,000 apiece.

There was no way De Lorean was going to meet the first deadline. But the Puerto Ricans willingly pushed it back seven more times over the next year as the dealer-stock sale continued to bog down in red tape. They even permitted De Lorean to entertain offers from other locations. Their accommodation, however, did not make De Lorean executives feel any fonder about Puerto Rico. Concerned about language barriers and the island's work ethic from the start, they eventually found enough tangible reasons to relegate the deal from "most likely" to "last resort."

Their principal criticism lay with the site itself, the former

Ramey Air Base located in northwest Puerto Rico. Isolated from major roads, the location depended on either the airstrip or a small nearby port for heavy transportation. "When I was at the site during one negotiation," Dewey says, "they had a brownout. It lasted about four hours. I found out later there were brownouts a couple of times a month out there. Do you have any idea what that would do to assembly-line production?"

Other details of the original agreement also came unraveled. The government wasn't sure it had proper deeds to the parcel where the factory would be. Originally the land had been confiscated from local *campesinos* to make way for the air-force base, and government officials feared that the relatives of those refugees might return with documented claims to the site. Some officials involved in the early negotiations left the government, and their replacements were talking about a tax on each mechanical drawing. While De Lorean later charged that these bureaucrats openly solicited bribes, Dewey says, "I don't know how John could substantiate a claim like that. We certainly didn't have any blatant demands for payoffs. But we were told we'd have to work with certain suppliers, and I think that's something we heard in a lot of places."

The federal government's willingness to guarantee $40 million of loans for the De Lorean project did not go unnoticed by states and cities who felt themselves just as deserving of his plant. Early in 1978, after a four-month study of its own, Detroit offered De Lorean a $50 million financial package, most of it in loans leveraged from federal urban-development grants.

Shortly after the city made the offer, *Detroit Free Press* reporters Kirk Cheyfitz and Allan Sloan discovered the trouble De Lorean had had selling stock to dealers. During a lengthy phone interview, De Lorean explained that some of his plans had gone awry when he put his faith in a wealthy Arab financier who was ready to underwrite the costs of the entire project. According to De Lorean the sheikh backed out rather than be identified as federal securities laws required. "Back in the Sixties, any moron with an idea could raise capital," De Lorean told the reporters. "Now, it's impossible." If he did manage to raise the $100 million he needed, De Lorean exclaimed, "it will be the most incredible accomplishment of the last hundred years."

Detroit officials were not dismayed by De Lorean's problems raising private funds. "We had our own peculiar reasons for backing the project," then city-planner Anthony P. DeVito says, "and I don't think they would have applied to any other city. We saw De Lorean as an opportunity to build a new assembly plant on a prime piece of real estate. Even if he went under, we knew that in Detroit we could find an occupant for the most modern auto-assembly plant in the world. I don't think Puerto Rico had that option building something out in the middle of nowhere."

DeVito's prime concern was whether the Big Three auto companies would tolerate a competitor, tiny as it might be, cropping up in their backyard. "We wanted to be absolutely sure that nobody in General Motors wanted to sandbag the whole thing. Quite to my surprise, the auto executives we sounded out really didn't care. In fact, with all the talk of antitrust suits against GM, I think they would have welcomed the evidence that someone else can compete. I was somewhat new in town, and personally I couldn't gauge whether or not they were hostile. It just seemed to me that most of the corporate executives were not much for direct entrepreneurial action themselves and had no real envy of De Lorean, or even understanding of why he was going to all this trouble. My feeling was they didn't much care what happened to his venture."

DeVito says he did not feel the need to check into De Lorean's personal background. "All we were concerned about was the viability of the car company, and our consultants, who were some of the top people in the industry, felt it could work."

Although he met with De Lorean a few times, DeVito says most of their negotiations were conducted over the phone. "I could see that people like Dewey were not in a position to make the decisions. He seemed to have as much trouble reaching John as I did. Still, we must have spoken over twenty times. I had one conversation with [De Lorean] when he was in his San Diego ranch that must have gone on for over four hours."

Dewey admits that he was having problems reaching De Lorean

in those days, and often wondered whether De Lorean really wanted to settle on a site for the factory. "At times, I thought John didn't want to go anywhere. It seemed he was always afraid something better would walk in the door."

Dewey did not see the Detroit deal as any better than Puerto Rico. "In essence, [the Detroit officials] kept telling us that we could still get the car on the market if we downsized the plant and tooling. In that case all we needed was $45 million in outside financing, which coincidentally enough was the figure they were offering."

But some offers did crop up to compete with Puerto Rico, from another island-state, the Republic of Ireland. Again, an intermediary made the first contact for the car company. In this case, the go-between was the Canadian branch of a Swiss investment bank, Wood Gundy Limited. Having already invested in Bricklin, Wood Gundy should have been reluctant to get burned a second time, but director G. Edmund King had tried to get De Lorean involved in another project, and afterwards was impressed enough by De Lorean to take another risk on his car. Wood Gundy invested $500,000 in a deal similar to Johnny Carson's and offered to make introductions to Irish officials.

By this time, De Lorean's negotiating team had changed considerably from the time he had first dealt with Puerto Rico. Among the new members was legal counsel Alan Cohen—one De Lorean executive calls him a "Lou Grant" type—a senior partner at the New York law firm of Paul, Weiss, Rifkind, Wharton & Garrison, and a specialist in corporate negotiations. The other addition was square-jawed and taciturn, Walter P. Strycker, a former top financial officer at IBM and Pittsburgh's Wheelabrator Frye, who had met De Lorean through their mutual friend at Rockwell, Bob Anderson.

Together, Strycker and Cohen made a formidable combination. Both had played games of corporate poker with antes that could have buried casinos in chips. Both could operate behind curtains of icy calm. Unfortunately, their leader was not capable of the same reserve, and his impromptu comments made some negotiations difficult.

Strycker tells of a typical De Lorean outburst during a crucial meeting with Irish officials. "John had a habit of pontificating. He'd say things that really were not relevant to the proposals on the table. One statement he made continually was how he saw the company eventually becoming an adjunct of Ford or Chrysler, manufacturing a separate line of luxury sedans and sports cars.

"Now you have to realize Ireland had been hurt by multinationals like Ford and Chrysler, which, at the first sign of economic recession in America, closed their Irish plants. Before we went into the meeting, I told John that the last thing these people wanted to hear was that we wanted to sell out to a big multinational. But at a key point in our negotiations, when we get to the future of the company, John says, 'We'll then be in a position to negotiate for acquisition with Chrysler or Ford.'

"I think there were sixteen people in the room on their side, and in unison, their mouths dropped and their faces went white. They then asked to be excused and went out to caucus. When they came back, they wanted no more negotiating. They just said, 'Here are our terms.' "

The terms included government control over the company for seven years. They also wanted De Lorean to use a huge, antiquated facility in Limerick. Their terms were unacceptable. Strycker says, "We told them we can't live with that sort of a deal. We all but resigned ourselves to either Puerto Rico or Detroit."

But the Wood Gundy representative traveling with the De Lorean negotiating team reminded the others that there was still one more player on the Emerald Isle. Britain's protectorate, Northern Ireland, was competing furiously with the Republic of Ireland for international industrial development. It really couldn't hurt, the suggestion went, to at least compare notes with the authorities on the other half of the island.

Thirty days later, they were in Belfast talking to the Northern Ireland Development Agency (NIDA). "That day John was in one of his sulking moods," Strycker remembers. "He wasn't happy with the meeting and after a half hour, he just got up to leave. So it was up to me and Al Cohen to explain the project and the status of the Puerto Rico deal and the Oppenheimer partnership. Then we all hammered out the basis for financing.

"They made it clear we had to locate in Belfast, and that the worse the area, the more financing they'd give us. But there wasn't one person who said you have to hire somebody, or use someone else as a supplier. They were truly interested in creating jobs, and the social and economic impact of a major manufacturing facility. We were to be the momentum project that could get things going for them. They said, 'We have the people, labor, and money. You have the project, management, and market. We're willing to let you make a profit on our investment, so we can have the opportunity to do this with another manufacturer again.' "

When Cohen and Strycker mentioned the funding they would need, they didn't see the usual shocked expressions. Only nodding heads. They signed an agreement in principle before they left Belfast. "When Cohen called to tell John about the Belfast offer," Dewey says, "John wanted to know whether it was real. He told me, 'There was no way it could be better. It was too good to be true.' "

Nevertheless, some obstacles remained to the deal. British tax laws blocked any government financing from going directly to a foreign company. The only way to circumvent that barrier was to create a British subsidiary in which NIDA had a controlling interest.

NIDA officials followed Cohen and Strycker back to New York for a longer meeting with De Lorean. They expected their ideas about a British subsidiary to be, at best, politely rebuffed. But they would find a "comfortable and urbane" De Lorean who seemed more content to chat about the political situation in Northern Ireland than discuss the details of a plan. "To our surprise," one of the NIDA officials remembers, "he was happy to agree with everything we suggested. He had no problems with a subsidiary, or controls, or our demands for representatives on both the boards of the subsidiary and the car company in the States."

As the magnanimous magnitude of Northern Ireland's offer began to emerge on paper, what the officials requested in return looked less important to De Lorean executives. Besides the equity investment of NIDA, the car company was also offered grants and loans from the nation's Department of Commerce. "John got the best deal I've ever seen," Strycker says. The total package was worth $97 million. Of that, almost one third was an outright grant. An additional $20 million of loans could be converted to grants if employment goals were met. Another $32.5 million came in NIDA equity. A further $12.3 million was loaned on the factory.

"Almost all of the Puerto Rico deal was a leveraged loan," Strycker explains, "but in Belfast the only debt was the mortgage on half the factory, and that didn't start to bear interest until production started. So for next to nothing, you end up with a brand new facility, tooling, training, equipment, working capital, and money for marketing, research, and development. On top of that, John got one of the strongest partners you can get in venture capital—a government. Obviously it was fully capable of keeping him alive and helping him develop his business plan."

From that first meeting in New York, negotiations were carried on with NIDA and British officials in a white heat. The following weekend, De Lorean was back in Belfast with a business plan. At that time, he met Don Concannon, minister of state responsible for industry and commerce in Northern Ireland. A big, burly MP from a rough mining constituency, Concannon squired De Lorean around the Belfast area, showing him training centers set up for other incoming industries and the boggy field between Catholic and Protestant enclaves where De Lorean's plant would be located.

"I think he had a bit of conscience about the area," Concannon says, "and wanted to do some good. At one point some information about his project leaked out in the press, and the letters started to pour into my office—people begging for jobs and not even asking about the wage rate, and he found that impressive."

Concannon remembers that De Lorean's biggest reservation about Belfast was the security. "I told him the one thing terrorists didn't do was bomb their own people out of work. He also got a chance to talk to political, religious, and community leaders in this area. They were able to rid him of the complex that there's a bomb on every corner."

If anything, Concannon explains, the factory would have bolstered security in the area. "Creating new jobs was part and parcel of our security policy. We felt that if the young people getting out of school had an opportunity for a job, they wouldn't be hanging about to make trouble. My job was to scour the world looking for what we called feeder industries, that would not just provide job opportunities on their own, but create other jobs for the suppliers that would feed the factories."

Since the Fifties, the British government had used economic development to quell what they call the "troubles" in Northern Ireland. A renewal of violence in the early Seventies, combined with the worldwide fuel crisis, stopped whatever industrial growth had occurred and started the country sliding backwards. But the program was to be revived again with even more vigor as part of the overall carrot-and-stick policy of Roy Mason. Appointed secretary of state for Northern Ireland in 1976, Mason threw himself at the job with the same ferocious tenacity he had brought to other high level Labour cabinet positions. He showed no quarter to the IRA, whom he would only call terrorists, and continued a controversial campaign to intern suspected members under emergency powers. During three decades in Parliament, the onetime miner gained financial acumen that was respected by fellow members and ministers. His political views also shifted to the Right and, while his militaristic moves in Northern Ireland raised the hackles on members of his own party, they also found bipartisan support among the leaders of the Conservative opposition.

Mason was as anxious to establish industrial stability in Northern Ireland as he was to stamp out the IRA. Together with his junior minister, Concannon, he made progress attracting foreign companies, but the going was slow. As he later wrote in the daily *Times* of London, "De Lorean happened at a time when no private enterprise would have entered west Belfast without government intervention, government cash, and had bold decisions not been taken by ministers."

Accused of rushing the De Lorean project through without an adequate study of its feasibility, Mason replies in *The Times* that at least fifteen government departments took part in the decision.

He writes that they raised questions about the cost and trade implications of the project, and also wondered whether the plant might be better suited for Wales or Scotland. But he finally hammered the deal through with all of their support. There was further surprising acquiescence in Parliament. The most vocal critic was a member of Mason's own party. The secretary of state had enough respect among the Conservative MPs to hear only isolated complaints about the cost of the De Lorean plan and the economic wisdom of government economic involvement with a private business.

Less attention was given to De Lorean's own background. Concannon explains that he quickly dismissed the stories about De Lorean's flamboyant lifestyle. "What we did was checking [sic] on what he'd done for General Motors. Here was some investment that was going to provide a lot of jobs . . . and of course what we were more considerate [sic] of was his capabilities of doing that job. We have a lot of flamboyant persons in the House of Commons. That's not to say they can't do their job . . . What we were looking for was a fellow who could get things cracking in Northern Ireland and help us out with our policy of jobs and security."

When pressed, Concannon admits he did search further into the reasons why De Lorean left GM. At the time, he was concluding an agreement with General Motors to build a seat-belt plant in Belfast, and he had contact with a few of the company's high-level executives. "Basically [I] was looking for somebody to do the dirty on him at GM, but no one did. The only comments I heard were if one man in the world could get a green field into a plant that would start production, it was De Lorean. Besides, if anything were wrong with him, then why had Puerto Rico and Detroit all but signed him up?"

However, one lower-level official in Concannon's department remembers that a few people were willing to "do the dirty" on De Lorean. "We knew about that racetrack he ran with his brother, and the dealership in Kansas. But we didn't take those things very seriously. American businessmen always end up in court over one thing or another. I don't think it's unusual for an entrepreneur to have a few companies go bankrupt when he's starting up."

• FORTY-FIVE DAYS •

In just forty-five days after the British first met De Lorean in New York, a master agreement was signed. Throughout that time, De Lorean kept up negotiations on two fronts. One squad was based in Belfast rushing to adjust the business plan to the different demands of an Irish site. Meanwhile Dewey continued bargaining with Puerto Rico—not just to put pressure on the British, but also to keep their investment banker, Oppenheimer & Company, happy. The investment firm had already sold $20 million worth of units in a research partnership. But their solicitation was based on building a plant in Puerto Rico. If De Lorean did opt for Northern Ireland, the research partners could rescind their investments. The Oppenheimer executives did not relish that prospect. "They told John to stop screwing around," Dewey says, "and settle down in Puerto Rico."

The final agreement with NIDA would come as a crashing anticlimax. De Lorean signed the document at Al Cohen's office. No one bothered to break the news to Puerto Rico's contingents of lawyers still waiting at Stroock & Stroock & Lavan's suite for a De Lorean representative to appear.

"We never did celebrate the signing," Dewey says. "I think each of us had different feelings about it." Mentally and physically exhausted, Dewey just wanted to take the next flight back to Detroit. De Lorean was on the verge of his self-proclaimed, "most incredible accomplishment of the last hundred years," but when Dewey stopped by his Chris-Craft office to say goodbye, he found the miracle worker petrified by the prospect of an upcoming meeting. "John had decided to see Howard Phillips from Oppenheimer to tell him we had signed the British deal, and he wanted me to be there with him. John hated confrontations. I told John I wanted to go home and I had a five o'clock plane to catch. But he was like a little kid. He didn't want me to go and leave him alone to face Phillips. He kept saying, 'You can't let me down like this.'

"I told him that if he wanted company when Phillips came, he should call Al Cohen. Then I left."

De Lorean did not bother to meet with any representative of Puerto Rico. On the following Monday, the Commonwealth still couldn't believe the car company had actually backed out. An angry Governor Carlos Romero Barcelo told *The New York Times*, "Today, I tried personally to get in touch with Mr. De Lorean and he has evaded my calls. This demonstrates without doubt his bad faith to everyone."

Officials in Washington were just as angry. The director of the business development office for the Economic Development Administration never had a company turn down loan guarantees as large as the ones he offered De Lorean. "This does not sit too well with us," he told the *Times*. "We put a lot of time and money into this."

If both the federal government and the Commonwealth of Puerto Rico were hornswoggled, the feat was all the more amazing considering the scanty resources of the hornswoggler and the highly speculative nature of his enterprise. The eventual $97 million De Lorean culled from NIDA with the help of an unrequited Puerto Rico added up to the greatest triumph of his business career. However, his success was also a dangerous lesson that sometimes image can suffice without substance.

Despite the largesse of the British government, De Lorean's executives could see the long haul that still lay before them in taking a car company literally from the ground up and starting production a year and a half later, as the stock prospectus promised.

Concannon and the rest of Northern Ireland's authorities believed De Lorean to be "a fellow who could get things cracking." But as far as De Lorean was concerned, his job was practically finished once he signed the British deal.

In a *Business Week* interview after the signing he indicated that the NIDA agreement was the crest of the hill, not the bottom. After four years, his car company had raised barely $5 million. In a span of forty-five days, the coffers swelled twentyfold. "The hardest part is pretty well behind me now," he told the magazine. "I think our chances of making it are 95 percent. That's nearly double what they were a year ago."

12
GPD

On the morning of October 18, 1978, a junior executive in the 100 West Long Lake office of the De Lorean Motor Company received a summons from his chief executive. He took the next plane to New York City, and just before noon was standing beside John De Lorean's desk at the Madison Avenue headquarters of the Chris-Craft Corporation.

De Lorean had not brought him to Manhattan to discuss the revised business plan or to help with the company's impending move to its new Park Avenue location. Instead, he asked the executive to do no more than spend the day running an errand. The first leg of his mission would be a taxi ride downtown to the Wall Street branch of the Chemical Bank. He would then search out a bank officer and draw a check on the account of the De Lorean Research Limited Partnership. He was to have the check made out to a company called GPD Services, for the sum of $12.5 million.

After matter-of-factly issuing his instructions, De Lorean returned to his papers. His courier left the office in a daze. Within an hour he'd be holding more money in his hands than most people see in several lifetimes. "I don't care how honest you are," he says of the incident today, "but for that one moment you wonder whether you could get away with having the check made out to cash and taking the next plane to Rio."

He also wondered what De Lorean proposed to do with the funds. After De Lorean made his decision to build the assembly plant in Northern Ireland, Oppenheimer & Company had not been enthusiastic about going through with the research partnership. They consented, but the investors could drop out if they chose, and several did. Finally, after taking its 10 percent commission, Oppenheimer deposited what was left—$16.8 million—in the partnership account. Now, just one month later, almost 75 percent of the assets were going to GPD Services, a firm he'd never before heard of.

After getting the check drawn, the executive returned to Chris-Craft again for De Lorean to sign it, and then went back downtown to the bank for the appropriate officer to countersign. He finally handed over the endorsed check to De Lorean that afternoon in his Fifth Avenue apartment. De Lorean folded the bank draft as though it were an ordinary scrap of paper and slipped it into his wallet.

"It was a cool fall day," the executive remembers, "but that night, when I got home and took off my jacket, I saw that under my arms my shirt was stained with huge rings of perspiration. I looked like I had run a race."

GPD Services remains the most disturbing mystery of the De Lorean Motor Company. A large part of the mystery was what "GPD" stood for. The letters were not even decoded in the company's contract with De Lorean. More like a ghost enterprise than a shell company, its address is a post-office box in Geneva, Switzerland. The only employee of the firm ever to be identified is a Swiss woman, whom De Lorean referred to as a Mrs. Juhan. She does, indeed, exist, but she refuses to speak about GPD, John De Lorean, or anything else. Just a few weeks before De Lorean drew the check from the research partnership, GPD first registered in Panama. Its Panama City lawyers are just as silent as Mrs. Juhan. Within one year, two De Lorean Motor Company subsidiaries would pay GPD $17.65 million. No trace of that money has ever been found.

For De Lorean executives, GPD became the most unsettling aspect of their company's affairs. When Vice President Bill Haddad first looked into the matter, so he could respond to questions from British reporters, he found that in Belfast, "GPD is a hush-hush subject." Some executives, including Haddad, wondered whether the phantom firm was a way De Lorean diverted company assets to his personal holdings. Others saw it as an embarrassment with far-reaching consequences for the gull-wing car. In an effort not to call attention to GPD, they say, De Lorean bypassed vital engineering services that the Swiss firm was contracted to perform. Like an unhinged muffler, GPD dragged along throughout the brief, tumultuous ride of the De Lorean Motor Company, first shooting off sparks, then scraping louder and louder until it came clattering to the ground.

The most suspicious aspect of GPD Services is the failure of De Lorean's SEC files to mention it by name after 1979. From then on, the firm is called an "independent contractor" and no more.

According to that first and last reference in the 1979 De Lorean Motor Company stock offering, GPD was to assist the company in "completion of product-design development." Although Collins had already made two prototypes, there was still a great deal of design work to be done. In effect, his work to that point was a film script. The property still had to go into production. Someone had to cast suppliers, design the set for the factory, choreograph the assembly, and, most important, build the props—tooling—needed to fabricate the various parts of the car. Very few companies in the world are capable of performing this transitional service. Detroit car companies have trouble doing it on their own. De Lorean claimed that he had made a desperate search for such help on both sides of the Atlantic. The German company Porsche, which is the leader in the field, asked too high a price and too long a lead time.

His salvation came, he says, when he was "suddenly contacted" by GPD in the early fall of 1978. According to De Lorean, besides providing its own engineers, GPD also subcontracted Lotus Cars, Limited, along with its celebrated founder, A. C. B. (Colin) Chapman, to supervise the transformation.

Exactly how De Lorean and Lotus decided to join forces is a matter of dispute. De Lorean has said that GPD was the matchmaker. The man who was then Lotus' finance director, Fred Bushell, agrees. He told the *Sunday Telegraph*, "[GPD] personnel travel the world looking for deals. . . . They found Mr. De Lorean for us. After all, in 1978, who was De Lorean? It didn't mean anything much then."

But there is plenty of evidence that, prior to GPD, De Lorean meant more to Chapman and Lotus than Bushell admits. First of all, Chapman had a long-standing relationship with Chris-Craft—where De Lorean was on the board—to make boat hulls out of the plastic process he had patented. Furthermore, early in the summer of 1978, De Lorean had contacted Chapman's engineering director, A. C. Rudd, about a job in the engineering squad he was going to assemble. Rudd turned him down but, according to several Lotus executives, then asked De Lorean to consider subcontracting the Lotus staff.

During all of his deliberations with Lotus, no one ever saw a trace of GPD. "All I knew was that in September 1978, Chapman and [Lotus managing director, Michael J.] Kimberly spent a day testing the car while it was in Phoenix," Bill Collins says. "That was the beginning of their involvement with the company. They were then supposed to issue a report suggesting the best way to get the car into production. I never met anyone from GPD, and I never heard that anyone else from the De Lorean Motor Company met anyone from GPD."

The relationship between Chapman and De Lorean lies at the heart of the GPD enigma. Once again, De Lorean had found a doer and, in this case, a certified winner as well. An aircraft engineer by training, Chapman started building race cars in the garage behind his house during the late Forties. Over the next two decades he revolutionized the sport, single-handedly creating the Formula One–Grand Prix event we know today. He was the first to incorporate aircraft techniques to harden aluminum and reduce the weight of the coffinlike car body he called the Monocoque. Later he'd master the use of plastic for structural material and learn to harness the force of air rushing under a race car to increase its speed and control around curves. As a result of his constant innovations, Team Lotus captured the lion's share of victories on the world racing circuit during the Sixties and early Seventies.

"He can be a prima donna sometimes," De Lorean once said of Chapman, "but he really is a genius. He's just one little guy and he beats these racing teams that literally have governments backing them."

In 1957, Chapman brought out his first touring car for the public. This limited-edition luxury vehicle would not find nearly the success in the showroom that his racing vehicles had had on the track. But when Chapman took his company public in 1968, he became a millionaire overnight.

In the mid-Sixties, Chapman moved out of London, and settled among the flat, farming fields of Hethel, some fifteen miles of winding, treacherous road west of Norwich. Ironically, the car maker chose the relatively isolated area so he could take over an abandoned RAF facility and have a private airport for his fleet of planes. His home and corporate headquarters were the nearby Ketteringham Hall, a rambling, castlelike mansion that once served as a boys' school. "I think John was instantly enamored with Colin [Chapman] as soon as he saw the setup he had in Norwich," Bill Collins says. "Maybe he was the type of guy John always wanted to be."

A short, debonair man with a precisely trimmed moustache, the balding Chapman was usually seen with a jaunty cap or porkpie hat. Some considered his distant manner to be almost regal. Others thought it was just arrogant. "Chapman always looked down on the rest of us in racing," says Smokey Yunick, a veteran of the American stock-car circuit. "You couldn't talk to the man. He always knew it all."

Chapman didn't treat Bill Collins any better than he treated the racing engineers. Lotus' appropriation of the DMC-12 came as an abrupt shock to the man who had created it from the seating buck up. Bivouacked in England, Collins was preparing to assemble his own team of engineers to do production engineering in Coventry. He thought that his years at General Motors had prepared him well for the task of guiding a new car into production, and he believed he could recruit similarly suited sorts from the auto companies of Europe. But with Chapman suddenly on the scene, Collins was denied the chance to deliver his own baby. De Lorean assured Collins that he would be able to consult with Lotus and direct the company's progress, but Collins found that he wasn't wanted. Lotus' overlord was an aloof, demanding man who could be just as hard on his employees as on strangers. "Chapman," Collins says, "didn't have time for anyone else."

Colin Spooner, the Lotus engineer put in charge of the De Lorean project, sympathized with Collins's predicament. "I don't think De Lorean ever bothered to define a specific role for Bill," he says. "John always tended to let things like that sort themselves out."

Collins sorted himself out of England and back to the States. He had devoted almost four years of his life to De Lorean's dream and made it his dream as well. His immersion in the project nearly wrecked his twenty-year marriage. He worked alone on designs when everyone told him the car would never get off his drawing board. He spent nights and weekends in the workshops helping mechanics assemble the prototypes. Now, when the impossible project was finally on the verge of fruition, De Lorean considered him expendable. "I was pretty much stranded in England with people I had convinced to go out there," Collins recalls, "and we found ourselves with nothing to do. John just wouldn't intercede with Chapman.

"I think I made the mistake of trusting John. He always said he was interested in people. But he never was—even in those people who did the most for him. My wife saw that from the start. Unfortunately, it took me a little longer."

Several auto-industry experts questioned whether the Lotus staff was equipped to help De Lorean with a production vehicle. While he planned on eventually turning out 30,000 cars a year, Lotus had never produced many more than a thousand annually.

Its procedures were considered more hand-tooled than assembly-line.

But Chapman did have one important qualification that set him apart from any other automaker. He, too, used a plastic molding system for the body panels of his car. He variously called his process Vacuum Resin Injection Moulding (VRIM) or Vacuum-Assisted Resin Injection (VARI). The plastic was one of Chapman's greatest achievements. "It was Colin Chapman's inspiration that brought us VARI," says Colin Spooner. "In two short years we went from the impossible to a fully developed process that could produce the quality of moldings necessary for a car."

Like De Lorean's ERM plastic, VARI produces a hard, light substance. But it requires tools that inject heated resin into a mold—a far more expensive and time-consuming process than the one De Lorean had licensed. VARI, however, had been tested for years in Lotus cars, and it seemed adaptable to mass production. De Lorean didn't have the same confidence in ERM (Elastic Reservoir Molding). VARI was a convenient alternative if De Lorean's subsidiary, Composite Technology Corporation, was unable to develop ERM in time. Once De Lorean brought in Chapman, his uncertainty about ERM became a self-fulfilling prophecy.

Considering that De Lorean did have good reason to use Lotus, one question remains: Why was so much money directed through a middleman?

It is a question that only John De Lorean, Tom Kimmerly, and Fred Bushell can answer. Chapman died of a heart attack shortly after De Lorean's arrest, and we are left with only one cryptic comment about GPD that he made to the press.

There was no reason for any third party to intervene, and all the evidence suggests that none did. The executive who drew the check from Chemical Bank asked De Lorean what the $12.5 million was for. He remembers, "De Lorean said that he was negotiating with Lotus and their subsidiary, GPD."

Then chief financial officer Walt Strycker says, "I was excluded from the deal. At the time, I was told that John and Tom Kimmerly were going over to Switzerland to negotiate the acquisition of

Lotus, which was in precarious financial condition. I was under the impression that a few NIDA officials would be there as well."

Almost three weeks after De Lorean drew the check (and three weeks of lost interest to the research-partnership account), he and Kimmerly took the draft to a hotel in Geneva where they met Chapman, one of his aides, and the elusive Mrs. Juhan. The result of their session was a sloppily prepared contract, which spelled out two areas of responsibility for GPD: vehicle engineering to be conducted with the research-partnership payment of $12.5 million; and development of Chapman's VARI process to adapt it to the DMC-12—that task was underwritten with a $5.15 million fee paid for by the new British-backed subsidiary, De Lorean Motor Cars, Limited. At that time it was decided that the partnership's initial payment be reduced to $8.5 million. De Lorean wired the $4 million back to New York. But two months later it all went back to GPD again.

Even after the payments were made, no one mentioned GPD to Strycker. "John told me they couldn't make a deal to acquire Lotus, that Chapman wouldn't sell. Instead, he demanded two payments—one for licensing the VARI process, and then another for product engineering."

Consisting of ten pages, the GPD contract was apparently printed with two different typewriters, and copies that were released to other car-company executives look to be authentic. They show the signatures of De Lorean and Mrs. Juhan on the bottom of each page. All blank spaces are crossed out to prevent any addenda from appearing after the signing.

The contract provided that Lotus would be paid any costs above the $17.65 million. While Lotus' records show that they received over $24 million directly from De Lorean Motor Cars, Limited, there's no mention of any payment from GPD. No trace of the $17.65 million can be found in the books of Lotus or any other firm.

De Lorean has not just tied GPD to Chapman in private comments to his executives, but in a few public statements as well. In a statement he issued to the press about GPD, he wrote, "GPD has the rights to, and markets the patents and technology for, the VARI process by which we produce our car body."

In fact, De Lorean was prohibited by British and American tax laws from contracting with GPD, Lotus, or anyone else for the rights to a developed process. The whole tax write-off for the research partnership required that funds go to legitimate research and development of untested processes. Licenses requiring no further development are not included in that category. The same tax benefit existed for the British subsidiary as well. The GPD contract specifically gives away its rights to Lotus' plastic process under a section that reads, "[De Lorean Motor Cars,] Limited will be entitled to the royalty-free use of all patents, shop rights, and know-how related to Vacuum Resin Injection Moulding solely for use in the De Lorean sports car, the subject of this contract, and other De Lorean automotive products."

Chapman strongly objected to the suggestion that he had anything to do with GPD. He raged to the *Sunday Telegraph*, "De Lorean wanted the deal done like that—ask him why GPD got the contract and then subcontracted to us."

Of course, Chapman did not add that he had other dealings with GPD Services, or that Marie-Denise Juhan had been associated with Lotus before. The *Sunday Times* of London's Insight team has since deciphered the acronym. At one point, De Lorean declared that the three letters stood for General Product Development. Actually, they meant Grand Prix Drivers. Chapman, who was reputed to have a maze of offshore companies to evade the stiff British income tax, reportedly used GPD as a conduit of prize money to his Formula One racers.

The very wording of the GPD contract indicates that someone British had a strong hand in its preparation. Anglicized spelling is used throughout the text, in words such as fulfilment, programme, whilst, practise, and endeavour.

If Chapman and GPD were connected, as most of the evidence suggests, a nagging suspicion persists that De Lorean also walked away with a piece of the missing $17.65 million.

The possibility concerned senior members of the De Lorean

staff, especially Strycker. "When we finally heard about GPD," Strycker says, "some of us thought about the possibility that John and Chapman put their hands on that money. But, just as quickly, we dismissed the idea. Here John had the opportunity to make hundreds of millions with the car company. Why should he risk that before the thing had even gotten off the ground? It would be such a goddamn stupid thing to do, we just couldn't believe that John would have done it."

De Lorean categorically denies that there was anything wrong with the GPD contract. As he pointed out in his press release on the subject: "The contract with GPD was submitted to, approved by, and is on file with the Bank of England (Exchange Control), the Department of Commerce, and the Northern Ireland Development Agency. Each of the agencies reviewed, approved, and consented to the arrangement before any payment was made. The only benefit I or anyone else in our company has received from this contract is a truly outstanding automobile design delivered in less than half the normal time at a fraction of the normal cost."

But De Lorean's own behavior after the GPD payments draws more suspicion to his participation in the deal than anyone else's accusations. Suddenly, during the spring of 1979, he was on the lookout for what he'd later call, "an income-producing investment."

It was a time when the De Lorean Motor Company had reached a critical juncture, so the chief executive's search for new investments seems all the more unusual. Never did his young company need his energies and resources more: the car had to be prodded through Lotus, the factory had to be built, scores of top executives hired, and the dealer-network finished. In the early days of General Motors, William Durant went on his own buying spree, but he did the buying for the corporation, and then picked up only companies that would complement the existing GM divisions. After he lost control of General Motors for the second time, in the early 1920s, he started the Durant Motor Company. It was another boom-and-bust effort, but this time Durant's fatal flaw was spending only part of his time on the car company and dissipating the rest on unrelated matters—especially playing the stock market. De Lorean, familiar as he was with Durant's career, did not learn any lessons from it.

Among the outside interests he pursued was the First Bank and Trust of Palm Beach County, but his efforts would be frustrated by an amazing coincidence. The bank's owner had turned to Wichita lawyer Paul Kitch for advice on the sale. "He called to tell me that this Washington bank expert claimed to be representing a very wealthy individual named De Lorean," Kitch remembers. "He told him De Lorean wanted to buy a bank in Florida, any bank in Florida. He was prepared to make an offer, and all my client had to do was name a price and deliver the stock."

But upon hearing De Lorean's name, Kitch warned his client to beware. As counsel for the Kansas State Bank and Trust Company, the lawyer was still in the process of suing De Lorean in connection with the Dahlinger Pontiac-Cadillac dealership. It was one of the rare occasions when the auto magnate's bungled entrepreneurial past came back to haunt him. Kitch says, "I told my client that this guy De Lorean was a crook, and I offered to be there at their first meeting. He called back De Lorean's lawyer to tell him that their appointment would have to be rescheduled so I could be there. I guess all De Lorean had to do was hear my name. He never showed up for the meeting." To buy the bank, Kitch estimates, De Lorean would have had to offer $15 million.

Undismayed by that one bad experience, De Lorean took his search for an investment from the Florida beaches to the snow-capped mountains north of Salt Lake City. There, in a little compound of gray aluminum buildings, he found a company that manufactured off-track utility vehicles. It was owned by the Pennsylvania chemical conglomerate Thiokol. De Lorean had been familiar with the parent company back in his GM days when they supplied windshield sealants and the chemical inflating components of airbags. Years later, one of the company's retired executives let him know that the company was divesting itself of subsidiaries unrelated to chemicals. The Logan division had long been such a Thiokol aberration. It was first formed as a favor to nearby Utah State professors who had patented a huge tank-tread that wouldn't get stuck in snow. The company's best-selling vehicles groomed the top of ski slopes, and although Logan dominated the domestic market—"a little GM," De Lorean called it—the division turned only a $1 million profit on $16 million of sales.

Because the bulk of Thiokol's contracts are defense-related, the company is able to veil much of its financial activity. The year it sold the Logan division, it lumped the proceeds in with other divestitures. But some Logan employees have seen De Lorean's purchase package and they put its total at $13.4 million. It included $7.5 million in cash, a $1.25 million note to Thiokol and a land swap, done for tax purposes, involving 450 acres of De Lorean's San Diego avocado groves, valued at $4.65 million. Beyond that expense, De Lorean also brought in another $7.5 million line of credit from the Continental Bank of Illinois to supply operating capital.

To facilitate all these moves, Kimmerly changed the title of the John Z. De Lorean Corporation to the De Lorean Manufacturing Corporation—providing a new name for the Logan division, but also a DMC acronym that could be confused with the De Lorean Motor Company. In just 1979, the year of the purchase, company records would show the assets for Manufacturing jumping from $616,464 to $15.8 million.

When asked about his purchase of the Logan firm, De Lorean explained to reporters that it was financed solely with the land swap. But those close enough to know otherwise wonder where he got the $7.5 million cash and the collateral for the $7.5 million credit line.

Coincidentally enough, the same executive who first drew the $12.5 million check for GPD would field a call from the Continental Bank of Illinois in the New York headquarters one day shortly after De Lorean purchased the Logan division. He was the only financial officer available during the lunch hour. The bank called to confirm that the necessary funds had been transferred from the Swiss bank account. Without knowing what the message meant, he passed it on to Walt Strycker. Since he had first suggested De Lorean go to the Continental Bank to finance a loan for Logan, Strycker was well aware what the call referred to. His suspicions were further aroused a few months later, he says, when he and De Lorean were discussing interest rates on export loans. "John said we should try to do it through a Swiss bank. Then he said he had just gotten a loan from a Swiss bank."

Continental Bank officials had told Strycker that they were ready to loan De Lorean more money for the purchase of Logan, but that he had given the business to another bank—a "foreign source." It was hard for Strycker not to start putting two and two together. GPD had been a Swiss transaction. Shortly afterward De Lorean had bought Logan and secured credit for the acquisition with the help of a foreign bank. Then his assistant got the call confirming the wire of funds from a Swiss bank. "When you looked at that chain of events," Strycker says, "you didn't have to be overly suspicious to realize that something was very wrong."

13

Belfast

"It was fantastic. It was unbelievable."

Billy Parker sits in the narrow wooden booth of a Belfast pub and remembers the first time he'd ever heard about the new car factory. At twenty-six, he's a thin, pale man with the long, straggly beard of an Old Testament prophet. He's been married ten years and has three children.

In the beginning, he didn't see how talk of De Lorean's deal would do anything to help him. Getting a paying job had never been easy, and it became even harder after the troubles, when his opportunities to paint and do maintenance work were restricted to impoverished Catholic housing projects. "There was massive publicity," Billy Parker says, "all about this American businessman and his movie-star wife and a strange new automobile. You really couldn't believe it."

Northern Ireland hadn't seen any new industrial development since major civil strife erupted in 1971, and before that, most new plants ended up in Protestant areas anyway. But most amazingly, this plant was supposed to go up in the industrial town of Dunmurry, in a marshy field that was a no-man's-land between the

Twinbrook Catholic housing project and Protestant neighborhoods.

There were still skeptics, even when the political dignitaries and local priests joined De Lorean and his executives for the sod-turning on October 2, 1978. A few of these skeptics gathered by the police cordons and shouted, "Yankees go home."

But then the trucks and land-movers came, and the first few hundred men from the area were hired to clear the field, reroute the little muddy streams that passed through it, and fill the swamps with stones. From the Protestant side, a railroad-track embankment screened out the construction. But in one spot, near a high-rise apartment house, the locals wore a footpath up a little knoll. There, among the saplings, they watched the steel canopies rise up out of the ground and then, patch by patch, get covered over with a metal skin. These were not your typical factory buildings pocked with grimy windows or studded with smokestacks, but new industrial creatures: long, rectangular, and sleek, with neat gray bricks on the foundation, a darker gray corrugated metal above, and gleaming, furrowed aluminum roofs.

From the Protestant vantage point, the new landmark stood in stark contrast to its surroundings. Two shabby housing projects spilled down the hills behind it, and to the other side, just as depressing, were the grimy and mostly abandoned shops and factories of the Dunmurry Industrial Estate (the sort of thing Americans call an industrial park). Built in the Fifties, the complex was the wasted vestige of another era's attack on high unemployment in Northern Ireland.

Before the De Lorean sports car, the most famous product to come out of Belfast was a luxury vessel called the *Titanic*. The linen industry, another mainstay of the economy, was just as doomed when the world turned to man-made fibers and the low-cost competition from the Orient.

By the Fifties, Northern Ireland was an enclave of unemployment unequaled in the Western world. The British solution was to build—right in the midst of the jobless—spanking new "advance factories," and then scour the globe looking for some itinerant multinational corporation to fill them.

Going after the man-made hair of the dog that bit them, Irish development officials concentrated on the synthetic-fiber conglomerates and managed to lure some of the biggest, including Courtaulds, Monsanto, Dupont, and ICI. From 1950 to 1970, over 300 new plants opened up in Northern Ireland, and of the 170,000 total employed in the country, over 70,000 worked in the new industries. But the so-called "footloose" industrialists who were so anxious to move in had few compunctions about moving out. When their tax abatements ended or recession hit their home markets, they started to look for greener and cheaper pastures outside Ireland. Sectarian strife complicated matters further as the nation shook itself into even-more-segregated pockets of Catholics and Protestants. The composition of a factory's workforce often fell in line with the surrounding neighborhood—a development that ended up helping Protestants more than Catholics. The conglomerates, however, did not like being caught in the middle. During the Seventies one out of three manufacturing jobs in Northern Ireland would be lost.

The waves of both economic and social devastation washed over the Catholic neighborhoods behind the De Lorean plant. The Dunmurry Estate, which had once employed 3,000, only had 300 workers by the time De Lorean set up shop. With unemployment estimated by some local officials at 80 percent, the area is a hotbed of IRA activism. A huge cement-block building with narrow windows and a ten-foot-high steel-slat fence serves as the local grade school. Up a barren asphalt road is the area's first public housing, Cherry Hill. Nearby is the newer project, Twinbrook, created to catch the overflow of Catholics fleeing the eastern sections of Belfast. The houses are drab one-color affairs, built in step-up clusters of three, and hastily scattered over the hills. Backyards are a maze of fences and clotheslines. Political graffiti are painted on the walls. From the Catholic side there was a more direct view of the factory site, but it was over a boggy dump, littered with tree stumps, garbage, and the occasional hull of a burned-out car. Two rings of barbed wire separated the plant from the housing complex. The Protestants and Catholics would each have their own entrance.

BELFAST

For first-time visitors to Belfast the signs of the deep national division are hard to ignore, starting with the stringent baggage checks at the airport. People bustle through the city, and at night young people mix in the pubs without any obvious regard for religious background. But barricades seem to be at every other corner downtown, sealing off the city center entirely. Each little roadblock means a search through any bags you carry and a quick frisk by policemen for handguns. Soldiers suddenly appear to dash down the center of the street, assault rifles braced in their hands, and then push through the oblivious shoppers to press themselves against the side of a building. Smoky gray armored vans are as ubiquitous as milk trucks. Each carries at least four soldiers sitting in the back, rifles upright by their knees.

The carcasses of some half-demolished buildings still stand behind fences. Scaffolding covers government buildings. Neatly lettered on bare expanses of brick are either "IRA" or "UDF."

Even on solitary residential lanes, far from downtown Belfast and a mile from the nearest housing project, barbed wire curls around the branches of a tree like some indigenous natural growth. It's difficult for a solitary male stroller to walk very far before he's stopped by an armored van and asked where he's going.

"I can remember my first visit to the Conway Hotel across the street from the plant site," one former De Lorean employee says. "I came in directly from the airport and, looking out the taxi at night, I wondered what all the fuss was about. We went by some very nicely kept-up Georgian-style homes and then came to the hotel entrance. It's up a winding, treelined driveway—like a little version of San Simeon. On the way you pass a garden house with a pool and fountain. Then the taxi stops and you're in front of a hotel that's surrounded with barbed wire eight feet high, and enough floodlights to light up a ball park. After you get out of the cab, you go through a little trailer where they frisk you and look through all your luggage. Just so you remember that you're a guest, there's a big sign over the entrance that says, WELCOME. When I checked in, I asked why they went to all these lengths for the security. Then they told me that this was the *new* Conway Hotel. The *old* Conway was blown to pieces ten years ago."

No one would be more concerned about security than the car company's namesake. During the entire life of his plant in Belfast, De Lorean never stayed in the city's hotels more than a handful of times. He preferred to spend the night in London's Connaught or Savoy hotels and shuttle on the plane. At one point, he put Bill Haddad in charge of security, and throughout their discussions on protecting the facility and executives from terrorist attack, De Lorean constantly brought up his desire to find a floor-length bulletproof leather trench coat. He had heard that Henry Kissinger had had such protective armor tailored and he kept after Haddad to do the same for him. Haddad's security expert quickly got in touch with Kissinger and discovered that the raincoat ended up being so heavy, he'd never bothered to wear it. Bill passed the information on to De Lorean, thinking that was the end of the matter, but soon after, when he sent a memo suggesting that they "work out the long-overdue local security system (office, homes, procedures, etc.)," De Lorean returned the memo with a note scrawled on the bottom: "OK—where's my raincoat?"

While De Lorean got his raincoat, he did not take too many opportunities to wear it. In the early days, the top job in Belfast—managing director of De Lorean Motor Cars, Limited—became the key spot in the company. To fill it, De Lorean turned to a man who knew how to cope with unusual locales. For years, Charles K. Bennington had been building and operating overseas installations for the Chrysler Corporation. England, France, Germany, Italy, Turkey, South Africa: all were stops along his career path. Originally from Detroit, he became more landless than recognizably American. The clipped cadence of his speech sounded almost British. He kept his hair brushed back and his beard vandyked with the tips of the moustache twirled. He preferred a leather jacket and a turtleneck to a suit and tie.

Starting out with only six people, Bennington proceeded to move heaven and earth to build the plant on schedule. Bennington had faced tougher jobs before and, in places like Turkey, more primitive conditions, but Belfast still posed its own problems. The area's major contractor was near bankruptcy, and to get the project completed his finances had to be shored up by a temporary

• BELFAST •

merger with another contractor. The site proved to be far more marshy than anyone expected. Besides covering up the brook and diverting it outside the property, Bennington also had to bring in 500,000 tons of stone before the ground was stable enough to build on.

Despite the difficulties, as 1980 approached, Bennington had the plant progressing on schedule. Once again, De Lorean had found a take-charge guy, and he was willing to give him free rein. Two months before Bennington came on board, De Lorean had hired a management consultant to draw up a critical path (the step-by-step time-line) for getting the factory finished. Bennington did not bother to even glance at his work. "He didn't need a manual to tell him how to build a factory," Ken Gorf, then Limited's treasurer, says. "Chuck knew intuitively. He had done it before and he had the guts to make those hundreds of decisions that must be made each day on a project of that sort. Of course, a couple of calls might have been bad, but you cause more damage by delay. He was an energetic, enthusiastic pioneer, and a man capable of working extremely long hours."

But he was also a difficult man to work with, and another British executive explains, "Chuck didn't want to know what other people thought. In many ways he was a loner who didn't share the load, and he kept taking an increasing amount of pressure from De Lorean. There was a daily barrage of phone calls and memos, and Chuck tried to handle them all. He was living in a very intense way and it started to show."

Other De Lorean employees, especially those from the sales organization in California, were not as enamored of Bennington's abilities. By early 1980, they needed information for parts catalogues and service manuals to prepare for the car's arrival in the States, but they had trouble getting Chuck's attention. One emissary cooled his heels in the Conway for two days before Bennington found time to see him.

"To me," one of the California executives says, "he was like the Bob Fosse character in the movie *All That Jazz*. He even looked like the guy. He was working and playing his way into a heart attack, and nobody else but God could butt in."

Other Bennington detractors pointed to his extravagance, especially in remodeling a home near the factory compound that was meant to be the guesthouse and residence for the managing director. Over $30,000 was spent on the bathrooms alone, part of which went for gold-plated faucets from Harrod's—a move that De Lorean later characterized for the press as "stupid, dumb, and indiscreet."

But Bennington's harshest critics were those who didn't work with him. While his colleagues in Belfast found him reclusive and occasionally arrogant, they respected his energy and looking back today most doubt whether the plant could have been put up as fast as it was without him.

The big delay did not come in building the plant, but pulling the car out of Lotus. Here Bennington could not be solely to blame. Chapman wasn't content to just work from Collins's prototype. Instead, he practically redesigned the car from the ground up. He was partly encouraged by De Lorean. Ten months after Lotus took charge, De Lorean sent the car back to body stylist Giugiaro for a few "minor" alterations to keep his original design up to date. Chapman and De Lorean liked to refer to the changes he made as "tweaking" the car. But for some others in the car company, the changes were more like splats than tweaks, and ignored many of the parameters Bill Collins and De Lorean had at first set for the car.

Instead of designing the car from the inside out, as Collins had first done, Lotus worked from the outside in, adjusting to Giugiaro's new, more stylish look. While the car eventually moved even lower to the ground, the interior became much more cramped. There was more than enough headroom for the shorter Chapman, but De Lorean was to find his own car a much tighter fit than he had ever intended.

Whatever anyone's view of the changes, they were keeping the company off its timetable. Pilot production was to have started in May 1980, but by October Lotus still had the car and several design decisions had yet to be made—from the suspension to the car windows. More important, time-consuming tests needed to be done on the few prototypes in existence to determine whether the car could meet U.S. safety and exhaust-emission standards.

One of Bennington's solutions for getting the project back on track was the creation of an Engineering Policy Review Committee—in essence an excuse for a group of De Lorean executives to make forays into the Chapman domain in Norwich and politely pass on their sense of urgency. Bennington would tell his aides, "It's like massaging the belly of a pregnant woman. You know the baby's there. All you can do is ease it along until it comes out."

But he found himself interposed between two jealous and anxious fathers—De Lorean and Chapman. Neither one was ready to confront the other, but that didn't prevent them from venting their frustrations on subordinates. The difficulty of Bennington's situation would be illustrated all too clearly on film. De Lorean permitted filmmakers D. A. Pennebaker and Chris Hegedus to make a documentary on the company's early stages, which was eventually shown in the United States with the title, *Start-up*. In one scene, De Lorean is squired through the old aircraft hangars where Lotus is making the car. Later, he's shown finishing up a leisurely lunch with Lotus executives at Hethel Factory. They sit on French-provincial chairs at a long table covered with a sumptuous spread of fruit and cheese. Light streams through the window. De Lorean is not talking about the delays that have mired his car at Lotus. Instead he gossips about Ford's troubles with the Pinto fuel tank—"a stupid design issue," he says, his voice dripping with disdain.

But the next day, at a board meeting for De Lorean Motor Cars, Limited, he speaks with similar loathing about Lotus—again for the camera. "We've got to get out of Lotus now," he tells Bennington. "What are you going to do to get us out of there?"

Unhappy with Bennington's answers, De Lorean continues to ask other needling questions about fees from the engine maker, Renault, and methods to convert the cars to right-hand driving. Nothing is being done fast enough for De Lorean. The camera captures a man who has aged decades since his departure from GM. He has let his hair go gray—a suggestion of his investment counselors, press reports said, to make him appear more distinguished. The lines are returning to his face, especially around his mouth. His contact lenses are no longer enough, and he's seen here wearing a pair of half-lens reading glasses, which he pulls off and tosses on the reports in front of him. He repeatedly tells Bennington, "This is asinine." The camera cuts to the Belfast managing director nervously chain-smoking cigarettes.

In just the few minutes of the October 1980 board meeting that Pennebaker and Hegedus got on film, it seems as though something is very seriously wrong with this infant company—even before cars are rolling off the line. Amazingly, the chairman of the board ends the meeting by an admission that, even when the sports car is in production, sales in America won't be enough to keep DMC afloat. New markets and another product must be developed first. "You cannot support this kind of overhead with one car," he tells the board, "and we've known that for a long time. We've really got to keep this moving. No matter where, we've got to steal the money to do it. This is not a matter of something extra. This is a matter of pure survival."

Of course, De Lorean didn't consider stealing, as long as he had the British government behind him, but he quickly found that he could go to the exchequer's well once too often. His relationship couldn't have been better with the Labour Party ministers he first dealt with, and, looking back, MP Concannon agrees. "At first, what was going on was a partnership between us and De Lorean. Both sides wanted to make it work and we were more than willing to cooperate. As far as we could see, he was delivering everything we asked for in getting the plant up."

If anything, the relationship got a little too clubby for some bureaucrats when De Lorean tried to hire NIDA executive Shaun Harte. More than anyone else in his agency, Harte had spearheaded the negotiations with the car company. He was later NIDA's designated watchdog on the boards of both the De Lorean Motor Company and De Lorean Motor Cars, Limited. The offer to chuck his government job for five times the salary was a strong enticement indeed, and it most concerned his immediate superior, NIDA's chairman Ronald Henderson. "At first Ronnie refused to let John hire Shaun," Walt Strycker says. "But the whole job offer just put everyone in a bad position. Shaun was left fuming at Henderson and obviously not happy about staying with NIDA. In any case, the whole thing cast doubt on Shaun's ability to be an impartial auditor. None of us doubted his integrity, but you had to wonder what outsiders thought about it. Eventually Ronnie had to let him go to us and the whole thing just left a bad taste in everyone's mouth."

But not necessarily in Concannon's; he expected such exchanges and even found them palatable. He explains, "That's what usually happens in Northern Ireland. Once these international companies start coming into Northern Ireland, they look for good local people, and the very fact is, the best people they can find are the ones who helped them get a good foothold there. I find this to be part and parcel of the process. It didn't worry me at all. In fact, it was very helpful that I knew somebody was in there who had Northern Ireland at heart. I was only concerned because I lost some good men."

Accommodating sorts, like Concannon and Roy Mason, however, were not long for the British government. In May 1979, the Labour Party fell from power to be replaced by a Conservative cabinet and a prime minister, Margaret Thatcher, who eschewed government involvement in any private-sector business—especially on the scale of the De Lorean deal. It was a state of affairs that John De Lorean later commiserated about with his Labour mentors. "If you talk to De Lorean," Concannon says, "he sees [the change of governments] as the turning point of the project. Before that point, he was working with a lot of ministers who only wanted to see him succeed. Then, suddenly, overnight—as the British custom has it—they disappeared and he gets a set of ministers who couldn't care less whether it succeeds. In fact, in their basic philosophy, they don't want it to succeed."

When offered Concannon's assessment of how conditions for the company changed when the Conservatives came to power, Limited's onetime treasurer, Ken Gorf, who is also British, responds, "That's a lot of crap. We had as much support from the Tories as we did from the Labour Party. And it lasted until the Tories said, 'Enough is enough.' I should know, because I negotiated a lot of the extra loans we did get from the Thatcher government, and they were substantial. The fact is, the day-to-day contacts in the Northern Ireland Department of Commerce did not change. They continued to be helpful. We did end up with a new chief executive at NIDA, Tony Hopkins, but he wasn't hostile. He just wouldn't give John everything he wanted. He tried to get the best deal for NIDA, as he should have done."

De Lorean first went to Hopkins in the summer of 1980 when development costs with Lotus were skyrocketing and he could see that it would still be months before the company could market the car. There were several loopholes in the contract that could have permitted De Lorean to ask for more support. One stated that the Department of Commerce should "be prepared to consider" the needs for money in such cases as inflation, construction delays, or fluctuations in the exchange rate between dollars and pounds. "We figured we were entitled to over $47 million in grants," Gorf says. "Hopkins was not ready to give it to us and it looked like we'd have to go through some hard bargaining to get what we wanted."

De Lorean ended up going over Hopkins's head to the new secretary of state for Northern Ireland, Humphrey Atkins. Leaving NIDA and Department of Commerce officials in the waiting room, the minister and De Lorean went into a closed-door meeting. They emerged with an agreement to loan the car company some $33 million. The British press played it as a coup for De Lorean, but the other car company executives were astounded that he was willing to settle for so little, and in the form of a loan to boot. "The last thing we needed was a loan at high interest rates," one of the Belfast executives recalls. "Here we were, all expecting a grant. Instead, we got a millstone with no benefits."

To make matters worse, in return, De Lorean let the British strike the inflation and exchange-rate adjustments that were in the original deal, preventing him from going back for additional funding again.

Over the next few months, De Lorean would realize how little he did get from Atkins. In a September memo sent to Haddad and Kimmerly, he saw a way he could force the British to turn over all of their equity in the project by "rattling the saber" and threatening legal action. If Americans controlled all of the stock, De Lorean hoped, the car company would look more appetizing when he went to Wall Street. In concluding the memo, he wrote, "Obviously this is an idealized scenario fraught with potential pitfalls and problems, but one we must pursue aggressively."

But his British executives in Belfast did not think such hard-nosed tactics would pay off. "We were trying to convince John that he had to start being more diplomatic," one says. "When Thatcher first came into office [during May 1979], I warned him that he needed some Conservative contacts, and he didn't listen. After the summer I thought he had started to see the importance of politics. We set up several meetings for John with committees of Parliament, and we tried to arrange a few informal gatherings too. John can really shine in those situations, and I felt it wouldn't take much to put some of his back-bench critics at ease. But he never kept the appointments. For some reason he just didn't want to do the diplomatic thing. He believed the politicians couldn't let him go down and lose all those jobs in Belfast. Looking back, I wonder whether he was scared of the questions they might have asked him, in particular about the Lotus cost overruns and the payments to GPD."

After he left General Motors, De Lorean never expected to have to answer to any higher authority, but suddenly, with his own corporation, he found himself in the hot seat again, and some of these governmental overseers were far more demanding than the committees on the fourteenth floor. In response, he was to be as rebellious and insouciant as he had ever been at GM. In December, he dashed off a Telex to NIDA's Tony Hopkins that bordered on blackmail. Forgetting his agreement with Atkins over the summer, De Lorean claimed he still deserved $28 million of "inflation adjustment." He further demanded that he get the $19 million the government was ready to give him during the original negotiations, when it looked as if the Oppenheimer limited partnership wouldn't go through.

Summing up his bill of fare in the Telex, De Lorean bluntly charged, "You owe us £20 million. If you give it to us we have enough money to finish the job in proper fashion." Earlier De Lorean had promised to raise further capital by going to the American stock market, but in this message he claimed that the British were blocking off Wall Street as a funding option. "Unfortunately," he wrote, "it is not possible to raise external financing unless the government financing is complete—no one will put $10 million into a company that is $50 million short of having enough funds to complete the job. We now have a legal opinion from our U.K. counsel indicating that, as DMC and DMCL directors, we are verging on fraud to continue to place purchase orders [with American car buyers] for which we have no identifiable means of payment."

As he would do many times in the future, De Lorean closed his missive with the specter of laying off his Irish workers. "It is squarely up to NIDA. If you cannot or will not provide the balance of the funding you owe us, we plan to shut down our operations on both sides of the Atlantic immediately. We cannot incur obligations without means of payment. If you have decided to shut us down for whatever reason, let us do it in a manner that will allow us to salvage the expenditure to date and eventually repay the government. To do this we need a coordinated, planned effort."

De Lorean would not get tuppence of further grants out of the British government. However, he did get Department of Commerce guarantees on over $40 million more of bank loans from Barclay's and New York's Citibank, which in time turned out to be as good—or as bad—as a grant. But De Lorean's Christmas Telex set the tone for his future strained relations with the Conservative government and NIDA officials.

His upper hand would be Belfast workers like Billy Parker, who continued to flow through the factory gates, unaware of the apocalyptic warnings to the government that continued to issue from New York headquarters. At first Parker never expected the plant to be built. When he lined up behind the hundreds of others who applied for work, he never expected to be hired. But the morning came when he and thirty other men walked into the brand-new factory building for their first day of work. It was unlike any factory they'd ever seen, with scrubbed white-linoleum floors and freshly painted gray-steel girders. And there on the floor, right in front of them, was the sleek, silver car they'd be building. "I had never seen it before that time," Parker says. "We all just stood and looked at it, our mouths hanging open. We would have sworn the car was real. The body looked just like stainless steel. But when we touched it, we found out it was wood."

It was fantastic. It was unbelievable.

14

New York

Walter P. Strycker was a hard man to stare down. John De Lorean could see that the first time he met him. With Bob Anderson's help, he convinced Strycker to help him raise money for his car company and then push through negotiations for a plant site. After Bob Dewey left in August 1978, De Lorean prevailed on Strycker to become the next chief financial officer. He was just the sort of tough-minded comptroller that wary bank officers and investors wanted to see. In the 1979 SEC filing, he'd be listed as a vital cog in the De Lorean wheel, "the loss of whose services could have an adverse effect on the Company."

But before the year was out, De Lorean found himself increasingly subjected to Strycker's piercing gaze, and he didn't appreciate the experience. "John doesn't like confrontations," Strycker says. "He tries to avoid them. Rather than shout you down, he excludes you from the important decisions."

It was not the first time De Lorean had to face down his chief financial officer. Disputes with Dewey had led to his early departure from the company. De Lorean later attributed Dewey's resignation to his unhappiness with the selection of Belfast as the assembly-plant site, but Dewey says, "I made up my mind early in 1978 that I'd leave. It was just more proper to wait until the financing was in place. I realized that John and I couldn't work together. There were too many tiffs over the way he was spending the money."

Dewey says today that if he had first read *On A Clear Day You Can See General Motors*, he never would have gotten involved with De Lorean. "Financial guys like me come out as the villains in that book simply because we look at the bottom line. I think the major accusation is that GM paid too much attention to the bottom line, but where else do you look? I never realized how much he resented us until I read his book. In many ways the comptroller is the corporation's conscience. In some situations that isn't a pleasant role to play."

For months before he left, Dewey battled De Lorean and General Counsel Kimmerly over expenses he felt were unwarranted. "Tom would start off my day calling with crazy invoices for services and supplies that had no connection to the car."

The arguments increased when the decision was made to move the corporate headquarters to Park Avenue. At first Dewey objected to the costs of living in Manhattan, recommending that a Detroit location, closer to consulting engineers, might be more useful. But De Lorean insisted that he needed to be near New York financiers to raise further capital. He also managed to secure the penthouse of the Bankers Trust Building on a sublease from Xerox at a bargain-basement price by Manhattan standards.

But as part of the move, De Lorean charged the company $40,000 for the old furniture in his 100 West Long Lake office, which never did find its way to New York. Although he had been living in his Fifth Avenue duplex with Cristina, Zachary, and their infant daughter for two years, De Lorean also took a $78,100 stipend for moving from Detroit—what the company decorously called a "Locale Adjustment."

When Dewey objected, De Lorean told him he didn't want to argue over "petty bullshit." The comptroller says he warned his chief executive, "When you only have $100,000 in the till, $1 looks like a lot, especially when you're talking about other people's money. Investors want to see a start-up be as bare-bones as possible."

Dewey continues, "It got to the point where John said, 'Do it my way or else.' I told him that orders like that remind me of the Nuremberg trials. His name was on the door, but I had fiduciary responsibility too. I could see that as the dollars got bigger, this sort of thing would get worse. I felt I owed it to the other people to ease out quietly. When John wanted some help over the next few years, I'd come back on a consulting basis."

As Dewey predicted, the improprieties grew exponentially with the influx of money from the British government. Ken Gorf, serving as treasurer for the Belfast subsidiary, watched incredulously as the costs of the headquarters office mounted. "At their peak, New York had over thirty people and an annual budget of $8 million. Before we could transfer funds overseas, we needed approval from NIDA and the Department of Commerce, but at best they gave the invoices a cursory glance."

One good chunk of the expenses went in salaries. Although De Lorean did not take a salary, his private company was getting over $300,000 in consulting fees. Kimmerly ended up with both a $108,000 salary and a $180,000 retainer for his law firm. Brimming with six-figure contracts, the entire executive payroll, including fringe benefits, was well over $2 million a year.

Beyond the high salaries and expenses, Gorf and other skeptical DMCL observers wondered what the executives in New York were doing. "Fundamentally," Gorf says, "I saw headquarters contributing very little to the sports-car project."

Strycker had the same impression from inside the beehive and, unlike his predecessor, he was not ready to back out quietly. In December 1979, he turned over his criticism to both the Audit Committee on the board and the company's certified auditors, Arthur Andersen & Company. The Audit Committee was composed of Johnny Carson's lawyer, Henry Bushkin, Wood Gundy's director, G. Edmund King, and NIDA's representative (soon to be a DMCL employee), Shaun Harte. They chose to defer to the decisions of the auditors. To the shock and dismay of Strycker, Arthur Andersen dismissed the bulk of his complaints, asking for only a few minor alterations from De Lorean. When Strycker brought up the Swiss loan transactions concerning GPD and the purchase of the Logan division from Thiokol, the auditor replied that the approval of the British government was sufficient certification for the transaction. Shortly afterwards, Strycker resigned his position as chief financial officer. "With John," he says, "you end up playing the policeman and I didn't want to do that anymore."

At the time, the De Lorean Motor Company account was being handled out of Arthur Andersen's Detroit office, under the supervision of managing partner Richard L. Measelle. Measelle has refused to comment on any specific parts of his audit. But two years after he looked into Strycker's criticisms, Measelle did volunteer his high regard for John De Lorean to one reporter. "I think the world of him. He's one of the greatest individuals this city has ever produced, and my association with him has been one of the best professional experiences of my career."

The irregularities Strycker reported to the auditors focused on several different areas, but many could be grouped in the category of John De Lorean's personal extravagance at company expense. "He had a high burn-rate," Strycker says. "Obviously with his wife's taste and his homes all over the country, he was tied to an expensive life-style, but a lot of his traveling and socializing was done on his company expense account. There were some quarterly reporting periods where he was going as high as $28,000. Everything he did was first-class. Only the best suites in any hotel he stayed in. No restaurant was too expensive and the stockholders picked up the tab. When you questioned John on this, he said you were nickel-shitting him. He felt he was entitled to a certain extravagance."

In California, the company purchased a $53,000 Mercedes that C. R. Brown delivered to Cristina at her favorite San Diego fat farm with a ribbon tied around it. Another company car, a Mazda RX7, was being driven around by her younger brother. De Lorean later explained that these cars were "evaluation vehicles" to compare with the sports car and the future luxury car. Top executives in New York got credit cards to Tiffany's and the 21 Club. De

Lorean regularly dined at the exclusive Boardroom Club in his building.

The royal life-style included a company-paid entourage. Strycker reported that two young men who worked as chauffeurs and servants for the De Loreans were on the company payroll. The comptroller liked to remind other executives that such improprieties caused serious SEC inquests for the late Gulf & Western chairman, Charles Bluhdorn (De Lorean later reimbursed the company for their payment).

The chief courtier was not on the payroll, but a paid consultant on interior decoration, named Maur Dubin. For some of the auto executives he was an incongruous and irritating presence. Eastern regional sales manager, Bill Morgan, says, "I remember when Dubin first came tripping into the office with his full-length mink coat. I said to John, 'Who is this guy?' And John said, 'I think he likes you.'"

As time went on, Morgan says, the little man became a more noticeable nuisance. "He had some sort of antique business. I know because the company would lease vans that Maur and his friends would use to haul furniture and objets d'art around."

Occasionally those vans were found wrecked or impounded. Morgan spent a day bailing one vehicle out of the police pound after it had been involved in a hit-and-run accident. "Once Maur claimed that the police had impounded one of our vans because the dealer we had leased it from hadn't properly registered the vehicle. He then went and blistered the dealer's office manager over the phone. The dealer called me up and told me he didn't need this guy's lip. I called Dubin and told him that either he'd leave my dealers alone or I'd come over there and throw his ass down the forty-three stories of the Bankers Trust Building."

Strycker had his own run-ins with Dubin. He estimated over $40,000 in company funds had been spent on office artwork—so much artwork that paintings lay stacked against the walls in hallways for months. Other less-visible pieces were never located. He adds, "Maur snuck an invoice through for $20,000 of antique furniture while I was on vacation."

Both Strycker and Dewey were to glimpse the different worlds of John De Lorean in the ledger books. People like Dubin were collecting consultancy fees along with the old Chicago Bears linebacker and dealmaker C. W. Smith. The expenses of another shadowy figure, known only as Mr. Rodrigues, also showed up on the books. He was allegedly working on a Venezuelan oil deal with Kimmerly and De Lorean.

"Sometimes I felt we were all stuck in the middle of a play," Dewey says. "Only one actor knew who was going to come on stage next, and that was John."

Strycker felt he never got a satisfactory answer from De Lorean about the precise role that Nesseth played in the car company, but De Lorean told Measelle that Roy was the marketing "backup" for C. R. Brown. Brown vehemently denied working with Nesseth when Arthur Andersen accountants called to confirm that information.

What concerned Strycker most was the staff time and money spent on projects he called "crazy tangents"—none of which had much to do with getting the sports car into production. The NIDA agreement specifically prohibited the De Lorean Motor Company and De Lorean Motor Cars, Limited from either "acquir[ing] any other company or enter[ing] into any joint venture except with each other." But within months of his deal with the British, De Lorean contemplated leveraging his assets to buy the ailing Chrysler Corporation. "I told him that Chrysler had just shut the doors in the U.K. leaving a billion-dollar debt behind," Strycker says. "There was no way the British government would support buying the parent company. But John kept working on the idea. At least $300,000 worth of salaries and legal fees went into preparing an offer. He actually made a presentation for Iacocca, who probably got a big kick out of the whole thing. John never heard from him again."

Even before De Lorean had turned out his own car, he envisioned using his dealer network to distribute other sports cars. He engaged in protracted negotiations with Alfa-Romeo and Citroën. He even offered a deal to Lotus, although Chapman wasn't enthusiastic about the idea.

To the amazement of the executives, De Lorean continued to

pursue his fascination with cheaply built Eastern European vehicles. Two weeks after he closed his deal with the British, he flew off to Russia to discuss distributing Ladas once more. He also contemplated manufacturing a flatbed utility vehicle currently used by the French military and to be called the DMC-44. He had his special-projects director in California assemble a few promotional films featuring the bizarre little truck.

Roy suggested he consider going into the replicar business—selling kits to assemble vintage cars. The company borrowed a Bugatti for preliminary studies. As early as 1979, with his car still in developmental stages, De Lorean was talking to Mattel and other toy makers about producing pint-size replicas.

Then there were the inventions: a gas sniffer capable of searching out deposits of natural gas in the desert floor (this deal fell apart when a private investigator discovered that the inventor had established a distinguished record as a scam artist on the West Coast); De Lorean took an option on a three-cylinder engine that his old friend Smokey Yunick developed; and he tried to raise venture capital for a group of engineers working on a Stirling (external combustion) engine in San Diego. For the latter project he enlisted the aid of a former secretary of the treasury, William Simon, who today laughs off the failed engine effort as a "nonstarter."

Still the list doesn't end. De Lorean tried his hand at auto leasing, and nonmechanical endeavors such as boat chartering and shipping. "John had the ability to recognize a good opportunity," Strycker concludes, "but he didn't know how to make it happen."

Strycker could not make out where official company business ended and De Lorean's private affairs began. At least three top executives, he believed, were working practically full-time on extracurricular activities. For Strycker, the most flagrant violation of the stockholder's trust was the De Lorean Manufacturing Company, his personal firm that built the off-track utility vehicles in Logan, Utha. "It was a definite conflict of interest. I told John he and every executive involved with Manufacturing should keep meticulous records of the time they spent working on it, and that John should then reimburse the car company for their time. Then

I got a letter from Kimmerly telling me that 100 percent of his time was devoted to the car company, and that he did no legal work on Logan."

But corporate records showed Kimmerly as both treasurer and vice president of the De Lorean Manufacturing Company, and Strycker found it unlikely that he played a passive role on a three-member board. Further, while Kimmerly did not perform all the legal work on the Logan division acquisition, the law firm of Paul, Weiss, Rifkind did. While it's not known whether the firm billed Manufacturing, Strycker found that during the last half of 1979 Paul, Weiss, Rifkind was billing the car company.

Shortly after Strycker resigned, De Lorean began implying to other executives that he had been fired at the request of the British. In fact, NIDA officials made no such demand. One month after Strycker's departure they echoed his concerns about the extent of De Lorean's outside interests. In June they again emphasized that the company shouldn't be working on any project other than the sports car. Claiming that all the noncar activities had never cost more than $277,978, De Lorean nevertheless promised to stop. However, all evidence suggests that his special projects continued at an even more fevered pitch.

When Ernest (Gus) Davis first tried to contact John De Lorean in December 1980, he thought he was applying for a job in the car company. A former production executive for Harley-Davison, he felt he could fit in well with a small manufacturer like De Lorean. "But De Lorean told me he didn't have a position open in the car company. He said he was having troubles in [his] Logan [division], and that things had to be straightened out there." Other car-company executives ate lunch with Davis in New York and filled him in on the troubles at Manufacturing.

After investigating the problems in the Logan division and writing a report recommending diversification and expansion, Davis was hired to run the factory—or so he thought—with a mandate to expand the facilities. Instead, over the next year he'd watch helplessly as money was drained from the operation to banks in Michigan and New York. "John or one of the car-company financial officers would call and have me wire the money. It would go out in $400,000 shots. On top of that De Lorean was taking a salary of $200,000 [from the Logan division]. In barely a year, he took $3 million from the assets." Further complicating matters for Davis were sporadic visits to Logan by Roy Nesseth—a man, De Lorean said, who knew a great deal about marketing. Roy was paid by Manufacturing on a consultant's-fee basis that brought him as much as $100,000 in 1980.

Manufacturing and the car company sometimes pursued the same objectives. Davis remembers being called in to help evaluate the ill-fated DMC-44 and, at one point, car-company executives prepared a prospectus for Manufacturing that would have offered a research-and-development partnership for the vehicle. Both the car and the snow-grooming machine wore the same DMC emblem, and at industrial shows, the stainless-steel car was often driven in for promotion to pair incongruously with its hulking cousin.

De Lorean, however, rarely made personal appearances with the off-track vehicle or at Manufacturing's plant in Logan. Most of the executives in his New York office were not aware of what was going on in Utah or of its connection with the car company. But another noncar venture—a bus company—was much more visible and controversial inside headquarters, and at its helm was the equally visible and controversial Bill Haddad.

At first officers like C. R. Brown could not understand what Haddad was doing on the De Lorean payroll. At the age of fifty-two, he had spent much of his life fighting the good fight for causes that were a bit too liberal for most auto executives' blood. A Kennedy political operative, Haddad was the first associate director of the Peace Corps. He later served in the Office of Economic Opportunity, lost a race for a congressional seat on Manhattan's West Side, and was an outspoken member of the New York City Board of Education during Mayor John Lindsay's decentralization campaign. As an investigative reporter for the *New York Herald Tribune*, he railed against the price-fixing policies of the international pharmaceutical conglomerates and spearheaded a campaign to promote the prescription of cheaper generic drugs. Later, as an aide to the speaker of the New York State

Assembly, he continued his crusade against big corporations, sponsoring inquests of utilities, oil, and pharmaceutical companies.

In the past, Haddad had recruited De Lorean's aid for some of his causes. While still at General Motors, De Lorean wrote the opening chapter in an anthology dealing with black enterprise that Haddad edited. Haddad believed De Lorean was sincere when he talked about corporate responsibility to society. For him, De Lorean's attempt to build his own car was one more fight pitting the little guy against the big bad guys. "I didn't go to work with John for the money," he says. "I believed his talk about the ethical car, and I wanted to help him show big business it was possible to make a good product and a good profit without ripping off the consumer."

Trying to dissuade De Lorean from hiring Haddad, Brown had someone peruse his voluminous file of New York clippings. The resulting report characterized him as "left-wing," "racially divisive" and "antibusiness." Brown later concluded that De Lorean expected Ted Kennedy to be the next president, and had hired Haddad to have an "in" to the White House.

But Haddad quickly showed his detractors the valuable role he could play in generating public relations. His gregarious nature and his own experience as a reporter helped him pull the press onto the car company's bandwagon. While De Lorean had played down his animosity for the GM system for fear the company would discourage its dealers from signing on, Haddad showed him how such conflict could redound to his advantage. When Pat Wright finally went ahead and published *On A Clear Day*, De Lorean refused to endorse the book, calling Wright's version of his interviews too severe, but that didn't stop Haddad from copiously Xeroxing newspaper articles that followed publication. There wasn't much juice to an article about another entrepreneur trying to make a quick buck. It was much easier for a reporter to get wrapped up in a story about a maverick fighting back against an entrenched, self-serving industry. For all the press attention De Lorean generated on his own, it surged noticeably when Haddad started to beat the hustings.

Haddad was not content to remain the company spokesman.

He spurred De Lorean to diversify the car company further with a bus-assembly plant, and to make him the division's president. Strycker still laughs at the prospect. "It was ridiculous. What did Haddad, or De Lorean for that matter, know about buses?" But for some time De Lorean had seen the American bus industry as ripe for competition. By then, General Motors held a virtual monopoly in the market with minimal competition from Grumman. When the Federal Department of Transportation put out bids for a product they called Transbus, which could accommodate the handicapped and achieve certain fuel-efficiency goals, the American companies declined the offer. Haddad and De Lorean tried to step into the breach with a German import that came closer to meeting the DoT's standards. Once again, in the fall of 1979, De Lorean started talking to cities about a prospective plant site—this time for bus manufacturing.

The improbable venture would end with an improbable backer backing out. An impoverished section of Miami had been selected as the site for the factory and, according to Haddad, *Star Wars* director George Lucas, looking to invest in a good cause, was ready to put in $5 million of seed money. But the deal unraveled during a dinner with Lucas's lawyer and the president of his film company. "Out of nowhere, John started talking about them putting the money into the car company, instead of the bus. It just came out of the blue and you could see them shift gears. It made the whole bus deal look like some sort of scam to lure car investors. That was the last talk we had with them and that's probably the point where I started to go sour on John."

Throughout his tenure at the car company, Haddad, as did the other top executives, clashed with Tom Kimmerly. No one spent more time with De Lorean than his trusted lawyer. Besides the raft of De Lorean's personal affairs, Kimmerly was conducting what was probably the major enterprise of the New York office: preparation of a public stock offering for the car company. "We must have had a prospectus for every day of the week," one of the executives who worked with Kimmerly remembers. "As conditions in the market changed we were constantly updating and changing our registrations with the SEC. I often wondered about all the business we were giving the company that printed up our prospectuses."

Working up a stock offering for Wall Street, and the resulting reorganization of the company, proved to be a much more complicated affair than a limited sale to car dealers. At times over thirty lawyers would be jammed into a room, and small, quiet Tom Kimmerly—the tax lawyer from Detroit—would be in charge.

According to Strycker, Kimmerly's role in management grew with the company. "Until the company was funded by the British, he stayed in the background. But afterward he surfaced as the general counsel and then started showing up on the payroll. From what I knew of the personal deals he had with John, his motive was to buffer him from documentation as the corporate officer and secretary."

According to some executives, Kimmerly was reluctant to sit on the board and become an officer of the company, and did so in March 1979 only at De Lorean's insistence. While his influence was felt in almost every area of the company—from marketing and financing to production—he still seemed content to remain behind the scenes. "We called him the corporate snake," Brown says. "If we had a disagreement with Tom and we came to New York to argue our side, as soon as we left John's office, we'd see him slither back to John so he could get in the last word."

At times, Kimmerly's executive assistants created more friction in the office than he did. Kimmerly was extremely protective of the two overbearing middle-aged women who served successively as his administrative assistant. "At first, when we moved into New York," Strycker says, "this one woman wasn't even on the payroll of the company. She was paid through his law firm. But one week while I'm out of the office, she tried to fire my secretary. I didn't appreciate someone who didn't even work for the company firing my employee—especially while I was out of the office. I called this woman up to find out what the story was, and she told me to talk to Tom. Well, I told Tom to take his so-and-so secretary and send her the hell back to Detroit."

But however close Kimmerly may have been to his assistants or any other members of the staff, all relationships paled next to his monastic devotion to John De Lorean and the company. His workday often reached into the late hours of the night and weekends. From the office he would walk back to his small one-bedroom apartment on Central Park South. On rare occasions he might stop by Harry's Bar in the Waldorf-Astoria for a beer, but it was usually back home to bed. There's no evidence that his mentor tried to introduce him to New York's night life or that Kimmerly would have taken him up on it if he had. At most, the two could be seen having lunch at the 21 Club. "When John came into a crowded room," one executive says, "Tom would almost visibly start to recede. He didn't just step back or into the corner. He became less noticeable—like a snowman melting away in the light of the sun with a little smile on his face."

Bill Morgan says, "Kimmerly impressed me as a guy with an inordinate admiration for John. He just got extremely defensive about the least little comment you made about John. I remember having dinner with him and Dick Brown one night. Brown is a very religious guy and he was wondering what De Lorean was doing getting married three times. You could see that comment really upset Tom. He got very huffy and said, 'Why are you so interested?' "

Haddad found that his own disputes with Kimmerly were not necessarily rooted in business disagreements. "I think he was jealous of John's attention. If some new person came on the scene and John showed interest in him, Tom would be there behind his back trying to cut the guy down."

For young executives new to 280 Park Avenue the De Lorean Motor Company headquarters were a classic anomaly. On one hand, they seemed to glow with the possibilities of a thriving company. By 1980, total employment went over 1,000, and it continued to grow by the hundreds each month. Mailbags were overflowing with letters from expectant car buyers seeking more information about the car or requesting the name of the nearest dealer they could order one from. Telexes went off like buzz saws with messages from Belfast and California. Almost every day members of the press trooped in with tape recorders or cameras in hand.

And yet, behind the façade of bustling prosperity, the warren of offices on the penthouse floor seethed with corporate intrigue. Serious questions remained about the state of the car's development and whether there was enough financing to keep the company afloat until cars came off the assembly line. To make matters worse, the corporate staff seemed riven into factions. There was first the Strycker camp and then the Haddad camp. All were at odds with Kimmerly and the group of young lawyers and accountants surrounding him. Secretaries were scouts and spies. Memos to John reporting who said what were the most potent weapons.

"When I first came into the company," one executive says, "I figured it would be as rigidly regimented as GM. That's where De Lorean cut his teeth and I thought he'd duplicate their system inside his own company. But it was exactly the opposite. There was practically no direction or there was too much direction coming at you from all sides. I expected De Lorean to provide that leadership. Instead he'd wander into your office in his shirt-sleeves, very friendly, but no help at all. He'd nod and say, 'How are you doing?' or 'What are you up to?' and sit there and listen. At most he'd tell you some anecdote that had nothing to do with the matter at hand."

From what his executives could see, De Lorean was toiling away at the center of the cyclone he created, but he seemed as buffeted by the winds as everyone else. His mornings could start as early as 6:00—the crack of dawn by New York standards. Much of the rest of the day was spent on the phone or hunched over his desk. "He wrote constantly," his onetime executive assistant Marian Gibson says. "Every little thought that came into his head he had to put down in a memo. Some were about the car company. Others were about people. Some seemed to be just stray ideas. I suppose that was what they taught him at General Motors. We had a typist going full time just typing up all his notes. There were times when he'd just disappear for a few hours in the middle of the day without warning anyone and sneak over to the New York Athletic Club and lift weights."

His employees rarely got a glimpse of his social life. Occasionally the papers and gossip columns made mention of John and

Cristina at some benefit ball. He talked of dinner parties with Herb and Ann Siegel, or the chief executive of Norton Simon, David Mahoney, and his wife, Hilly. They also occasionally dined with Fifth Avenue neighbors such as *60 Minutes* producer Don Hewitt and his wife, TV reporter Marilyn Berger.

On rare occasions, the two worlds would mingle. Some employees remember a Christmas party with several of the New York celebrity friends in attendance. Maur Dubin was at the door acting as maître d' and Cristina was in the kitchen doing most of the cooking. But the onetime swinger would complain to his older executives that Cristina wanted to do too much partying. He preferred spending quiet evenings at home with her and the children. At least once, he took Zachary with him on a trip to Belfast, but he tried never to be away from the family for an extended period of time. He was especially enchanted by his first natural child, Kathryn, born in 1978. As she grew older, she would look more like her father than her mother. During one interview with a reporter, the nurse stopped by with the two-year-old and left her with De Lorean. He propped her on his lap behind his desk and continued talking to the reporter, unmindful as she grabbed the nearest pen and scribbled over every piece of paper in sight.

A few years later one New York businessman explained why he first got involved with De Lorean. "My father was driving down Fifth Avenue early one morning and he saw John walking his daughter to nursery school. I figured that, with all the concerns of his company, if he could still find time to walk his kid to school he had to be all right."

There were some nights when De Lorean brought his workday world home with him. One executive remembers following the boss home for dinner. The elevator of his apartment house brought them right up to the foyer of the duplex. A winding marble staircase led up to the bedrooms and the two sleeping children. While Cristina prepared dinner, De Lorean took the visitor on tour, showing him the seventeenth- and eighteenth-century pictures hanging on the walls. Most of the furniture was French provincial. Expensive-looking antique clocks and vases sat on the mantels and tables. "I was more impressed by the wallpaper behind the dining-room table," the executive says. "There was some pastoral scene hand-painted on the paper. You don't see something like that very often." He remembers an "elegant" meal followed, with poached fish, pasta, salad, and wine. At times De Lorean's conversation could wander to contemporary subjects and on this night he discussed the wisdom of legalizing marijuana.

Both he and Cristina were in their jeans. After dinner, she put a Barry Manilow record on in the den, and he took a letter out of his pocket that an old army buddy had written. "It was one step removed from a fan letter," the executive says. "Basically, it went, 'Now that you're famous, you've probably forgotten me, but remember the time when . . . ?' "

At one point in the evening De Lorean walked over to the living-room window and drew open the blinds. A picture-postcard scene of Central Park in the evening spread out before them, complete with the horse-drawn carriages cantering along by lantern light. "Isn't this spectacular?" he asked.

But in just another year he was negotiating to buy an even more spectacular sight in Bedminster, New Jersey. This twenty-five-room home sat in the middle of 430 acres and was valued at $3.5 million. De Lorean claimed to have swung this deal with the proceeds of the Pine Creek ranch Roy had unloaded in Idaho. Deeds show the official titleholder to be a syndicate headed by Tee-Kay International, Tom Kimmerly's private corporation. Just down the road lived millionaire publisher Malcolm Forbes.

These were all the trappings of America's capitalist elite, from the estates to the international company. The boy from the grimy Eastern European neighborhood had become a name, and as an added fillip to his manufactured persona, he even changed his name. During the mid-Seventies, as graphic designers fooled with letterheads and emblems, they continued to have difficulties with his unusual surname. De Lorean willingly consented to a space between the "De" and the "Lorean," further emphasizing his bogus claim to French origins. And after his car moved close to production, he discouraged the use of anything as anonymous as "DMC-12" on the nameplate, opting instead to call the car simply "De Lorean." The contemporary, rounded calligraphy for the logo would be designed by the car's stylist, Giugiaro.

The personal identification of the car was complete. Advertisements followed that continued to stamp the product with the personality of its maker. Cutty Sark Scotch started a campaign with De Lorean's face superimposed on a frontal view of his silver beauty with the doors opened. The legend above the ad reads, "One out of every 100 new businesses succeeds. Here's to those who take the odds." The copy repeats the mythos of De Lorean "on the way to the presidency of General Motors when he quit to build his own car company" (here forty-four patents with GM are cited—again, the actual number was thirty-one). The hook is that Cutty Sark is "the Scotch with a following of leaders." (C. R. Brown scoffs, "Imagine a safety car being advertised with a bottle of Scotch.") Supplier Goodyear Tires started another campaign featuring De Lorean leaning against a car in a field.

And yet, the regal serenity that emanated from the still photographs did not come through in life. Documentary filmmaker D. A. Pennebaker was to find De Lorean an uneasy subject for his motion-picture camera. Over the years anxiety had begun to creep through the look of superior calm. He seemed to be constantly adjusting his head on his long, slender neck, cricking it backward and from side to side. His flaring, curved eyebrows no longer arched for emphasis at the end of a sentence, but seemed to rise and fall of their own accord. He could press on a forced smile, but the sparkle and focus would go out of his eyes.

"He was so tight," Pennebaker says, "he twitched."

· 15 ·

Irvine

C. R. Brown would rather not be called by his first name, Cecil. Instead he prefers his initials, his middle name, Richard, or just Dick. But he does not shy away from talking about his namesake, Uncle Cecil Brown, who died on an evangelical mission to the jungle when he was attacked and eaten by a band of cannibals.

It is a fitting piece of ancestral psychohistory. Throughout his career in the auto industry, Brown has displayed missionary zeal, but he has also worked with the intensity of a man who expects the cannibals to arrive at any minute. At times, he's heard them knocking before anyone else has, and just as often they've barged in on him without warning.

Raised in Detroit, of middle-class origins, he, like De Lorean, cut his teeth at the Chrysler Institute, but was directed toward the marketing side of the business. Over the years, he became a troubleshooter for the company's dealer network, and when he took over as assistant regional manager for the San Francisco area, he moved sales in his region from last place to first in just four years. Frustrated by Chrysler's slow promotion rate, he jumped to American Motors as president of the Canadian division. His move was to coincide with a catastrophic downturn in the company's fortunes, and he watched for a year as AMC racked up unprecedented losses. A chance encounter with a bank official in 1970 had him meeting a team of executives from Mazda who were looking for ways to expand sales in America. Brown says he intended to do no more than give the group some advice as a favor to his banker friend, but after one session, the Japanese hired Brown as their general manager for Mazda Motors of America.

Today, one former Mazda executive says that the Japanese only intended Brown to be a West Coast regional manager. Whatever their intentions, he soon annexed the rest of the country. The kinder auto-industry analysts labeled Mazda's marketing strategy for America insane. Franchises went only to dealerships that carried Mazda and nothing else. But in a matter of two years under Brown, the number of Mazda dealers went from 31 to 412.

Brown's idiosyncrasies made him a difficult man to work for. His employees soon learned of his propensity for late hours, and few could keep up with it. "Brown would fly into our regional office for dinner meetings," one former Mazda executive remembers. "There'd be a long dinner and then, for a couple of hours, we'd have to listen to C.R. hold forth over a glass of wine on the state of the auto industry. At about one in the morning the meetings would start. Brown would be grilling guys into the dawn hours while they were practically falling asleep in their chairs."

Many found his temper fearsome, and even worse when they attempted to argue back. "There was just something in him," another former employee says, "that made him want to kick you one more time after he'd already made his point."

In contrast to his ferocity with co-workers, Brown maintained a deep religious devotion. He had a soft spot for a man with a wholesome family, and often overlooked faults in breadwinners that he would have picked apart in more rootless sorts. Many believed his moralistic attitudes were best expressed in his own home. Married for over twenty years, he raised his three daughters and son in a gatehouse community in Long Beach. His daughters went to the state college at the bottom of the hill.

Brown's last days at Mazda were to be steeped in controversy. During the fall of 1973, just in time for the oil crisis, the EPA released mileage figures showing that the little Mazda cars with their rotary engines got only ten miles to the gallon. Convinced that the test had been improperly conducted, Brown engaged in a heated debate with EPA officials, only further publicizing the embarrassing results. Meanwhile, over 100,000 1974 Mazdas sat on the docks. Brown says he left the company of his own accord, and he takes credit for some of Mazda's currently popular product line.

Despite his difficult working habits, when Brown joined De Lorean he was able to recruit several of the men who had worked with him at Mazda. As one of them explains, "For all the crap Dick dished out, he was at least a man of his word and exactly the sort of driven son of a bitch who could make something as crazy as the De Lorean Motor Company work."

If Brown was not overly impressed by De Lorean, he adds, "I took it for granted that he knew what he was talking about. John was supposed to be an excellent engineer who could get a car from the drawing board to the highway. I had great respect for the executives around him like Bill Collins and Bob Dewey. We felt we had the horsepower to get the job done. We just wanted John to be what he said he was, and since we were representing him, we wanted him to play it straight."

But quite early in the game, Brown discovered that De Lorean did not always play things straight. He recoiled at De Lorean's tendency to exaggerate at dealer meetings. He was more distressed when De Lorean permitted Roy Nesseth's minions to sell the stock with boiler-room tactics. "John used to tell me that my problem was trying to be purer than the driven snow," Brown recalls. "He'd say, 'Real successful people have had to cut corners and manipulate. That's the way things get done.' "

But if De Lorean had turned out to be a less savory person than Brown would have preferred, the question of why he stayed on remains. "I was hooked," he admits. "At a certain point I got too many of my friends involved as investors, dealers, and employees. I couldn't let them down and just back out."

If anything, Brown continued to dig in deeper. At one point in the course of his tenure, when it looked as if the company couldn't make his California office's payroll, he dipped into his own checking account to tide things over. During the first week of August 1978, both he and De Lorean were in Hollywood, Northern Ireland, to sign the NIDA agreement. Only a few days before, De Lorean's putative plant manager had quit, disgusted with his boss's high-handed treatment of an architectural firm that had contributed over $300,000 of services in preliminary design work on the factory. After the ceremony was completed, De Lorean took Brown into a corner. "He put his arm around my shoulder and told me he had no one around who knew about launching the company. He asked if I could stick around in Belfast and help set up the procedures to get the plant going."

For the next few months Brown spent most of his time in Dunmurry. He made the rounds of the Belfast public relations circuit in De Lorean's stead, visiting schools and business groups. Coincidentally, he discovered he had a long-lost uncle living nearby—not a bad development when he was trying to win the local community's acceptance. To start initial ground clearance, he brought in a California building contractor. To help him recruit European executives, he turned to the brother of a next-door neighbor in Long Beach who had once handled personnel for Chrysler Europe. This man suggested Bennington, and they built the rest of the team around him.

From the first moment he started working for De Lorean, Brown expected to be appointed president of the company. In the early, developmental days, De Lorean talked about moving the headquarters to southern California to be close to the market where he would sell most of his cars. But in time, he made it clear that his headquarters would remain in New York and that he expected his company's president to reside there as well. Brown refused to move east, but he still held out hope that De Lorean would come to his senses and relocate the headquarters to the West Coast.

"In the spring of 1979, after things had been set up in Belfast," Brown says, "I came back to California, and the employees had organized a lunch where I was presented with a plaque as a memento of the Belfast start-up—a very nice affair. Afterwards, as we were leaving the restaurant, they told me that John had sent something he wanted me to have. I went outside and there was a new Mercedes 450SEL. When I called John, he said, 'I know you'll be upset hearing this, but I'm bringing in Gene Cafiero as president. I didn't want you to be upset.' I told him I appreciated the thought, and I guess it was a nice gesture. John was capable of nice gestures."

Like so many other De Lorean operating officers, Eugene A. Cafiero had come from Chrysler. Paradoxically, Cafiero's record at America's third-largest car maker was both more and less auspicious than those of the new company's other Chrysler veterans. In 1975, at the age of only forty-nine, he became the corporation's president and chief operating officer. But, during his tenure, Chrysler reeled towards bankruptcy, and whether or not he deserved it, he got all the approbation of the skipper on the *Titanic*.

From De Lorean's perspective, Cafiero had still been chief executive of a major American car manufacturer. It was the sort of distinction neither he nor Brown shared, and it was the sort of distinction that investors on Wall Street might appreciate. Brown strongly advised against Cafiero's hiring, a fact he didn't try to hide from Cafiero. "We first met in Turin on a trip to Giugiaro," Brown says. "He was there with Chuck Bennington and John. Later, in the hotel, I told him that I didn't recommend him to John. When he asked me why, I explained that I had been a Chrysler dealer during two of the three years of his tenure and that both the product and the production quality had suffered dramatically in that period. He then went into a one-hour dissertation on why that wasn't his fault."

A week later, Brown tried to make amends with a letter, telling Cafiero, "Just in case there was any doubt resulting from our brief conversations last week, I want you to know that you can depend on our support and best wishes for success in your new role." But his initial conversation set the tone for their relationship, and he found that his new superior could be just as caustic. Adding insult to injury, Cafiero started with a salary that topped out at $375,000 a year, compared to Brown's $155,000. To make up for the bonus provisions he had lost from Chrysler, Cafiero was also given a $164,800 payment.

De Lorean's announcement of Cafiero's hiring in the short-lived company newsletter (only two issues were published) would be as interesting as the appointment. To some extent his column reflected the qualms employees were having about De Lorean's ability as an entrepreneur. The "Word from Mr. De Lorean" began as follows: "Not all successful executives in large corporations can adjust their talents to beginning a new company, and so, in our search for innovative executives, we needed those with a full range of automotive experiences and skills, necessary not only to build a new car, but also a new corporation. Gene Cafiero is one of those talented professionals. During our meetings, I found that Gene's impressive background was not a barrier to that entrepreneurial quality we needed to direct our automotive operations."

Despite those kudos, Cafiero's role in the company would at best be ineffectual. Unwilling to contend with the palace intrigue, the president settled back and collected his lavish salary. When De Lorean insisted that he take control of the factory in Belfast, Cafiero recoiled and looked instead for someone to replace Bennington. In his first year he issued a handful of memos, the lengthiest concerning paid holidays. "See this memo," Brown would tell his California executives. "It cost about $375,000."

For his part, Brown needed no prompting to get involved in the company—as far as De Lorean and Kimmerly were concerned, too involved. When an Arthur Andersen official called to check out De Lorean's explanation that Roy Nesseth was working for the company, Brown denied it. Another of the auditor's questions dealt with the vintage gull-wing Mercedes Roy had taken from Gerry Dahlinger. According to the books, DMC bought it from Nesseth for $20,000—a transaction Brown had wondered about. He was keeping it in storage and had learned that it would cost $40,000 to restore. Brown also confirmed that he had delivered the Mercedes to Cristina, and picked up the Mazda sports car at her brother's house.

His honesty brought him a curt memo from John De Lorean a few weeks later. "Roy Nesseth is a consultant to me," he wrote. "I talk to him virtually every day on various DMC projects and concepts. I find his advice invaluable. As you know, he saved our company when it was obvious we were going to miss our 150-dealer target." De Lorean went on to praise Roy's ideas about the Bugatti replicar and a Canadian distributor (whom the company never did secure). "Again," he added, "since you and he don't get along, I keep you apart." De Lorean then denied that he ever told Arthur Andersen's Measelle that Nesseth was Brown's backup.

The first major rift between Brown and De Lorean was to come during the cash crunch of summer 1980. The delay in the car's production had been difficult for Brown to handle. His restive body of dealers was starting to wonder whether their money had been thrown down the drain. But Brown was also nervous about the overhead in the New York office. The original business plan had never envisioned so many people in headquarters earning so much money. Further complicating matters, the British government had commissioned a report from the auditing firm of McKinsey and Company that raised questions about the costs of the New York office—predicting the U.S. operation would be $2.5 million over budget in 1980—and suggesting that De Lorean was never going to meet his sales projections.

Brown helped De Lorean prepare his reply and offered his own experience at Mazda as an example of how sober market estimates could be exceeded. But Brown was not ready to cooperate in a bizarre bail-out plan that De Lorean and Kimmerly concocted in the middle of July. They presented a resolution before the board that permitted the company to borrow $600,000 from De Lorean's private firm, Manufacturing. The loan was collateralized with virtually all the assets of the car company.

When the resolution reached Brown's desk in Irvine, he was shocked. "The way John was spending money in New York," he says, "I figured that $600,000 wouldn't last thirty days."

The resolution had been signed by De Lorean, Gene Cafiero, Johnny Carson's lawyer, Henry Bushkin, and Wood Gundy's director, Edmund King. Brown suspected that, except for De Lorean, no one of the group had read the loan agreement closely. "I called Gene and told him that we had fiduciary responsibility as board members to protect the minority stockholders. This resolution would give away the company for $600,000."

They agreed to call Brown's lawyer. He advised that Kimmerly first issue an opinion letter. Tom told Brown it wasn't necessary. "He said the documentation was already on file."

But Brown went ahead and called Bushkin and King. A member of the audit committee, Bushkin was himself becoming far more involved with the company and John De Lorean than he had ever intended when he'd first advised Johnny Carson to invest. He performed legal work for De Lorean in California and tried to finance some of his private deals by using his influence at a bank in which he and Carson had an interest. In return, De Lorean at one point had Brown and his employees search for a suitable car dealership in the L.A. area that Carson and Bushkin could buy.

The car company also got entangled in the production of an auto-theft alarm system. The product's unlikely inventor composed music for *The Tonight Show*. Although De Lorean had yet to prove himself out, NIDA took his advice and bankrolled another Belfast venture to manufacture the alarms. Two Irish businessmen were to handle production, but they never managed to turn out any alarms that reached the States in working order. During its short life, De Lorean and Brown were on the company's board and Bushkin was chairman.

Despite Bushkin's other contacts with De Lorean, Brown felt that the lawyer remained one of the few independent and influential powers on the De Lorean Motor Company board. When the lawyer was alerted to the resolution, he was grateful for Brown's vigilance. "Bushkin told me, 'Thank God somebody in this company is thinking. I was in a hurry when I signed this, and I didn't read it closely first.' "

The next morning, a Thursday, De Lorean called Brown in a rage. He started out by saying that he deserved $46 million from the British and just needed time to collect it. He couldn't understand why Brown wouldn't sign the resolution and he went on to accuse him of running Bennington down to the British. Brown shot back that the only person in the company denigrating other executives was De Lorean himself. "After we got through all that, John said, 'Come into New York Monday and let's talk. You really haven't participated in the management of the company.' "

Later in the morning he'd hear from Kimmerly as well. "Bushkin had called and scared the daylights out of him. Evidently he said that if the 84 percent stockholder doesn't have enough confidence to loan the company $600,000 without tying up all the assets, then that worries everybody."

When Brown arrived in New York, he was told a board meeting had been called for Thursday. De Lorean asked him and Dewey to work on a survival plan that would get them through the cash bind without further British aid. On Tuesday, Brown first heard that De Lorean had reconstituted the board, leaving him off. De Lorean had given no hint of the move when they had met earlier. Brown also learned that NIDA, furious over the board change, had summoned De Lorean to Belfast.

At Wednesday's management meeting, Brown and Dewey presented their proposal for halving expenses in the New York office. He was interrupted by De Lorean. "John just took our proposal and tossed it aside. He stated he had called a meeting with NIDA for next week—of course I knew they called him—and at that meeting he would tell them that they owed us $46 million. 'Either they come up with the money,' he said, 'or they could stuff it.'

"From there he went into a diatribe, calling the British 'cowards' and 'dumb fucks.' He said, 'A $2.5 million shortfall for the U.S. is peanuts. I'm not going to be nickeled and dimed by those bastards. I'm not going to run a nickel-shit company. We're going to keep California, Detroit, and New York at their present spending levels and continue to do all the things we think are necessary, and if they don't like it, I'll close it down next Friday.'

"He finished by saying, 'Our car is a $30,000 car and there is no way we can proceed without the diversified programs.' Then he left the room."

The next day, a calmer John De Lorean walked into the office Brown was using in New York and perched himself on the arm of a chair. He had talked with Hopkins, and NIDA was willing to advance some money to tide them over for another month. He added again that he was serious about shutting down the company if he didn't get the rest of the money they owed him.

But then, Brown says, De Lorean abruptly shifted gears. "He told me he knew how some of the things the board was doing bothered my conscience. He said he wanted me to keep a clear conscience and not to worry as much as I did, so he had dropped me from the board. I told him that action was all too indicative of his character. He couldn't bear having anyone disagree with him, so he had to stack the board his way.

"John just nodded and said, 'That's right. It's my company and I'm going to do what I want to do—when you get your own company, you can do the same.' "

Brown shot back that De Lorean's problems came from "listening to the scum of the earth, then making your business decisions based on a premise of bad information, including rumors, lies, and innuendo. In the final analysis, these people are your nemesis."

Brown says De Lorean replied, "There isn't going to be a final analysis." However, he added that he hoped they could try to start a new relationship with "a clean slate."

Among those De Lorean had "stacked" on the board were Kimmerly and his own wife, Cristina. SEC files subsequently identified her as "self-employed in the advertising and entertainment fields since 1965." The résumé neglected to add that, in 1965, the board director was fourteen years old.

Disconsolate, C.R. returned to California, expecting his days at the company to be numbered. "Dick never hid the fact that he believed De Lorean had no moral fiber," one executive says, "[and] he held it against everyone in the New York office. The crazy thing was that we worked for the De Lorean Motor Company, but if we said a complimentary thing about De Lorean himself, we were in the doghouse with Dick."

Yet, in the first few weeks following his return from New York, Brown would again work his way back into the good graces of De

Lorean by supplying a vital piece of the distribution network. Brown had already put De Lorean in touch with the shipping company he had used with Mazda, Pasha International. At De Lorean's request, Pasha studied the feasibility of flying the cars over from Northern Ireland, but eventually settled on a system of ocean freight. Loading cars with gull-wings on and off a ship and then onto truck carriers was a complex process. But Pasha proved to be sophisticated enough to overcome those obstacles.

Both the shipper and De Lorean's manufacturing subsidiary required payments before the cars reached the dealers. To provide those funds, De Lorean needed an interim credit line known as a "bridge financing." It was crucial to the survival of the company. As the date for the first delivery of cars loomed, De Lorean still had no arrangements for the bridge. "Kimmerly kept telling me he was going to take care of it," Brown says. "He went to Chemical, Continental, and Citibank and was turned down by all of them. I could see in the summer of 1980 that the cars were only months away from delivery, so I asked to try on my own. I know Kimmerly was laughing up his sleeve, and never expecting me to do it. I went first to the Japanese bank that Mazda had used. Then I went to Bank of America."

In October, Brown secured a $31.2 million loan agreement from the Bank of America for the cars, and an additional $2.3 million for parts. "Tom called me up to say he didn't know how I did it."

During this same period Brown was engaged in building his own western version of De Lorean headquarters in a 50,000-square-foot warehouse building in Irvine. It was, he says, a bargain that rented for only $14,250 a month—compared to the $80,000 a month the New York headquarters were paying for their offices. But in decking out his domain, Brown would spare no expense. He had the cement-block building carefully painted in a two-tone gray and black to match the corporate colors. When he didn't like the look of the carpeting he'd bought for the first floor, he had it torn up and replaced for an additional $5,000.

Office decoration was no small matter for Brown. He thought

nothing of walking into an executive's office, straightening the pictures on the wall and sometimes replacing them. Over $70,000 was spent on office furniture—some $8,000 on Brown's office alone, including a $2,000 desk and a $600 chair. The walnut conference table, stretching ten feet by four feet, was bought for $2,550. There wasn't a metal desk or piece of composition board in the place. De Lorean's office, next to the conference room, had only one narrow vertical window. It overlooked the end of the little visitor's parking lot on the side of the building, so Brown had that piece of asphalt torn out and replaced with grass and some landscaping. When he didn't like the landscaper's choice of bushes, he had those torn out and replaced as well.

In a textbook case of the pot calling the kettle black, Kimmerly reprimanded Brown for his lavish expenditures. "Our auditors," Kimmerly told Brown, "feel that someone is building their own rec room out there."

"Are you serious?" Brown says he replied. "Do you mean using the funds personally?"

When Kimmerly answered yes, Brown asked that they come out and conduct an audit.

But the squabbles over office furniture were quickly forgotten when the first cars started to roll off the assembly line. "Suddenly John and Tom saw how much they needed Dick Brown," one New York executive says. "If he couldn't sell their car, they were in big trouble."

When Brown saw the first pilot vehicle, however, he had his doubts. "It was flown in and delivered in a truck," one of Brown's assistants remembers. "It was partially disassembled, and we were like little kids at a Christmas tree, putting it together as fast as possible to see what had hatched. Unfortunately, the car looked nicer disassembled. There were poor body fits. The trim was falling apart. Water leaks all over—through the roof and window. It scared the crap out of Dick."

Brown dashed off a memo to Belfast with fifty suggestions for improvement touching on everything from the license-plate holder (Lotus had forgotten to include one on the designs) to wiring that dragged too close to the ground. However, when Brown wrote dealers announcing the arrival of the first pilot car, he enclosed a copy of a decidedly different Belfast memo: "We have spent the last three days in rather intensive evaluation from the standpoint of technical features, appearance, appointments, and on-the-road handling characteristics. . . . My personal feeling as well as the feeling of all the people at DMC-California is that: 'It's a Winner!' "

·16·
The Ethical Car

Few American automobile buyers have ever had the chance to receive a thank-you letter from the name on the grille. But such was the added distinction of owning a De Lorean. The car maker's message read as follows:

> I am pleased to learn that you have purchased a De Lorean automobile. I wanted to write you myself because the purchase of a revolutionary new product, particularly one as significant as a car, is an act of faith, perhaps even courage, qualities very much at the heart of forming and developing the De Lorean Motor Company.
> It has now been several years since we undertook to bring another kind of automobile into being. The goal was to design and build a car that would be as safe as possible, reliable, comfortable, handle and perform well, be enormous fun to drive, and unmistakably elegant in appearance. We wanted people to be able to buy a car which they truly liked and then keep it year after year, much as one does one's home.
> If, as you come to know your car better, you want to comment on how well we have achieved our goals, or how we might even improve, I do hope you will do so. You can be sure that we are

concerned about the attitudes and experiences of our owners and your comments will be valued.
Warmest personal regards,
John Z. De Lorean, Chairman

Some De Lorean owners who had come to know their cars better did send in their comments. But they did not all come with the warmest of personal regards. One, an industrialist from Long Island City, New York, wrote:

> ... due primarily to your poor quality control, I am embarrassed to be the owner of a De Lorean.
> The car is a showpiece and is always on display. When it doesn't start due to a short in the inertia switch, I am embarrassed. When the headlights don't turn off, I am embarrassed. When the signal lights don't work, I am endangered. When the fuel gauge doesn't work, I get stuck. And when the roof leaks, I get wet. I could enumerate many other problems. I should also state that my [Ford] Mustang was delivered with fewer defects.

Some of the complaint letters were incredibly forgiving. A Chicago-area lawyer reported that he "noticed a number of small problems," and lists a few:

> 1. Side window sticks in the up position.
> 2. Fuel pump is excessively noisy.
> 3. Dye from the optional floor mats comes off and stains clothing, shoes, and skin.
> 4. Interior body fit of the door is not excellent.
> 5. Owner's manual does not state the type of light bulbs to use (several were burned out on delivery).
> 6. The radio is terrible—especially in the FM stereo position.
> With the exception of the above I have found the car to be great.

Other correspondents were not as accommodating. A Laguna Beach developer wrote:

> I have had my De Lorean for three and one-half months. During this time it has been in the shop for repairs a total of six weeks. It was towed in three times ...

The problem is that on five occasions I have been unable to start the car in the morning and keep it going. It starts and remains at 1000 rpm. When you depress the gas it doesn't go any faster, and when you release the clutch it jerks forward and kills. At the same time a loud humming noise comes from under the gearshift lever . . .

A second problem is the driver's window. Three times I have put it down and the glass has fallen out. [The dealership] cannot get a replacement part. They glued the window in and told me not to use it. . . .

The car is of no use to me because I cannot be sure when it will run. If you cannot fix this automobile in five days, my attorney has been instructed to file a class-action lawsuit to recover the money I paid for the car as well as the inconvenience I've been through. Enclosed is a copy of a $90 towing bill . . .

One of the De Lorean executives who had to field complaints like these quickly came to a sorry conclusion: "Those cars were literally scrap when they rolled off the boat," he says. "You get warranty claims on all cars. Car companies average three or four claims for each car produced in the course of a year. But the De Lorean was pulling three or four claims per car per *month*."

The quality-control problems were apparent to Brown from the first pilot vehicle he saw. His fears were heightened further when Belfast air-freighted more cars for the February 1981 Los Angeles National Auto-Dealers Convention. When a pilot car arrived in Detroit, Midwest technical manager Jeffrey C. Synor was dispatched to the airport. Both gull-wing doors were jammed shut and the shippers were unable to get the car off the wooden palate. "You had to be careful not to cut yourself when you opened the hood," he says. "I used to say it was a British car with body by Wilkinson Blade."

Belfast, meanwhile, was making over 500 cars ready for shipment in the next two months. Brown immediately started to wave the red flags. Up to that point, De Lorean was not concentrating on problems of assembly. The major fear in New York was that the engine wouldn't pass emission tests. An alternate plan was to ship the first batch of cars to Canada, where pollution standards were lower. The move sounded very familiar to an incident De

• THE ETHICAL CAR •

Lorean relates in *On A Clear Day* when, after a strike, GM was left with 400 Camaros and Firebirds that were one year old and didn't meet EPA guidelines. "At one of the GM [board] meetings," he writes, "somebody suggested that we sell the cars in Canada where the safety and pollution laws were less stringent.

"So we set out to peddle these cars in Canada. The only trouble was that some public-spirited guy at the Norwood plant leaked the plan to the Canadian press, which jumped all over 'giant General Motors' for trying to sell in Canada cars which were too dirty and unsafe for the United States. At a time when Canadian nationalistic spirit was rising and 'ugly American' ownership of Canadian industry was under attack, the decision to try to sell these Camaros and Firebirds in Canada was the worst thing we could have done."

But it was not a bad enough experience to teach De Lorean a lesson. Instead, it gave him ideas. This time, however, a "public-spirited guy" wasn't necessary to blow the whistle. Other executives realized that it would take so long to pass Canadian import requirements that nothing could be gained by unloading the cars there.

Brown turned everyone's attention away from the engine and toward the rest of the car. De Lorean put Cafiero on the spot to stop the problems at the gate. By this time C. K. Bennington had been yanked from his post as managing director of the Belfast plant and brought back to New York. In his place, Cafiero hired the retired chief executive of Chrysler Canada and Chrysler International, Donald H. Lander. A benign, balding man with an easy smile, Lander was to be one of the few people in the entire company who would win praise from all factions. But he came in only two months before production started. On April Fools' Day De Lorean flew in to see whether any progress had been made on the condition of the cars. Apparently satisfied after test driving a few, he flew back home. He sent Cafiero to make the final inspection before the cars left. On April 14, the president Telexed back to New York and California: "Inspected this A.M. 216 okay cars at Stormont dock and additional okay units at plant. Quality and appearance level much improved since my last visit. In my opinion these units with U.S. prepping are satisfactory for shipment to U.S. dealers."

That assurance was not enough for an anxious Brown. The boat arrived in Long Beach in the middle of May. "Fortunately," Brown says, "the press stayed just long enough to see the first cars come out. Of the 250 on board we had to roll out 150."

De Lorean and Cafiero flew to Long Beach to see what he was complaining about. One executive remembers, "Cafiero looked at the cars and said, 'These are perfect. Better than Cadillac.' We all just stood there and tried not to laugh."

De Lorean dashed off his own urgent Telex to Belfast with two columns. One was headed, "Must be corrected before any sales." In that list:

> Door seal, poor quality, falls off getting out of car; must be replaced and mechanically fastened in customer contact area.
> Radio interference must be corrected. . . .
> Shim out rear wheel to avoid tire interference.
> How do you enter locked car with dead battery?

De Lorean also had problems with the key fitting into the door lock, the way the doors shut, and the way the stainless steel stained even before the cars hit the road. Among his items that did not need to be corrected immediately, he referred to the poor visibility out the rear window and wrote, "Car does not park. Is this legal?"

"I think the poor state of the cars became a moment of triumph for Dick," one of his executives says. "He had given everyone warning and it was clear the cars couldn't be sold in that condition. De Lorean gave him carte blanche to do anything that had to be done to get those cars to the dealers."

Brown used his mandate to create what some executives called his own little kingdom—Quality Assurance Centers. He set up three processing points in Santa Ana, California; Troy, Michigan; and Bridgewater, New Jersey. Brown told the press that the QACs only performed dealer prep, no more than for the Japanese imports—shine the body and tighten any little bolt that came loose in transit. In fact, Brown was reassembling the cars.

The big push started with the very first boatload. One executive remembers, "Brown called in every district manager and technical expert he had. At that point we did all the processing in Irvine. We were working twenty hours a day. Some people fell asleep under the cars. For dinner Dick would spend $200 or $300 on pizza and chicken. While we were eating, he'd come down out of his office and give us pep talks. Here we were—big-time auto executives stuffing our faces with Colonel Sanders and up to our shoulders in grease."

One of the staff members mimeographed a cartoon drawing entitled, "Be a POG for De Lorean!" It defined a POG as someone who worked like a dog and looked like a pig. Qualifications included: "A Ph.D. in automotive technology with heavy emphasis on finance, education, and accounting. Your own metric hand tools helpful but not essential."

Brown alternately badgered and sweet-talked the troops, at times telling those who had left the building that they had just as well quit their jobs. A few wondered whether he was striving for unattainable perfection. "We spent more time on the body than anything else," Jeff Synor says. The fascias—the plastic bumper material on the front and rear of the car—were often not flush with the rest of the car. "We could work two days readjusting the other panels of the car so the fascias would fit. Then they'd sit out on the lot and expand in the sun and we'd have to do it all over again to pass muster with C.R. He used to take a little metal gauge to the edge and if he could slip it behind the fascia it wasn't good enough."

However much Brown frustrated his staff, they all knew he was putting more hours in than anyone else. During the day he was on the phone with his dealers, trying to assure them that the cars were on the way. At night he sat at his desk, working on memos, or paced the halls railing against the idiots in New York and Belfast. For his workers he became as fearsome and tortured as Ahab, but some wondered whether the "great white" he was out to harpoon was none other than the man with his name on the door. "C.R. was obsessed with turning out a good car," one of his senior staff members says, "and it eventually turned into overkill."

Forced to get cars to the dealers as fast as possible before financing ran out, Brown spared no expense to bring in the necessary parts to finish off the cars. Orders went out in a frantic and often wasteful fashion. According to Synor, "C.R.'s favorite expression was: 'I don't care what it costs, just get the job done.' We Federal Expressed everything—from tires to slips of paper."

One of his hastier decisions was to replace the hidden radio antenna embedded in the windshield with an inexpensive, noncollapsible whip antenna. "The problem with the hidden antenna was the wire they were using," Synor explains. "It was more suited to defrosting the windshield than picking up radio signals." Rather than try to improve the wire and keep the hidden system—a De Lorean trademark at GM—Brown insisted on an external antenna.

Brown's alternative meant drilling a hole in the fender. When De Lorean later offered car owners a more discreet power antenna, the fenders with the antenna holes had to be replaced at a cost of $200 apiece.

What distressed senior staff most about Brown's alterations was his unwillingness to defer to his trained engineers. He was more likely to ask the hourly Mexican mechanics for advice while his executives fumed nearby. "The whole problem," one concludes, "is that Brown was making mechanical decisions and he wasn't an engineer."

But Brown was the only man in the company making decisions, and that was a vital role to fill when the company faced intense pressure to deliver cars as fast as possible. There would be no more nagging memos from Kimmerly or De Lorean during those launch months. In fact, one of the dealers most chagrined that he hadn't received cars was limited partner Chuck De Lorean. Finding that he had no special influence with his brother, he threatened—for at least a few weeks—to give back his franchise.

By August, Brown had still not met his goal of getting out at least one car to every dealer. Only ten cars were leaving the

THE ETHICAL CAR

Quality Assurance Centers each day. Eventually he geared up his QAC kingdom to include almost 250 hourly workers in all three locations. "When we started out," Brown says, "we spent an average of 150 man-hours per car. Eventually it got down to sixty-eight hours. Finally ten. When you added up all the expenses, we spent between $1,500 and $2,000 in additional labor on each car."

Ideally, the QACs should have withered away after the first few bugs were shaken out of the production process. Brown continually sent expeditions over to the Belfast plant to track down where the errors were coming from. His envoys found one of the most modern and sensible assembly lines in Europe. The initial assembly of the doors and the body was done on lines where the work was pulled by overhead carriers. Along the way, the body was married with the chassis and put on a robotic moving platform—first pioneered by the Swedish car maker, Volvo—that followed wire tracks embedded in the floor. If a car presented problems, the platform could be taken off the line and pushed to the side.

No matter how good the system was, it took men to run it. In the critical days when production was first gearing up to speed, Irish Republican Army conflicts heated up again as interned prisoners died on hunger strikes. One of the dead was IRA activist Bobby Sands. Elected to the House of Commons as a symbolic sign of Catholic sympathy during his fast, Sands had lived just behind the De Lorean factory in Twinbrook. The strikes provoked the first pronounced absenteeism at the plant. When the British Army marched in to quell the violence that followed Sands's funeral, they used the De Lorean grounds as a shortcut—a move that made the plant site a target of two fire bombs. One touched off a fire in a small prefabricated building where engineering drawings were kept. The company later claimed £10 million of damage—an amount that De Lorean executives privately conceded was inflated. A skeptical government has yet to settle the claim.

The civilian strife that roiled around the plant did not find its way inside. Brown's staff encountered willing workers who reported early and seemed truly dedicated to putting out a good product. But many were still adjusting to their first industrial jobs. Some had never even held a screwdriver before, let alone worked on an assembly line, and very few owned cars. "I was watching one guy putting in water seals around the door," a California executive says, "and he was having trouble making it all fit at once, so he was cutting it into pieces, and fitting one little piece at a time. He just had no idea what the seal was for and how it worked."

But one of the Irish shop stewards, Malachy Higgins, says the workers were well aware of the defects. "These people came in from California to watch us, and we weren't supposed to know who they were. I think they were worried about insulting us. But we knew who they were, and we knew there were troubles with the car. But we were told to let those things go and not slow up the line."

Limited's managing director, Don Lander, liked to tell the visiting delegations that every new car program has to cope with first-run gremlins. He had seen several in just as much trouble when he'd run Chrysler in Europe and Canada. Adjustments to the line, he warned, could only be made gradually. Eventually, he said, all the kinks would be straightened out.

But until they were, the company had to go through the onerous cost of Brown's Quality Assurance Centers, and cars still went out with serious defects. The car's most prominent feature—the gull-wing door—was just as prominently prone to failure. The two latches were on either side of the door (instead of on the bottom as Collins had originally designed them), and occasionally both didn't engage at once, which ended up jamming the mechanism and making it difficult to pull open the door. A double-lock system—intended for convenience—kept both doors locked when one was jammed. The most notorious incident involving a broken gull-wing occurred at a Cleveland auto show, where a spectator was trapped for over an hour until he was pried out. During the interim, the event's sponsor notified Brown that a De Lorean car had taken a hostage. Brown was ready to send Synor to the rescue on the next available plane.

THE ETHICAL CAR

Part of the door problem would be solved by one of Brown's homemade solutions—a metal guide over each latch. But until the molds for the guides were made in Belfast, he had an elderly machinist in Irvine make them individually out of metal. Each week, the man showed up with the latest batch in a paper bag, taking $40 cash for every set.

Cold weather created other problems with the door. Moisture gathered in the seal on snowy nights, freezing the perimeter of the gull-wing shut. One employee manning the complaint lines says, "I remember getting a call from a guy in a phone booth in Chicago on some miserable Sunday afternoon. He had just come out of the stadium after watching a Chicago Bears football game and couldn't get his door open."

The car's incompatibility with cold would be proven in laboratory tests, but these weren't conducted until the car had been on the road for seven months. In extreme cold, the windshield didn't defrost and the struts in the door jammed. At intervals the door stuck shut or didn't shut at all. In his regional headquarters in Michigan, Jeff Synor discovered that moisture gathered within the throttle cable and froze overnight. "I know of one incident where a woman rode up over a curb and into a gas station parking lot when she tried to rev her engine. It's a miracle no one was injured." The solution was a rubber boot around the cable, but it took, Synor believes, an unconscionably long time before Irvine recognized the severity of the problem.

Winter weather was also unkind to the striking stainless-steel coat. Salt on icy roads left lingering white spots. In warmer climates, cars could be tattooed with finger- and handprints. De Lorean executives recommended a variety of waxes to keep the cars clean, but most owners found it didn't take long before their silver beauty looked like the smudgy toy of some giant four-year-old.

Even the car's most public owner and investor, Johnny Carson, would fall victim to the gremlins. Brown took care to deliver his car personally, but on the comedian's maiden voyage down to the drugstore the battery failed in front of an appreciative crowd.

"Some of that initial word of mouth on the car was disastrous,"

Brown sums up. "I don't think you can calculate the damage it does, but you know it's considerable."

Brown tried to make up for the difficulties by promptly replying to complaints. His executives took turns manning a complaint line during evenings and weekends. "I don't think any company was ever more eager to please," Synor says. But in many cases, the help came after the fact.

No one was more aware of the product-quality backlash than John De Lorean. In his own understated way, he offered Brown a solution—buy back the first 5,000 cars off the assembly line, giving customers the option of getting a new-model De Lorean instead. It was the sort of grandstand move, De Lorean told Brown, that could turn them from bumbling idiots to heroes. Brown convinced him to put aside his generosity. That one move would have shown up as a $115 million liability on the company's books.

Certainly, De Lorean did not deserve all the blame for production problems that showed up in his car. But De Lorean was responsible for all too many of the car's drawbacks. Somehow his personal dream car had not merited his attention—when it was most needed—to either details or overall concepts.

When he was general manager of Chevrolet, De Lorean was saddled with the disastrous Vega. It was a car, he says, designed by a committee that missed all of its announced objectives by a mile. In *On A Clear Day*, the chapter on the Vega opens with a press conference conducted by GM chairman James M. Roche. De Lorean relates Roche's overly optimistic assessments about the price and characteristics of the car that would allow it to compete with the cheap imports. He writes:

> A study of the conception and gestation of the Vega reveals not a lesson in scientific marketing and development, but rather a classic case of management ineptitude....
>
> When Roche announced the car, his information came from statistical abstractions. Not one prototype had been built or tested. There was no model to point to because the car existed only in financial statistics and blueprints derived from a consensus of the existing subcompact cars, all of them foreign and some of them

built by GM overseas. . . . All of this information provided a weight and price class for the car that became the foundation for the chairman's startling small-car announcement. Shortly thereafter, the first prototype was delivered from the central staff to Chevrolet. . . . Already the small, svelte American answer to foreign-car craftsmanship was putting on weight—twenty pounds in understructure to hold the front end intact. Thus began a fattening process of the "less-than 2,000-pound" minicar that would take it to ponderous proportions in weight and price compared to the original car described at the opening of the new GM building in New York City. . . . To be a viable product on the road, the Vega was going to arrive on the market heavier and costlier than the company's target because it was already close to 200 pounds heavier than planned.

De Lorean ends the discourse on the Vega by adding, "I hope the Vega lesson was learned well by GM management and that the knowledge gleaned from this lesson is applied in the development of future products. . . ."

It was another lesson De Lorean chose not to learn. If anything, he took GM's design duplicity to a higher degree. His goal was not to fight off imports but, as he told reporters, to make an "ethical car" that was durable, fuel-efficient, and safe. Like Roche with the Vega, De Lorean made wild claims about his car from no more than "statistical abstractions." But when his prototype came off the blocks, he continued to make the wild claims. As late as January 1979, he told *Newsweek* that the car would get thirty-two miles per gallon on the highway, and it would accelerate from zero to sixty miles per hour in under eight seconds. These performance goals he keyed to a prospective curb-weight of 2,200 pounds. "In theory," he told the magazine, "you could drive it for twenty or twenty-five years, and nothing should happen to it. It's not designed for early obsolescence." De Lorean put the price at $15,000. In other magazines, he said the price would come within $1,500 of a Corvette.

But, like the Vega, his baby would be overweight when it came off the production line. Not just by 200 pounds. The De Lorean weighed over 900 pounds more than the early projections, according to the motor magazines that tested it. The surge from zero to sixty miles per hour, *Road & Track* discovered, did not take eight seconds, but a lumbering 10.5 seconds—faster than a Cadillac, but nothing like a real sports car. As far as durability was concerned, De Lorean's statements about a ten-year, 100,000-mile warranty came crashing to the ground. The company offered the standard one-year, 12,000-mile protection. His Goodyear tires were recommended for 8,000 to 10,000 miles—not the 100,000 he had projected. Finally, the price came out close to $26,000—$7,000 over the comparable Corvette.

If the car neared any of De Lorean's promises, it was in the area of safety. Tests done for the National Highway Traffic Safety Administration found the car to be safer than most, but the tests were conducted with airbags—another feature De Lorean touted that never showed up in the final product. Gone, too, were bumpers capable of withstanding ten-miles-an-hour of impact. When Giugiaro's redesign lowered the car, the field of vision became greatly reduced. Beams on either side of the windshield grew wider and the view through the louvre-covered rear window became next to nonexistent. As the test driver for *Road & Track* wrote, "Looking straight back through the louvres is somewhat like being farsighted. You can see things off in the distance fairly well but up-close vision is limited, so parking can be a challenge."

De Lorean's unsupported hype for his car was a foolish mistake—especially with the example of the Vega in recent memory. And yet, maybe De Lorean sincerely felt he could meet his own extravagant claims—or at least inspire someone else to meet them. One of his senior executives says, "I spent more time with John chasing colored balloons than doing anything else. He believed anything you imagined was possible, and he gloried in the idea that somehow he could make it work. But he let other people come up with the somehow."

The real "doer" was better off at GM, clawing to the top of the totem pole. As De Lorean discovered, the price for being on his own was constant compromise. With a limited-production vehicle, he was at the mercy of component makers. His original desire for a mid-engine car had to give way to a rear-engine design when Renault became the only supplier willing to accommodate him. On his own, he was incapable of producing airbags and no company was then making enough of the safety devices for a production car. Cost exigencies also determined the choice of tires and several other important parts of the car. As president of GM, De Lorean could have produced his own airbags or ordered a new mid-engine model for the Corvette. The political compromises of the big-time corporate boardroom paled in comparison with the practical compromises a small businessman makes every day.

And yet, the tragedy of De Lorean's car is not the compromise that was forced on him, but the compromise that he didn't have to make. While De Lorean may have portrayed himself as a maverick and rebel, as a business leader he was much more the conformist taking the path of least resistance. No move demonstrated that more than his arrangement with Lotus.

"The De Lorean car never had a father," its original designer, Bill Collins, says. "It was a bastardized Lotus."

Although De Lorean officials vehemently denied the charge, it was apparent to the most novice auto buff. Except for the doors and the stainless steel, the car had the look of the Lotus Esprit. The Pennebaker documentary caught Colin Chapman admitting as much to a reporter at the Geneva Auto Show. "As you see," he says, "the chassis has a very Lotus-like design, but this is what we understand and what we believe works well. It's very nice to see John De Lorean productionizing it and producing it in such large volumes."

Statements like that were part of Collins's whole argument for not turning the project over to Chapman. "He wasn't going to make the car we wanted," Collins says. "He was going to use the process, the design, and the materials that he was the most familiar with. He also wasn't going to make a product that was any better than the one he was selling."

While Collins's statements could be dismissed by some as sour grapes, they are supported by his successor as De Lorean's chief engineer, Michael Loasby. Having worked in a similar capacity for sports-car maker Aston-Martin, Loasby was part of the British school of engineers. Yet, he is in complete agreement with Collins.

"Chapman tore Bill Collins's baby apart. They came up with a totally different car, and I don't believe the change was at all justified."

Colin Spooner, who headed the Lotus team, admits that the group had problems with De Lorean's most basic original concepts—the gull-wing doors, the rear engine and the stainless steel. "But John wanted us to adhere to those requirements," he says. "Evidently he felt they were important from a marketing standpoint. But we didn't see how they worked from a functional standpoint. The doors were complex and heavy, and the stainless steel was redundant. The Lotus VARI plastic can be painted. That's what we do with our cars. We didn't need a second skin. It only added further weight to the car."

Adding even more weight was the steel backbone required to hold the Lotus plastic underbody together. In keeping with his promise not to use any metal parts that would corrode (although the car did use standard fasteners, which tend to rust before anything else), De Lorean demanded that the backbone be dipped in a protective epoxy, which had the same effect as dolloping a comb with molasses. The molten material collected in every recess. "We couldn't get the coating thin enough," Spooner says, "so it added more weight in just the areas where you didn't want it."

De Lorean executives still argue that the ERM plastic process was not given enough of a chance. "From the moment John signed with Lotus he gave up on ERM," one says. "You can see that just looking at the budgets for Composite Technology, the subsidiary that was doing the research on ERM."

The major hitch in using ERM was creating a press so large that it could mold a big enough section of the car. "If you broke the underbody into too many pieces," Spooner says, "it would offer no protection in a crash. We felt you needed as few pieces as possible and that they had to be continuous."

Of course, there could be an acceptable, although charitable view, of De Lorean's relationship with Lotus. Perhaps the time element in meeting deadlines—set by his own prospectus and the British agreement—left him no choice but to opt for Chap-

THE ETHICAL CAR

man's proven engineering squad and plastic process. Even so, there was no excuse for not getting involved in some of the critical design decisions Chapman made.

No part of the De Lorean was so susceptible to damage as the front-end suspension. In essence, Lotus had put the torso of a weight lifter on arthritic and spindly legs. Chapman refused to permit adjustable caster and camber. Spooner explains, "His genius was in simplicity and economy of design. The idea of an adjustable suspension was alien to our principles. You build in adjustments and someone is likely to put it out of adjustment."

Such principles were fine for hand-tooled cars but, as Loasby argues, "In production cars you never can duplicate the dimensions that finely. You normally design adjustment in so you can cope with that imperfection."

The suspension eventually prompted three recalls when the De Lorean hit the road. Company engineers admitted that the fix was merely a Band-Aid. The real wound needed to be repaired on the drawing board.

"John did not want to argue with Chapman on issues like suspension," Loasby says. "He just didn't have time for the details of the project. But attention to detail is everything. I had understood that De Lorean made his reputation at General Motors as a man who paid attention to detail. But I suspect he had been away from the shop too long."

When De Lorean did get into the picture, it was with suggestions that seemed more like distractions than help. "He came in one day," Loasby says, "to say we should hook into the cooling system and make a little icebox for a six-pack of beer behind the driver's seat. Or, another time, he told us to work on a sixty-watt radio speaker that could be detached and hung outside the car for picnics."

Meanwhile, only months from production, electrical components had not yet been chosen, and details as significant as the car windows were yet to be designed. American engineers would later be shocked to see that De Lorean had permitted Lucas electrical supplies in his car—long the laughingstock of the auto industry, but still the preference of chauvinistic British engineers.

The most serious blunder would be using a weak British alternator that burned the battery out when more than a few accessories were going at once. Brochures had already been printed showing a window that slid manually to the side. But it was eventually redesigned to resemble a little mail slot—which added to the claustrophobic atmosphere of the car—and it was operated electrically.

"We'd get these visitors from De Lorean like Brown," one Lotus engineer says, "and he'd be full of suggestions. Everybody came with a suggestion, but nobody took any authority to sort those suggestions out—it was a case of too many cooks spoiling the broth. The first thing you usually design for a car is the wiring. But with [the] De Lorean, we put it in last and had to go around everything that was already in place."

Eventually, to force the car out of Lotus, Cafiero brought in four retired production engineers from Ford, a move that rubbed Chapman the wrong way. "At some point John lost confidence in Chapman," one Lotus engineer says. "You see these things happen so many times. Ambitious people who are easy to fall in love and easy to fall out—just to win."

But as the car rushed pell-mell to production, important elements of the process went uncompleted. No complete parts list or shop manual ever existed. The factory was in the position of an orchestra playing a symphony from a recording and not from a score. "It may sound incredible," Loasby says, "but we didn't have a specification for all the parts and tools for the car. Some parts didn't even have drawings. The first cars off the production line were not built to a specification."

Loasby had expected to oversee that work, but he found De Lorean unwilling to create an engineering staff. "I joined on the premise of ultimately taking over from Lotus, but now I realize John had no inclination to create an engineering department. Instead, he chose to abdicate total responsibility for engineering. I'm not entirely clear why. I would have thought that as an engineer, he'd be sensitive to the fact that the car still needed continued design work after it got out of Lotus. An engineering group should have been established in Belfast long before."

• THE ETHICAL CAR •

Loasby has his suspicions about why De Lorean could not justify any expense for more engineers. "His problem was that he had already paid $18 million to this mysterious Swiss company for his engineering work. If this company was doing its work, an in-house engineering staff would be redundant. I'm afraid that when you look at the whole thing, the letters GPD loom very large."

·17·
Out of Control

Everyone else had gone home for the night. Only Marian Gibson remained. Alone in a suite of De Lorean Motor Company offices, a shopping bag in one hand, she methodically flipped through the memos and documents piled on desks and spread out on file cabinets. After a quick look, she dropped them in the bag. At last, she turned out the lights and left.

It had not been an easy summer for Marian Gibson. For two years she had devoted her life to the De Lorean Motor Company and its chairman of the board, and suddenly, in June, she was being told by some young executive that she was no longer "a perfect fit," and might have to be phased out of the company.

An apple-cheeked woman with short blonde hair, she was born some forty years before in London. She had gotten her interview for the job as De Lorean's administrative assistant in September 1979, shortly after he had moved into his Park Avenue headquarters. Struck by her British accent and crisp manner, De Lorean had her come to work the next day. He had been especially fond of the capable secretary he had had in his 100 West Long Lake office, but he was unable to persuade her to move. As a result, he would let Gibson take charge of his daily regimen. She scheduled his appointments, typed up his confidential memos, and helped balance his personal checking account. In the process she got a glimpse of the varied and disparate parts of his life. There would be urgent calls to Roy Nesseth, which meant picking through a score of different phone numbers ringing anywhere from a steak house in Huntington Harbour to Logan or Boise before she could find him. She reminded De Lorean when Cristina wanted him home for particular parties and commiserated when he complained about his wife's hectic social calendar. At other times, she chatted with interior decorator Maur Dubin and his retinue of young male assistants as they sat waiting for De Lorean to get off the phone.

In October 1980 she got a raise, and promotion to the title of deputy administrator. She would be office manager, supervising the secretaries and ordering supplies. But in the course of the year, she'd find herself caught in office intrigue. Both she and Kimmerly shared the same maid and, according to Tom, Marian told the maid she didn't have to empty his cat's litter box. From this point of contention, Marian says, a feud would escalate and be taken to extremes by Kimmerly's obstreperous personal assistant. In June, Gibson was demoted from her job as office manager. Officially, she became secretary to Bill Haddad, but it was clear that she wasn't wanted. In the ultimate act of secretarial degradation, she says, they had her fill in during lunchtime for the young woman at the switchboard—the lowest spot in the office pecking order.

"They wanted to humiliate me," she says. "I'd worked too hard too long to deserve that treatment."

She found a sympathetic ear in Haddad. He too was on the outs with the inner circle. But his fight didn't start over Kitty Litter. In July, Kimmerly and his legal minions had registered a stock offering with the SEC. If successful, it would bring in over $22 million. But the issue did more than raise money. It also significantly restructured the entire organization, creating a new entity, the De Lorean Motors Holding Company, which would exchange stock on a one-for-one basis for De Lorean Motor Company shares. The initial offering price was to be $12 a share. By virture of his control of 84 percent of DMC, De Lorean stood to collect 9.95 million shares in the deal—on paper worth $120 million.

His executives did not come out so well in the plan. Although they had options for 1.79 million De Lorean Motor Company shares, they would not be allowed to exchange those options for Holding Company stock and a chance at a $22 million killing. In Wall Street parlance they weren't taken "upstairs." Kimmerly and De Lorean weakly explained there were tax implications that had to be considered first, but most of the executives—especially those in the New York office—didn't accept the explanation.

Haddad says that long before the options became an issue, he had been disillusioned with De Lorean's behavior with potential bus-company investors. He was also repelled by De Lorean's attempts to bully the British government. At times, he discussed the company's heavy-handed tactics with Marian Gibson. He mentioned the battles with NIDA during the fall of 1980 when De Lorean was first trying to get more grants out of the company and then opting for more equity. With the new stock offer, NIDA would get only 3.6 percent of the holding company, and stock worth just $8.4 million—not much of a deal, considering that the government had already poured into the company close to $147 million of grants, loans, and bank guarantees.

Haddad's talk, Gibson says, sent the Union Jack up the flagpole. De Lorean wasn't just doing her in—he was going after her homeland too. Marian had lived in America since 1960, but she still felt an allegiance to the U.K. and visited there often. "The whole thing had me in quite an emotional state," she says. "Sometimes, out of nowhere, I'd start crying. But I felt that if any good was to come out of my job at De Lorean, it would be to stop that stock issue."

She had already planned a trip back to Britain in mid-September, but the voyage was now going to be more than a vacation, and she assembled her brief for the prosecution. "I don't even know what all I picked up," she says of the papers she gathered in her late-night forays. A few, she adds, came from "disgruntled employees," whom she won't name.

Fate would choose an unlikely repository for Marian Gibson's revelations. Through the advice of a friend, she chose to contact Nicholas Raymond Winterton of Macclesfield. Until he met Gibson at the Chelsea home of their mutual friend, Winterton had spent an otherwise sedate and obscure tenure on the Conservative back-bench. All that would change now. Marian let loose a welling tide of accusation against her former employer, touching on everything from De Lorean's original investment and NIDA equity to fancy bathrooms in Belfast. Winterton understood little of what he heard, but as he told the London *Times* later, he believed his informant "was genuinely concerned about the interests of the country and the long-term prospects of the people who worked for De Lorean."

The MP asked for some documentation to support her charges, and six days later Gibson appeared at his office door with two file folders stuffed with letters, documents, and memos. "Nicholas is really a very nice guy," Marian says, "and I told him I was sorry for putting a bombshell on his doorstep, but he replied, 'Look, if you lift the rock and maggots are under it, you've got to sweep them out.'"

Although Winterton found the files a little too long and too obscure for his own perusal, he still put in an urgent message to 10 Downing Street for a personal appointment with Margaret Thatcher. But the prime minister—not known to be a fan of De Lorean's or of his project—had just left for Australia and a meeting of Commonwealth officials.

Meanwhile Marian Gibson returned to New York, expecting the transatlantic news wires to start chattering with stories of the De Lorean inquest as soon as she reached the airport. But no word came, and one of Marian's first assignments on returning to work was to retype the prospectus for the stock offering. "They were telling me it was coming out any day."

Gibson put in a frantic call to England, and her friend, after talking to Winterton, told her nothing could be done until the PM came back from Australia. "I could see nobody was going to move," she says, "and I had to do something on my own. I had to call in the press." Before the evening was over she'd phone

London free-lance journalist John Lisners. "I told him I had a great story that could make him a lot of money."

For three days the reporter stayed in Marian's apartment rummaging through documents. He saw enough to burn up the cables back to Fleet Street trying to sell his story. His best deal came from the country's best-selling paper, the *News of the World*, a sensationalist tabloid that has never prided itself on accuracy. But Marian was not upset with Lisners's choice. She wanted the widest coverage she could get. She only asked that her lawyer look at the story first.

She says Lisners did not pay her that courtesy. Early on Saturday, October 3, after wiring the story to London for the next day's paper, Lisners called De Lorean to ask his reaction to Marian's charges. "Later in the morning," Marian says, "Maur Dubin delivered a letter to my apartment building. It went something like, 'Dear Marian, what are you doing?' He wrote that John wanted to see me, and then he ended it saying that Jonathan sent his regards. Jonathan was one of his young friends, and we used to enjoy chatting when he was up at the office."

Before the day was over, one of the De Lorean Motor Company lawyers was in the lobby of the apartment house. "He told me again that John wanted to see me. I asked him to go away."

The story would not run in the *News of the World*. According to British press reports, it was killed at the last minute by publisher Rupert Murdoch. Also the proprietor of the *New York Post*, Murdoch was a Manhattan neighbor of De Lorean's. Reportedly he found Lisners's submission, with liberal references to Dubin and his gay crowd, too scabrous for even his scandal sheet. Reportedly, he also gave De Lorean warning of what was in the works.

After his interview with De Lorean, Lisners met up with Marian again and played her a part of the tape. "Just hearing the voice made me very fearful. There's something very penetrating and deep about his voice that's beyond description. As I heard that tape in the cab, I decided I had to get away. I left on the next flight to England."

Marion had warned Winterton that a news story was coming, and he in turn tried to warn the prime minister. This time he told her personal secretary why he had tried to reach her, and a message was sent to Australia. The prime minister asked that the attorney general take a look into the matter.

Fleet Street was still looking skeptically at Lisners's story, but when the papers called Winterton, he confirmed that an investigation had begun. Later, he'd tell *The Times*, "I regret it has become public."

The day after her arrival in London, Marian was suddenly a tabloid celebrity. Without warning her first, Lisners had placed her story in a more respectable tabloid, the *Daily Mirror*. This paper chose to run solely with Winterton's reports of an inquest, and excerpts from a Bill Haddad memo dated December 1980. The memo read:

> I continue to be concerned about our efforts to set up a scenario under which the British relinquish their share of equity in the program. . . . I am also worried about what a Parliamentary inquiry will uncover about our expenditures on both sides of the ocean. There are the 'official' complaints which can be sensationalized even though the accountants, SEC, et al., will give a clean bill of health. The [former chief financial officer Walt] Strycker picture is a highly personal one of John Z. De Lorean milking the company for his private profit. Some of the discredited Strycker charges can be succulent journalistic morsels for the Fleet Street crowd, never overly concerned about separating accusation from fact. As you know, I am also troubled by some of the actions regarding the house [by the assembly plant in Dunmurry] and some of the expenditures appear to have been 'fuzzed' (like a £10,000 expenditure [actually £2,000] at Harrod's [for] gold faucets). I recently learned, for example, that we have hidden some of the capital expenses of the house in expenses for the project. In short, the books were altered. Silly, because the house can be justified. . . . Why wasn't JZD there [in Belfast] to oversee everything? Was he, as Strycker charges, pursuing other interests?

Claiming that they were doing no more than pursuing "routine" inquiries, Scotland Yard inspectors, under the solicitor general's orders, flew to New York to interview Haddad. The car company's first reponse had been that the memo was a forgery, and that

Marian had been no more than a typist. A press release further averred, "The company's affairs are a matter of public record and have always been open to the fullest examination and scrutiny to the satisfaction of the government." But Haddad confirmed his authorship and that he was engaged in a contract dispute with De Lorean. The next day Haddad was on a plane with De Lorean en route to Jacksonville, Florida. On the way, he says, De Lorean offered to settle the contract differences if Bill denied that he ever wrote the memo. "He wanted me to hole up in a motel in Atlanta and hide from Scotland Yard." But Haddad went ahead and saw the Yard in his lawyer's office on Friday.

Back in England, Marian decided to hide out on her own. She first stayed in a hotel under an assumed name, but finally took off for the Midlands and the cottage of an elderly aunt. To her surprise, she was starting to feel like something of a criminal herself. "At one point I was in a taxi," she says, "and without letting on who I was, I asked the cabbie what he thought about the De Lorean affair. He said, 'I think that secretary is wrong. She shouldn't have gone removing documents that way. It's a messy business.' I think a lot of people felt that way, although they didn't seem happy with De Lorean either. Like the cabbie said later, 'If they gave us ten quid apiece instead of giving it all to him, we'd be better off.'"

The *Sunday Telegraph* titled its account of the affair the DE LOREAN FURORE, and De Lorean decided to take on the "furore" in person. Looking natty in a double-breasted blazer, gray slacks, a turtleneck, and sunglasses, he arrived at London's Heathrow airport on a Friday night. He told reporters, "I still can't understand how a troubled, nervous old typist and an MP who was never known for his intellectual clarity can cause so much trouble."

De Lorean continued to attack Gibson and Winterton in interviews he granted from his suite at the Savoy Hotel. He also started to imply that some larger conspiracy was afoot. "There is quite clearly much more to this than we have heard so far."

But the rest of the press had started to ask questions beyond those raised in Haddad's memo. Some of those articles did no more than dredge up facts that were public when De Lorean had first made his deal. Winterton would express surprise to the BBC that De Lorean had put so little money into the venture, and *The Times*'s Insight team would take its first look at published SEC documents and realize that if De Lorean's company did succeed, De Lorean was permitted to buy back British stock before the government had a chance to make a big profit on its original investment.

Neither of these topics should have come as revelations. Far more explosive stuff was in a *Sunday Telegraph* story by reporter Stella Shamoon. One month before, she had looked at Lotus' involvement with De Lorean and mentioned the dreaded acronym GPD. In the first sentence of her article, two days after De Lorean's arrival in London, she asked, "Why should a Panama-registered partnership based at 'PO Box 33, 1211 Geneva, Switzerland' have received on behalf of Colin Chapman's Group Lotus some $18 million from the state-aided De Lorean sports-car concern in Belfast?"

Armed with a written statement, De Lorean flew to Belfast on Monday ready to respond to the allegations. "We didn't want John to shoot from the hip on this," one of his British Belfast executives says. "We told him to first meet with the city editors of papers and give them a chance to see that he wasn't a charlatan. But he really believed he knew best how to handle the press. He wanted to do it the American way and come on like a big whale. He called a press conference at four o'clock and then moved it up to two. He asked whether it would be feasible for him to hold it outside, so he could burst through the crowd of reporters in a car and get out to read his statement.

"He ended up doing it in normal fashion, but he was very tense and aggressive. He hadn't allowed us to read it first; and evidently it had been prepared by his lawyer. It was reported quite fully on television and the papers. But at that hour there weren't too many heavyweight journalists in attendance."

De Lorean offered a point-by-point refutation of what he called "charges that have virtually destroyed our company." In the case of his comments on GPD, his prepared text cited the company as a licensing agent for the VARI plastic, contradicting both his own previous comments and remarks that Lotus had made to the press.

But before De Lorean responded to the charges against him, he made his own accusations:

> I must say that I find it very hard to believe that a troubled, unstable typist, an unemployed writer, and a solitary MP could have damaged our company so severely. I must make note of the fact that no one bothered with us until the past few months when it began to look like De Lorean Motor Cars might succeed. . . .
>
> I have a strong feeling that the loud public alleging of these spurious and fictitious charges, each of which could have been easily answered to Mr. Winterton and his associates by our auditors or the government accountants without damage to the company and without destroying jobs in Northern Ireland is part of a wider conspiracy. I'm a car maker. Wiser heads than mine will have to seek out the motives of those who would destroy us and with us, Ulster's proudest achievement.
>
> I think all right-thinking people will share my view that the circulation of these lies in circumstances where they destroy a fledgling business and deprive 3,000 people of their employment is totally reprehensible.
>
> There is a conspiracy to bring down the De Lorean Motor Company. The allegations that have been made could have been made for political or economic reasons.
>
> A foreign country may have been involved in the plot to destroy Ulster's proudest achievement. I dare not name the country I have in mind. [Elsewhere he blamed the Republic of Ireland.]
>
> It is unlikely that a group of minor people of limited ability could have created the problem alone. Why did it all happen when we started looking like we were going to make the grade?
>
> I don't know whether a competitor in the car industry could have been responsible. That's certainly a distinct possibility.
>
> The company will be filing libel writs against the most serious perpetrators of this terrible crime against the company.
>
> Early on October 3rd, rumors reached me that an unemployed writer, Mr. John Lisners, and Marian Gibson, a former typist at De Lorean's New York office, were negotiating to sell a story to the *News of the World* [whose] reporters contacted our public relations department, but eventually . . . decided against publishing

the story for fear of libel since they were not able to confirm its allegations.

De Lorean's executives listened to the rambling diatribe in stunned silence. To their surprise, the press was not much more vocal. One of the British staff says, "The reporters were permitted questions at the end, but almost nothing was said. I don't know whether they all sat there in awe or ignorance."

De Lorean followed through on his threat and slapped Gibson, Lisners, Winterton, the *Mirror*, and the two British television networks with libel writs. His lawyer was the formidable Lord Goodman—the man, one *Times* wag wrote, "who put junk in the word injunction." But libel laws are far more severe in England than they are in America, and the move had more than a chilling effect. For the next few critical months it froze solid all further close examination of De Lorean in the press. The one exception would be the gadfly investigative magazine *Private Eye*, which continued to report on stories breaking in the States about the "high-living motor man."

For its part, the British government did all it could to put a lid on the commotion. The day of the press conference, the attorney general and the director of prosecutions announced, "No evidence has emerged to support any of the allegations of criminal conduct on the part of Mr. De Lorean or the company. . . . [We] are agreed that there aren't any grounds for continuing the police investigation."

From her country cottage hideaway, Marian Gibson saw a cover-up. "When the police came to interview me, I could tell they weren't interested at all in what I had to say."

One government official agrees that Her Majesty's legal legions were not eager to turn too much up. "I think the greatest argument De Lorean had for quelling all this talk of allegations and investigations was that float. The feeling of everyone involved—pro and con—was let him go to Wall Street and suck the fool Americans into his bloody project, and Godspeed. If he were capable of raising scads of dollars and got rich to boot, that was fine. Just as long as he got off our dole."

• GRAND DELUSIONS •

Among the few political officials jumping publicly to De Lorean's defense was Roy Mason. In a *Times* op-ed column, he proclaimed that the car company had already met the five-year goal of employment and that the "breakthrough" product was in heavy demand in the States. The title for his column—"De Lorean is a winner, damn it!"

And for a few brief moments in the early fall of 1981, it looked like De Lorean was a winner and that his stock issue would be a hit on Wall Street. At last cars had gotten to the dealerships, and from Anchorage, Alaska, to Portland, Maine, local newspapers were treating the arrival of the eye-catching wedge like the visit of an extraterrestrial. A few greedy dealers took the lid off the suggested retail price of $27,000 and were getting as much as $35,000. One of the Texas limited partner-dealers was offering a $5,000 premium for every De Lorean his fellow dealers would rustle up. In October, monthly sales shot to a new high of 710, more than the previous two months combined.

But the warm glow coming off the De Lorean Motor Company was only the first sign of the flames convulsing it from within. Even if the company continued to sell 710 cars a month, production in Belfast was going at twice that rate. "In July," one of Belfast's British executives says, "John came to Belfast to tell us that production had to be up to eighty cars a day [a rate of 20,000 a year] by the fall season. It was a decision he made against the recommendations of the entire team here and a decision he made in the teeth of adverse political conditions. But John had the power to make those decisions."

As for Brown, the Belfast man remembers him backing De Lorean's stand. "He told us he could sell every car we could make."

The move to press production to those limits was probably the single most disastrous decision De Lorean made. Absolutely no marketing data he received supported the increase. It was exactly the sort of wishful thinking he excoriated GM superiors for in *On A Clear Day*. There he said, "Where modern industry prepares an overall marketing strategy which scientifically ascertains customer needs, designs products to bring the need, the product, and the consumer together, GM relied on little more than rah-rah sales pitches and hard-sell techniques."

De Lorean purchased the best expertise in the automotive industry from market-research consultants J.D. Powers & Associates, and then chose to ignore their advice. Back in 1980, Powers' volume projections showed the company, at best, selling over 20,000 cars a year if each was priced below $18,000. Over $21,000, cars would sell at a mean of 16,000 a year. But those figures dropped dramatically after the price went above $24,000. Then the company could hope for only 10,000 a year. At $28,000—under 4,000.

The introductory price for the De Lorean cars, with taxes and shipping, was dangerously close to $28,000. Both Brown and De Lorean hoped to make up some of the slack with foreign exports, but that was years away. De Lorean wanted the best of both worlds—high price and high production. In September he wrote to Brown, "In our planning and analysis, it is important to realize that we are tooled to produce efficiently in the 25,000-unit to 30,000-unit range. At 11,500 units we become a relatively expensive manufacturer . . . join[ing] the Lotus and Renault Alpine camp—again we can't win. This financial analysis also demonstrates the urgency of bringing our sedan on stream. We probably cannot sustain this volume beyond two years. If we don't have a sedan by then, we will have to reduce our overhead by 50 percent in both the U.K. and the U.S."

In fact, De Lorean had no evidence he could "sustain this volume" for one year, let alone two. Ken Gorf remembers the process the chairman used to delude himself. "He had Powers do a study a second time and found that we might be able to sell 16,000 cars if the price was close to $20,000. So John took that figure and said, 'You have to factor in the glamour quotient associated with my name. That should bring it up to 20,000 at least.' So then he raised the price of the car to $26,000 and told everyone he had hard figures from J.D. Powers to say he could sell at least 25,000 cars."

Nothing made that projection more foolish than the trend lines Brown had charted. The bar for the hoped-for volume of the De

Lorean stuck out next to the actual sales figures of similarly priced sports cars like a skyscraper in a field of anthills.

To some extent, executives explain, De Lorean was committed to the higher production. Long-term contracts with suppliers like engine maker Renault called for certain numbers of orders, and those suppliers were not interested in figures of less than 20,000. He was also committed to employment goals to convert the Department of Commerce loans into grants. However, he was already overshooting those goals. "I'm afraid any business that stays slow and steady wins the race," the Belfast executive laments. "Our figures showed that this was a viable company with half the production. If the extravagance had been cut out of New York, we could have broken even making just 6,000 cars a year. But that wasn't fast enough for John. First he had to build his paper empire in the stock market. A creditable success was not enough for him. He wanted to be an overnight sensation."

Going beyond all reasonable optimism, in early fall De Lorean started talking about outstripping the 20,000 unit ceiling. At an Irvine business-forum luncheon on October 28, while Brown sat in attendance barely believing his ears, De Lorean jubilantly rattled off his production goals. "We have 3,000 highly motivated employees [in Belfast] who are producing eighty cars per day. The consumer and dealer reception has been spectacular. In fact, on the basis of public reaction, we have raised our production targets up to 30,000 for 1982. In thirty years in the business, it's the first time people have told me our price is too low—and we're sold out through the end of 1982."

Back in Belfast two of those motivated workers could already tell that the bubble had burst. "In October new workers were just pouring through the doors," Malachy Higgins says. For him, the new recruits on the trim line meant extra money. Rather than create a training force, the company paid experienced workers like Higgins to help another worker adjust to the job. "A day after you were hired you were on the assembly line."

More crews also trooped into the powdery mist of the Body-Press Building where shop steward Billy Parker molded the VARI plastic underbodies. "It was amazing. The work was just piling up. We had enough molds for 100 cars. We had nowhere to put it all. They didn't tell us, but we could see all around us that their cars weren't selling in the States. It was a cruel thing to see all these people coming in to work and knowing that they'd all be laid off in a month or two."

The wisdom of market reports would come crashing home to Brown in November. Car sales dropped to just 654 for the month, and winter was setting in—traditionally the slowest time for sports cars. He remembers, "The month of December started with a sudden influx of notices from dealers to hold shipments until further notice."

Meanwhile, in the middle of the month, De Lorean made a rare trip to Belfast to meet with the secretary of state for Northern Ireland. James Prior was the "wet," or liberal, in Margaret Thatcher's cabinet. Booted out as employment minister for not cracking down on the unions, he publicly proclaimed that the last job he wanted was secretary of state for Northern Ireland. That said, he took the post—at least going in equally despised by both Catholics and Protestants. After the initial faux pas, he showed himself to be more activist than his two Tory predecessors in the office. A maverick in his own party, Prior might have been the one Conservative best able to get on with De Lorean.

They were to first meet at the Dunmurry plant early in the day, and De Lorean would lead the royal tour. Stout and ruddy, with an unruly mane of white hair, Prior trudged through the snow to arrive on time. Hours went by before De Lorean showed up. His tardiness did not necessarily set the stage for the asking of favors, but De Lorean went ahead and tried. First he asked for £4 million, which was rejected, and then for an extension of repayment for £10 million of loans that were coming due at the end of the month. That request was granted. "When he asked for the loan renewal," a Belfast executive says, "John went overboard telling Prior how good things were going to be next year. He told him sales were over projections and that new shifts would start soon. He just needed time to renegotiate his bridge loan with Bank of America and put the stock on Wall Street. Prior looked pleasantly surprised by the news. I have to say that some of us couldn't believe the news. We instituted a new bonus plan for the workers if they met production goals. But only days after John left, a very gloomy Dick Brown showed up. It hadn't been more than a few months before when he was telling us he could sell every car we made. But now he said he couldn't even handle the cars we were producing. The bottom fell out of the market."

Brown went into urgent meetings with managing director Don Lander. Brown would be "shocked" to hear they'd added another shift. "I thought we had only one choice," Brown says, "and that was to cut back on production immediately, and I convinced Lander as well. We then placed a call to John in New York over the speaker phone. When we told him the plan, he was his typical vulgar self. He said, 'That's bullshit. You cut production now and all you do is blow the [stock] offering.' "

But the offering was already in serious trouble. The sole underwriter, Bache Halsey Stuart, Inc. (then, the brokerage firm of last resort), was getting leery as each week passed. The stock issue was cut in half, to $12 million, and the warning was added that "investment in the units involves a high degree of risk and should be considered only by those who can afford a total loss of their investment." While the prospectus estimated that capital projects would cost $41 million beyond the money raised on Wall Street, it admitted that the company "currently hasn't any funds available, or commitments from outside sources, for any portion of such $41 million."

A bitter winter, a lousy car market, a soft stock market: all seemed to strike together with the force of one sudden knockout blow. Executives were already bailing out. Cafiero resigned, claiming he had been cheated out of his stock options by the new offering. Anxious to hush up any acrimony, De Lorean settled for $1 million before his former president could file suit. The third chief financial officer would also quietly take his leave. (The parting with Bill Haddad was the most acrimonious. Eventually he charged that De Lorean opened his mail in the office and tried to break into his apartment. De Lorean replied that Haddad had engineered a press campaign to destroy his company. There would be no settlement of this rift. Haddad sued for $18 million in damages, claiming breach of contract, slander, and fraud. De Lorean threatened to countersue for $30 million.)

Despite the bad press, De Lorean still tried to muster another nationwide dog-and-pony show to sell his amputated stock offering. He and the executives met with brokers and potential investors in some seven cities, complete with another slide show and closing remarks from the chairman. De Lorean, Brown says, was as enthusiastic as ever, but also as hyperbolic. Although Brown felt they were well received, when they returned from the whirlwind tour, their broker announced that the issue was being pulled from the market. In the newsletter *New Issues*, the publisher called De Lorean "a classic case of go public or go broke."

The executives agreed. Ken Gorf says, "Everything was riding on the stock offering. When it didn't go through, we all knew it was over."

Failure loomed everywhere. Only 259 cars would sell in January. While some De Lorean spokesmen claimed that over 5,000 cars had been sold—in fact, over 5,000 had been shipped to dealers. Only 3,300 were actually sold. Over 1,800 cars languished in showrooms or the lots out back. No matter how the company fudged the figures, the stark reality of the poor sales was there to see in the auto sections of most major newspapers. Already panic-stricken dealers were offering the car at fire-sale prices.

Meanwhile the bills had begun to pile up—from niggling to gargantuan. Dealers forced to service the cars on practically a monthly basis were sending in warranty claims. "We never did get a computer service in place to process warranties," one California executive says. "So at first we made neat little stacks on a counter about fifteen feet long. It was like a little garden. You'd walk by each day and watch it grow, until it got to the point where there were no more neat piles, just one huge mound of paper."

For a few weeks Brown optimistically anticipated orders from the better-selling dealers. As soon as cars were shipped, he could tap their credit lines. But now dealers were reluctantly accepting cars and asking for no more.

Over $18 million was due the Bank of America and over $22 million was owed the British subsidiary for some 1,500 cars. Renault had $25 million coming for its engines. Some Bank of America financing was still available for parts, and overnight a team prepared an order for virtually every part in the Belfast plant. De Lorean would send Roy over to expedite what was to be the last boatload of stainless-steel cars bound for California. Brown says, "I heard him tell Roy to get every car out of that plant and on a boat."

For his own part, Brown had the ignominious task of calling back the company cars given out to VIPs and investors like Sammy Davis, Jr., who had one of the $150,000 De Lorean Research Limited Partnership units. "Davis didn't want to give the car back," one of the Irvine executives remembers. "We had a hell of a time tracking both him and the car down. I guess he was under the impression the car was his as part of the bargain for the investment. C.R. had to get on the phone with his secretary and threaten to send out a tow truck before we could get them to cooperate."

Yet, even as car sales in the States slowed to a standstill, De Lorean was careful not to fire the 2,600 workers in Belfast. They were the last bit of leverage he had. The plant went on a three-day workweek instead, and a few hundred of the least senior employees received notices that they might be laid off.

As before—as always, the last hope lay with the British government. With the Bank of America unlikely to extend the bridge financing, De Lorean turned instead to the British government's Export Credit Guarantee Department, and asked for a $65 million line of credit. Once again, there was the problem of a government agency directly funding an American company, but over the fall, Kimmerly had restructured the company to overcome that obstacle. The Irvine operations had been cloistered in a separate subsidiary called De Lorean Motor Cars of America, with Brown as president. If the British gave the go-ahead, it could be reallocated again as a marketing division of the Belfast factory.

But the British were not about to give the go-ahead. De Lorean later said the government reneged on its agreement. However, government officials say the export agency was never very enthusiastic about the idea. The plan could only have been hammered through by a cabinet minister, and Secretary of State James Prior was not in the mood to argue with bureaucrats for the sake of John De Lorean. "Why should he have stuck his neck out for this caricature of an American?" one of De Lorean's Belfast executives says. "Just remember, only four weeks earlier—before the Christmas break—De Lorean had promised that the production would go up; that the stock issue would go forward; that cars would start selling again. Well, then Prior comes back from holiday and he sees the plant's workweek reduced, the stock dead, and car sales worse than ever. He had been utterly betrayed. He could only come to one conclusion—De Lorean was an absolute liar."

De Lorean made it clear to the press that the Belfast jobs hinged on the export credit, but this time the government would not give in. In a brief meeting on January 28, Prior told De Lorean that there'd be no $65 million. But that wasn't his only bad news. He had also called in the London branch of the accounting firm Coopers & Lybrand to conduct a major review of the government's relationship with the car company. The inquest would be under the supervision of the estimable onetime lord mayor of London, Sir Kenneth Cork.

The mere mention of Cork's name could strike terror in the hearts of British businessmen everywhere in the empire. As a government-appointed receiver he had disposed of an imposing roster of industrial bankrupts, but Cork greatly resented his sobriquet, "the undertaker"; as he told any reporter who would listen, his reorganizations had often helped save companies, not only embalm them. But at sixty-nine, age had played a cruel trick on the lord, hunching his bald head forward. His stooped shoulders combined with his thick glasses and weak chin made him very much the human caricature of a buzzard.

At 5:00 A.M. the morning after the British government refused the export aid, Don Lander called in the shop stewards for an urgent meeting. "He told us that he had some bad news," Billy Parker remembers. "He said there was a slump in car sales—that America suffered its worst winter in thirty years. Then he said that within the week they'd let over 1,100 men go. We thought they were bluffing to force the government's hand. Under our

Employment Act, they were supposed to have a ninety-day consultation before they made anyone redundant."

Despite the violation of local work rules, reporters trekking to Belfast found the workers sympathetic to De Lorean's plight and more upset with the government. The *Daily Express* titled an article, WHY DE LOREAN IS STILL A HERO, and quoted one laid-off employee saying, "If the government came up with more money it would be seen as an important gesture to the Catholic people. Fair play to John De Lorean. He made a lot of money, but he has given a lot of people jobs."

De Lorean, however, was not ready to give Belfast fair play. After Prior turned down the export aid he returned to New York the next day. In an interview with the London *Times*, he dispassionately blamed Belfast for most of his problems. "We had a terrible time producing a management team because Englishmen would not work there. We grossly underestimated the magnitude of the problems." De Lorean went on to cite 140 fire-bomb incidents and added that his executives were constantly the targets of snipers. "Trying to keep a management team together under those circumstances, especially of people who are good enough to work anywhere, is difficult."

"Of course those statements about Belfast were unmitigated bullshit," one of the Belfast executives says. "He implies that he had to settle for a team of incompetents. But we weren't the ones who decided to increase production and increase it even when the inventories were bulging. The statements about the fire-bombings are just evil. We had the one incident during the hunger strike, but that was because the blasted army tramped onto our property. The fire did destroy that hut where we had some drawings, and it did cause some damage—not the £10 million John claimed [and that the British refused to pay], and nothing we lost was responsible for putting us in trouble. As far as snipings went—there was one stray bullet in a water tank. Period."

As all came crashing down around him, De Lorean appeared confident—even serene. Among his visitors in early February was one of his major service suppliers. "My contract was running out," he says, "and I was passing through New York, so I went in to see what John wanted to do. I knew termination would have a devastating impact on his business.

"The secretary met me in the lobby and showed me into John's office. From what I could see, the place looked pretty deserted. I guess he had let most of the people go. But there was John sitting in his office acting like nothing had happened—just as pleasant as always.

"He had quite a view up there and, when I sat down, he stared out through the windows and started telling me how his little boy had just been robbed. Someone on the street had grabbed his watch. 'It was just a Timex,' he said, 'but what are we going to do about the crime in America?'

"From there he just took off. I didn't say a thing. I just sat there listening. He was going on about our government, and then he was talking about the Russians. He said, 'Let Russia have Europe. They already have most of it. Just as long as we get Central America and South America. We'll give Asia to the Japanese. They can handle that.'

"I couldn't believe it. Here his whole business was disintegrating to ashes and he was solving the problems of the world. This went on for forty-five minutes. Finally I looked at my watch and told him I was sorry to interrupt, but I had to catch a plane soon, so we should start talking about my contract.

"It was like I had thrown cold water on him. He looked down at his desk and started shuffling through his papers. He said, 'I don't know about that. Talk to the lawyers. They know what's going on there. They'll handle it.'

"Then he stood up and looked at his watch and said, 'I've really got to be going.' "

·18·
Roy to the Rescue

By March 1982, like one of its defective cars with the throttle stuck open, the De Lorean Motor Company was careening down a canyon road—lurching across lanes, bumping off guardrails, barely making the curves—and at the wheel was Roy Nesseth. No longer did Roy have to lurk in corners or hide behind vague titles. Now he was out front. Big, bad Roy. Charming, "buddy-buddy" Roy. Screaming, fist-pounding Roy. Finally he had control of John Z. De Lorean's dream as it hurtled to destruction, and nobody but John was going to say anything about it.

In just one twenty-four-hour period Roy would send out armed guards on two coasts to flout the authority of a bank agreement and set in motion forces that would jeopardize another $18 million deal and definitively kill off a potential $100 million investor. By the time the smoke had cleared, Roy had fired the company's two most senior executives and negotiated settlement on a $278,000 debt with an exchange of worthless stock. Just another day for Nesseth. As one executive who worked with Roy explains, "Roy is the kind of guy who likes to show he's doing something by taking a sheet of paper, tearing it into little pieces and throwing it into the air. He only forgets that somebody has to come back and pick up the pieces."

Back in early February, De Lorean was ready to forget the car company and wave goodbye. Once the export aid was refused and Prior called in Sir Kenneth Cork, no one had any doubt that the plant was going into receivership. John De Lorean had not left General Motors to have some fusty old receiver looking over his shoulder and questioning his every move.

"From their first meeting," a Belfast executive says, "Cork and De Lorean hated each other. It was a classic case of 'this nation isn't big enough for the both of us'—two egos that would never be reconciled. John would start in about how the British government wasn't giving him a chance, and Sir Kenneth would talk about extravagant overheads. Each was out to cut the other down."

Court records show that, early in the month, Kimmerly called in Detroit's best bankruptcy lawyer, Lawrence K. Snider, to discuss a Chapter XI reorganization. But if he had contemplated a quick exit, De Lorean was not ready to leave without a door prize. On February 9 he proceeded to relieve the car company of a few assets, like office furniture and artwork. He also started assuming the mortgage on the old Bridgewater, New Jersey, car-dealership building that had been a QAC for the car company. The property was located near De Lorean's Bedminster home, and he had strongly recommended the site when regional director Bill Morgan was looking for a good location. "As far as the company was concerned," he says, "it was out of the way. But the place was in a prime development corridor and John said, 'It's a hell of deal. If we don't buy it, I'll buy it for my own account.' Then he said he knew buying a facility was a tough job. He said if I needed help, Roy was available to help with the details."

Without any request from Morgan, Roy was on the scene, screaming at movers, sending through orders, and giving Morgan more aggravation than help. Despite his genial manner, the barrel-chested Morgan was not ready to tolerate Roy's antics. "The man just wreaks havoc wherever he goes. I had enough of it. I told him that either he left the building or I'd throw him out." Roy meekly took the nearest exit, Morgan says, later complaining to

De Lorean about the regional manager's inclination to violence.

But De Lorean let Roy go ahead and handle the details of the property transaction for the Bridgewater facility. The landowner was in serious financial straits and, in the midst of negotiation, Roy turned to the bank with a lien on the property and found a better deal. It was just one more bank that, without knowing better, wanted John De Lorean's business. "The [landowner] went belly up," one California executive says, "and Roy just couldn't stop crowing about how he screwed the guy."

The mortgage for the property came to only $900,000—but when De Lorean became personal owner, the car company entered into a very sweet deal with its chairman by prepaying two years' worth of rent, which came to $200,000.

As De Lorean expected, the British placed the Belfast factory in receivership on February 19. While Cork said he felt the company could be made viable with an additional infusion of capital, the rest of his report was kept secret. Parts of it were critical of De Lorean's management style, though it wasn't the outright condemnation that some of his executives felt he deserved. De Lorean attributed the critical comment to Brown, who had spent a few days with the auditors. But, like so many previous British efforts to set De Lorean's house in order, the investigation was too little too late. "At the end of the day," one of De Lorean's Belfast executives says, "people will realize what a poor job Cork did on De Lorean. He was too tough and too easy at the wrong times. How could he have assessed the viability of the car company in just a two-week study? If he had really been intent on saving it, he would have booted De Lorean out in February."

If the company needed more capital, Prior made it clear that the British government was not to be the source. As he told the press, "I had to reiterate to Mr. De Lorean that there was no question of further public money."

It was a moment, Fleet Street thought, of utter humiliation for De Lorean but, to their surprise, the receivership left him ebullient. As he prepared to board the Concorde to fly home, he told reporters, "I am delighted by the outcome." He didn't have to worry about the plant being sold to anyone else, he said, and

Cork was giving him a chance to buy it back. Receivership, he explained, "ensures the continuity of production, sales, and service for the De Lorean car." He then told reporters that he was to put in $5 million of his own money, and in return the government was prepared to write off $70 million of investment.

When told of De Lorean's jubilant assessment of receivership, Prior replied, "That is what I might describe as a piece of De Loreanism. When someone buys the restructured company he will still be responsible for these debts on which the government will have first charge."

But later the government did admit that they had signed an agreement to forgive $70 million in loans after De Lorean put up $5 million first. But their generosity was not due to any renewed faith in De Lorean. Instead, out of the blue, an investor had appeared who was truly capable of saving the day. When De Lorean first approached the government with the offer, they had reason to be skeptical. For the last year, De Lorean had been turning Aesop on his head with cries of "sheepdog." Some new Arab sheikh or financier was always just around the corner eager to invest millions.

But Alan H. Blair was no figment of De Lorean's imagination. An international businessman who had a house in Los Angeles, Blair had built a fortune many times over in European manufacturing and pharmaceuticals. Introduced to the car company by a friend who was a client of DMC board member Robert Benjamin, Blair instantly envisioned a way he and four partners could save the De Lorean car and use the factory more efficiently. "We didn't think there was the market for the sports car that De Lorean saw," Blair says. "We had in mind adding another vehicle. Many countries these days are looking for a cheap utility truck, and we felt we could swing that in Belfast. We obtained about $100 million in private capital. Forty million would have gone to clear up the situation with the British government."

Blair adds that if he had taken charge, he would have radically restructured the company. "The underlying principle was that if De Lorean was there, it would be primarily to contribute his name—whatever underlying value that may have had. But he certainly would have had nothing to do with management. That was a condition we set forth among ourselves, and John seemed amenable. He simply was not a businessman himself. I could see that right off the bat. Of course things are different in General Motors—you have accountants and financial people giving you help, watching your spending. I think it was like being in the military and then trying to do something alone. He couldn't operate on his own."

Blair had only one condition. He wanted the British government to forgive the $70 million in loan guarantees and credit. De Lorean set off to London to get an answer from Prior on the day receivership was announced. Those around De Lorean remember him being unusually jubilant when he left. "I don't think he expected Prior to go along with it," one says. "And that meant he'd have the perfect excuse to wash his hands of the whole thing. It would be clear that, even with a legitimate backer, the British didn't want to make it work. He felt he could then leave with his conscience clear and his reputation intact."

But when Blair first contacted Prior, via Cork, he found the British were not about to scuttle his deal. "Prior," he says, "is the best man in the cabinet. Although he has the dirtiest job, he's unfailingly pleasant and low-key. He can still be a very tough man to deal with. It's hard to get a yes out of him. But he did have a chance to check me out first and, knowing of my arrangement, they were ready to cancel the $70 million of credit.

"They had yet to see De Lorean, and I asked him to come first to see me at Claridge's, where I was staying. I told him I was quite happy to say that they were forgiving the $70 million in loans. But then he turned to me and said, 'I want to put $5 million of my own money into the project.'

"I couldn't believe my ears. I told him not to mention that. 'Just let Prior say his piece, say thank you, and get out of there.' He sort of looked away from me and didn't answer.

"De Lorean then left, and soon after I received a phone call from Prior. I remember him saying, 'I can't work with the man. I just can't work with him.'"

Prior then told Blair that De Lorean's first words when they met were that he wanted to invest $5 million of his own money in the company. "After that," Blair says, "what could he have said but, 'Fine, we'll forgive $70 million when you deposit $5 million.' And both Prior and I knew he'd never put up that money. I was just livid. When De Lorean came back I asked him, 'Why did you do it?'

"Then he said, 'You don't think I'd take all that money from the British government without putting up my own money, do you? I don't want their charity.'

"I told him that now he had no choice but to put up his own money. He said that all he had to do was to go back to Citibank. Of course, he never did put up that money."

De Lorean returned to New York on Saturday, February 20, and upon his arrival met with Kimmerly to tell him he wanted to put $5 million of his own money into the company. He was ready to sell his Fifth Avenue co-op to raise it. Stunned, Kimmerly called one of his young executives and asked, "Do you think John is losing his judgment? Why would he want to put his own money into the company now?"

Tom turned to his occasional, uneasy ally, Roy, to talk De Lorean out of this spate of generosity. Roy's strongest ally in the struggle was Cristina, who, according to John, didn't want any of their personal assets involved with the car, and especially not her precious apartment.

Yet, while Roy and Tom were against investment, they were also against declaring bankruptcy. According to New York executives, after the British put the factory into receivership, bankruptcy lawyer Snider strongly recommended De Lorean declare Chapter XI for his side of the operations. One of the inner circle remembers, "Roy started yelling, 'What the hell do you think a bankruptcy lawyer is going to advise? It's his business to have people go into Chapter XI.' Tom's argument was that if they went into reorganization, all the assets would be gone. He and John weren't about to stick around to handle what was left."

And there were still 2,000 tempting stainless-steel assets left, with a street value of over $40 million. But there were debts over $43 million. At least $22.5 million was claimed by the receiver in Belfast. The plant never got paid on over 1,500 cars that had gone out. De Lorean countercharged that he was owed $22 million by the plant for product-quality repairs. Warranty claims were another $1.1 million chunk of the car company's debt, along with $1.7 million from various suppliers. But the most worrisome liability was the $18 million owed the Bank of America. Despite the crucial role the bank's bridge financing had played in the company's existence, De Lorean had always left direct contacts to Dick Brown, who had succeeded in getting the bank to extend the loan, but now De Lorean decided to handle matters himself.

On February 23, just ten days before the deadline, De Lorean flew into Los Angeles with Roy, Kimmerly, and Snider. They met first with Alan Blair in his Los Angeles mansion for a strategy session, and then it was on to the Bank of America. De Lorean talked of restructuring his car company much as Germany's BMW did when it had gone bankrupt. He had learned his lesson, he told the bankers, and he was scaling down his production goals.

But the bankers sat in glacial silence. They had gone as far with the De Lorean Motor Company as they were willing to go. A seething Roy would later say that Dick Brown was behind their cool reaction.

Although he was putting on a brave front for reporters, Brown was waiting for the other shoe to drop. For five years he had staved off the influence of Roy but, in the last few weeks, Nesseth had moved into De Lorean's Irvine office by the conference room and set up shop. Even with Brown's plush carpets, the halls rang with Nesseth's curses.

Nesseth, in another mission to save the company, had also brought in four friends. In this case "the henchmen"—as De Lorean employees called them—were renegotiating with creditors. Roy Nesseth, the best car-deal closer in southern California, had finally graduated to closing out entire companies. His men would get a creditor on the phone, and then Roy would lock him up on a deal for so many cents on the dollar. Before he'd left Roy's office, a hapless supplier had signed an agreement promising not to sue if Nesseth met the terms of the contract. To some De Lorean staff members the whole arrangement did not appear on the up-and-up. No supplier, though, has yet come forward and claimed physical coercion. However, the henchmen reprimanded one staff accountant when she took contracts with big spaces in the middle of a page and filled them in to make sure nothing was added after the supplier signed.

At times, Roy didn't stop his creditor negotiations with just cents on the dollar. He also tried to push some of John De Lorean's personal stock on suppliers. He succeeded in pushing the most stock on the company that had finally provided the car with a successful radio system. The vice president of finance for the Louisville company Audio Systems, Inc., accepted 25,000 shares of Motor Company stock in partial payment. Roy offered the stock even though he was not registered to do so, and even though he knew it was worthless as anything more than a novelty souvenir.

Brown had to bite his tongue and watch Roy's antics in silence. He kept in touch with Bill Morgan on the East Coast, and over the phone the two started noticing ominous designs on the 2,000 cars left in their care. The bank was ready to slap a lien on the entire stock any day. But De Lorean and his crew appeared to have their own plans for the vehicles. "One day in the middle of February," Morgan says, "I got a call from John asking me to find 450 of the latest models that hadn't been sold yet and get them out of sight. I told him that you just couldn't put that many cars in somebody's basement. You needed a few hundred thousand square feet. He just let it drop, but I left that conversation tucked away in my memory. Later it occurred to me that he was getting ready to steal some cars. At that point I told myself I was finding out more than I wanted to know and tried to put the thought out of my mind."

Occasionally on weekends Morgan would have a couple of cars driven the few miles to De Lorean's Bedminster estate so he and some visitors could "evaluate" them. But near the end of February, when he sent a man to bring back two cars, he was told that De Lorean had already attended to the matter. They were going to be shipped out to Ross Gilbert in Beverly Hills, the old friend Roy had set up in a Mercedes dealership. For Brown, the cars meant some $34,000 of badly needed income to meet the week's payroll, but when he had someone go out to pick up the payment from Gilbert, he returned with a check for only $4,000. When Brown called to ask what had happened to the balance, he says Gilbert replied, "You owe me for warranties."

In fact, the car company owed every dealer for warranties, but industry practice does not permit dealers to take those costs off vehicle purchase prices. Gilbert was not going to bother talking about it any further. Brown then tried to ask Nesseth to intercede, but he found that Roy was well aware of the transaction. Brown says, "He told me, 'You take care of your friends like Bank of America, so I can take care of my friends too.' "

The Gilbert transaction would only be the beginning. On March 3, the day before the bank loan officially went into default, the Telex machine snarled with disturbing messages about the company's fragile condition. For weeks Brown had been cutting back, but now even more workers would have to go, pushing the total number of layoffs to 67 out of 117. Brown had created a tight-knit crew—sometimes most united in its irritation with him—but that was something he understood and even fostered. After all the months of pep talks, he found it hard to announce that the efforts were all over.

Before the day was out, the most ominous Telex would emanate from board member Benjamin. "He wanted me to come to New York and talk to him. The day was so hectic, I ended up missing my plane. Now I realize that it was part of the scheme. They wanted me out of the city."

Soon after the New York office learned Brown was not on his way, he received a call from De Lorean. Brown knew that the ultimate showdown was coming, and he knew that when it came, it would never be face-to-face, but over the phone. "John started in about the Coopers & Lybrand's report from England. He said, 'You criticized my management.' I told him I didn't criticize anybody personally. I criticized the structure of the company. Then John said, 'I don't see how you could take someone's money and then criticize him behind his back. I think we should separate.'

"I said, 'It isn't your money. It's money from our dealers and our limited partners.' But I told him I'd send a letter of resignation."

Meanwhile, Morgan had his own problems with headquarters. Roy was holed up in New York and calling every few hours. "Roy told me he wanted to get fourteen cars outside the gate so John could make payroll that week." The cars had actually been ordered the day before but, anticipating the default, the bank had refused to let them go. Pasha International, the importing company, also served as the bank's agent and had a man on the premises in both California and New Jersey to watch over the cars.

Morgan called to ask Brown's advice and Brown told him the cars belonged to the bank—under no circumstances should they be let off the property. But that night, Morgan received an urgent call from the Pasha guard at the QAC. Five armed men had shown up claiming to be from De Lorean and demanding the cars. Spearheading the take-over was the nervous young office manager from De Lorean's New York headquarters. Morgan called the QAC and spoke to the office manager. "I asked him," Morgan recalls, " 'Do you know what you're getting into?' "

Almost as soon as Morgan put down the phone, it rang again. At the other end was Nesseth, the Patton of the De Lorean invasion. Moments before, he had called to congratulate his troops, only to find them in full retreat. Now he wanted to know what Morgan had told his field commander. "When I got on the phone," Morgan says, "Roy yelled, 'What the fuck are you doing?' I told him the cars belonged to the bank, and then he said, 'Who's your allegiance to—the bank or De Lorean? If it's the bank, then go work for the bank because you're fired.' "

The next morning, Morgan called to see whether he had actually been fired. He talked to one of the De Lorean lawyers who promised to put a call through to John. But finally it was Roy who got back to him to say that both he and Brown were fired.

That night, the Nesseth assault squad returned. This time a Pasha regional supervisor, Earl Hanson, was on the site. Hanson later testified that the De Lorean guards did not let him use the telephone. They told him instead that Pasha had been terminated by De Lorean and he should leave the premises. Hanson sent his man out to a pay phone to call the police and then went to telecopy the notice of default from the Bank of America, but the armed guards wouldn't let him use that equipment either. When the police arrived, the only documentation they saw was the deed that De Lorean held to the property. This time, Hanson was forced to retreat. But he kept his assistant posted in the parking lot. That night, the scout would watch in his darkened car while fifteen of the De Loreans were driven out of the warehouse and onto their namesake's property.

It was Brown who originally got George Pasha involved with the De Lorean Motor Company—a fact that caused Brown some acute embarrassment when Pasha called to give him the sordid details of the Bridgewater take-over. Brown promised he wouldn't let the same thing happen in Santa Ana. First he called his people in the warehouse and warned them to be ready. Then he called the police. By the time Brown arrived at the scene, the police had already barred four armed men from access to the QAC. Inside, Roy Nesseth was waiting on the phone from New York. He was calling from his favorite hangout, Peacock Alley in the Waldorf-Astoria Hotel. As Brown and his warehouse supervisor listened on the phone, Nesseth screamed, "If you want to stay alive and if you want your family to stay healthy, you'll cooperate."

Brown says he then asked if that was a threat. Nesseth replied, "You can call it whatever you want, but you know that I can back it up."

Kimmerly was also with Nesseth at the restaurant, Brown says. "He took the phone from Nesseth and he said, 'What are you doing there? You have no business there. You didn't have to be notified.'

"Then I asked, 'Does that mean I'm terminated?'

"And Kimmerly answered, 'Yes. You're terminated.'

"I hung up the phone and I went home."

Brown would be wakened at 6:00 the next morning by De Lorean. "He asked me where my letter of resignation was, and I told him my attorneys were handling it. He said, 'Fuck that. I don't want to deal with attorneys. I want it done quick.' But I told him, after six years I couldn't just walk away from the company. Besides, my situation had changed. Kimmerly had told me I was fired. Then I asked John, 'Don't you know what happened at the QAC?'

"He said it was all just one big misunderstanding."

For Roy, Brown's exit was a cause for celebration. Now he had the run of the Irvine office and he had eliminated his archenemy from the corporation. But Brown's loss would have an immediate and devastating impact on the company, by permanently alienating Alan Blair—the one investor who could have saved the plant. "While I was sitting there one day with Nesseth and De Lorean," Blair says, "they were talking about getting rid of Brown. The whole thing almost sounded as though they intended some sort of physical threat. Nesseth said something like, 'I'll knock his head off.'

"From what *I* saw, Brown was very good. He had done all the work with the sales organization. I respected his credibility and his past history. But there was just a terrible personality clash with De Lorean; I suppose to the point where De Lorean was ready to cut off his nose to spite his face.

"Now I didn't think highly of Nesseth at all. In fact, in all my experience in the business world, I had never met anyone like him. There seemed to be a relationship between him and De Lorean that I just couldn't fathom. Unfortunately, he had a tremendous influence over De Lorean, and that really didn't penetrate until I'd read about Brown's dismissal."

The warehouse escapade had other ramifications as well, which De Lorean discovered as soon as the United States Court for the Southern District of New York went into session on Tuesday, March 9. The Bank of America immediately brought suit to stop sales of all De Lorean cars in the United States and the Honorable Charles L. Brieant was ready and willing to cooperate. When De Lorean's attorney explained that his client's company was in financial difficulty, the judge shot back, "You don't work yourself out of the financial difficulty by sending people in with force and arms. . . . If the allegation be proved at the hearing that somebody came with guns in the 1980s, we don't allow that. I am very doubtful we would have allowed that in the 1880s. . . ."

De Lorean's lawyer was not in a very good position to respond. He had been retained only one hour before (and was just beginning to run up a $47,000 tab, which would never be paid).

After indicating that the seizure was considered a criminal act under most state laws, the judge restrained the sale of all De Loreans and demanded the return of the missing cars, adding, "Please understand: if the order is not complied with, somebody is going to jail—fast."

De Lorean returned the fifteen cars as the judge demanded. He could not comply as quickly with the bank's demands and a restraining order remained on the rest of his inventory. For Roy, the injunction was a blessing in disguise that stymied yet another deal De Lorean made the very night Nesseth ordered the armed guards to march on the QACs. In effect, the chief executive signed away every car in the supposed possession of the De Lorean Motor Company. While Roy had opposed the massive fire sale, and De Lorean himself regretted the pact as soon as he agreed to it, Tom Kimmerly argued that their only other option was bankruptcy.

The deal started innocently enough with a phone call from an elderly businessman in Columbus, Ohio who claimed that he and a partner could help De Lorean through his financial difficulties. "When these two little Jewish guys showed up from Ohio and said they'd buy the entire inventory," one De Lorean executive says, "Kimmerly and Roy were laughing themselves silly. They never really expected them to come up with much money. Whatever it was, they thought it would be like taking candy from a baby. Roy started off treating them like a couple of Joes in to buy one of his used cars—first slap them on the back, swap a few stories about Columbus, and then hit them hard and leave them ragged."

But anyone familiar with liquidation in America could not take Sol Shenk or Jerome Schottenstein lightly. From a personal bankruptcy in the auto-parts business, Sol Shenk has built an empire on the detritus of other men's broken dreams. Bricklins; Fiat

Lancias; Diamond Reo trucks: Shenk's Consolidated International is the garage in the sky for the failed oddities of the American road. He also specializes in more prosaic and profitable buy-outs of such things as appliances and auto parts, and a good part of his inventory appeared to be crammed into every available corner of his sprawling, but still cluttered one-story headquarters. Posted prominently on his paneled wall is an autographed version of De Lorean's Goodyear ad with the inscription: "To Florence and Sol Shenk, with my best wishes, John De Lorean."

A crusty man of advanced years with a bald head and thick, oversized glasses, Shenk likes to get quickly to the point. There are deals to be made and time can't be wasted on long answers. "Our business," he explains, "is buying excess inventory. Buying—not selling. When I read that De Lorean had 2,000 cars sitting around and the Bank of America was screaming for money, I gave him a call. He was desperate to stave off the creditors. My primary concern was buying the cars."

On most big deals, Shenk's partner is Jerome Schottenstein, whose cagey acquisition of failing apparel stores has made him one of America's largest clothing retailers. Together they went down to New York during the last week of February and, after days of solid negotiation, signed a letter of intent. "Nesseth was originally doing the negotiating with us for De Lorean," Schottenstein says. "And it was very tedious. He's a very excitable person and I tried to stay cool. Every so often he'd get up and bring De Lorean in. Usually when people do deals with us, they're anxious to finish. De Lorean seemed to be dragging his feet."

Shenk says, "De Lorean was acting the part of a big-time executive. You could see him in the office next door reading a magazine. I think he was pretty down. He told us he was prepared to step out, but he wanted to save face. He said he personally had a lot of money, so it wasn't a matter of him being forced to hang on."

After a week of negotiations, a brain-bending agreement emerged. De Lorean's bankruptcy lawyers would later say that Consolidated had taken possession of the gull-wing cars like a giant hock shop, but Shenk and Schottenstein would be careful to structure the deal solely as a purchase. If De Lorean went bankrupt, they did not want to share the cars with creditors.

The easiest part of the agreement to understand is the $14,887,500 Consolidated gave De Lorean for the 1,191 cars in the Santa Ana QAC. Much more complicated was De Lorean's option to buy them back and maintain the exclusive rights to sell his nameplate through his dealer network. To keep those rights, he had to buy at least 400 cars every three months. The price to get each one back from Consolidated would be $13,500 (Consolidated bought them for $12,500 apiece). On top of that, he'd have to pay interest on the total price of all the unsold cars in the Consolidated inventory and meet certain other payments at ninety-day intervals.

"Whenever we dealt with De Lorean and his people," Schottenstein says, "it would be very boring. Hours would drag by. Sometimes we felt we had to read his mind. I thought that, because he had an engineering background, he was never really much of a businessman. He needed people around him to conduct business—although he still wanted to be a part of it.

"When we finally finished writing the contract, he kept us waiting even longer." Schottenstein had no idea that during that night warehouses on both coasts were being stormed. "I just sat around drinking coffee. John would call me in and ask for a change [in the contract], and then he wouldn't sign it. Nesseth said he had to go to a quiet place and read the contract by himself. The whole office was empty. I really didn't understand what he meant by quiet.

"After an hour I walked in to see how Roy was doing. We're talking about a forty-page agreement and he's on page four. I come back an hour later. He's back to page three. It was ridiculous. I just took the contracts into John's office and spread them out on his couch. I told him he could either sign them or I was going home. After he signed, I yelled through the door at Roy that the contracts were signed. He never said a word."

Roy Nesseth had finally been beaten by someone tougher than

he was, and he didn't like it. Although he had done most of the negotiating, he blamed Kimmerly for letting De Lorean sign the deal. Beyond the conditions of the repurchase, the contract also called for a bulk-sale announcement to all of De Lorean's creditors. It was a risky proposition. Some creditors—especially the British government—might fear that all the company's assets would be dissolved in the transaction and try to force an involuntary bankruptcy.

Rather than go ahead with the bulk-sale announcement as they had promised, De Lorean's brain trust let the Bank of America's restraining order on the sale of the cars languish while they hunted up other sources of money. Shenk and Schottenstein soon got the picture and tried to intervene in court, since their deal with De Lorean could help him pay off the bank loan. "Roy tried to chase me out of the court during one of the Bank of America hearings," a Consolidated lawyer says. "He kept telling me I didn't belong there."

Meanwhile, De Lorean was actively pursuing other sources of quick funds. One would be with Budget Rent-A-Car. The company's chief executive, Morris Belzberg, had dealt with De Lorean back in the days when he ran Chevrolet. "Our deal went through two phases," Belzberg says. "The first would have had us purchase 1,000 cars. Those would be repurchased between four and six months later. Evidently he would take the dollars from our purchase to satisfy his loan requirements with Bank of America. But this deal fell through when my lawyers felt we could be involved in some sort of litigation if the company did go into bankruptcy. They felt we wouldn't end up with proper title to the cars and they were afraid receivers could then step in and take the cars back.

"The next deal involved a lease. They'd get so many millions for that. Each car would have a few months' lease and then they'd be turned back. But by then I got a call from Schottenstein. He had evidently read about the deal in the press, and he said, 'If you want to lease cars lease them from me.'

"I called Nesseth and he said, 'Don't worry. I'll handle [Schottenstein]. His deal is not a deal. We'll go ahead with our deal.'

But by then we'd decided we couldn't go ahead. We were concerned by our exposure, and when we called several dealers, they told us, 'We're not being paid for warranty.' That meant we ran the risk that if something went wrong with one of our cars, dealers wouldn't service them.

"Little by little I became unhappy with my treatment by Mr. Nesseth. He would make statements that caused some confusion when we got back to Bank of America. They told us they'd have nothing more to do with Nesseth and that if I did, I should proceed with caution. He really didn't accept no for an answer. At one point I was in San Diego for a meeting with our parent company, Transamerica, and I became ill with a bleeding ulcer. While I lay in the hospital, Nesseth kept calling me. I was really in no condition to get into arguments with him, and somehow he didn't understand that."

Nesseth and De Lorean were very candid with Belzberg about their unwillingness to go ahead with the Consolidated deal, and Schottenstein could see how reluctant they had become. He says, "They seemed to have a fear of completion. Sometimes details arose that De Lorean wasn't familiar with and then seemed reluctant to get."

Meanwhile, Roy was becoming more of a nuisance. "He kept giving me a distorted picture of what each party involved was saying," Schottenstein explains. "So I arranged for representatives from the bank, Budget, and the receiver to meet at De Lorean's office. Roy tried to put us each in a separate office and wouldn't let us talk to each other. When I saw what was happening, I started knocking on the doors and telling them to come out. Roy yelled back, 'You can't come in here.'

"The whole thing was so amateurish it was almost funny. We all finally got together in the lobby to find out what the real story was. I don't know what the relationship was between Nesseth and De Lorean, but from my point of view it wasn't doing John or the company any good."

At last, in April, with no other source of funds and the bank threatening to take in all the cars and auction them off, De Lorean went ahead with the Consolidated deal. To the surprise of executives and bankruptcy lawyers, the British government did not force an involuntary bankruptcy. Instead, the receivers made arrangements with Shenk and Schottenstein to purchase some of their excess stock.

But in the minds of the remaining few executives at the top of the company, the bulk sale was as good as a bankruptcy. "The night they shipped out all their titles to Consolidated," one insider says, "they were dead in the water."

·19·
Trapped in a Terrible Tower

During the last spring and summer of his car company's life, John De Lorean was spending an increasing amount of time at his Pauma Valley ranch. He often came alone, and for days conducted his business by phone out on the flagstone patio by the pool.

The four houses and fifty acres had been on the block since 1979, when he'd sold the avocado groves. Cristina never did like the place. She'd tell visitors she was worried about snakes in the grass. She didn't like being out in the middle of nowhere.

But as his life grew more complex and difficult, John appeared to love the solitude even more. He could no longer look out at the neighboring hills and say they were his. Still, as he lay sunning himself by the pool, there must have been some serenity in wealth. He could look down from the piece of mountainside he still had left, or watch his three Mexican hands move easily through their tasks, their little dogs chasing after them.

Back in college when he wrote, "Know you what it is to be an Engineer?" he'd answered, "It is to be trapped in a terrible tower of pure science." Evidently he liked that image, because he prac-

TRAPPED IN A TERRIBLE TOWER

tically repeated it later in the piece, writing, "It is to suffer a throne alone in your terrible Temple of Science. . . ."

By the middle of 1982, De Lorean was trapped in another sort of tower, and if he still sat on a throne, he did suffer its burdens alone. The way he reached these heights had nothing to do with "pure science." In fact, as he'd discovered long before, a mastery of physics or engineering was not enough to attain affluence in America. If he had remained only an engineer, the law of corporate gravity would have kept him back at Pontiac, poring over the drafting board during the day and going home to quiet evenings with his pretty blond suburban wife.

Real success lay in the hazy fields of finance and public relations, but the greater the gains, the more ignominious the losses. The cocky college student once felt he could design his way out of any engineering problem. The business tycoon would find his predicaments far more complicated and far more intractable.

Never before had John De Lorean's name been so publicly associated with failure. In all the other deals that went bad, like Saf-Gard and Grand Prix, he had been insulated from disrepute. But the car company was different. His greatest accomplishment had been to bring his dream to world attention. Now the spotlight wouldn't go away.

In the past, when the fortunes of his little companies turned sour, he could turn to Roy and Tom. But it became clear that neither one was capable of the big solution that would save the De Lorean Motor Company. Roy had not delivered his Boise dealer friend as the Canadian distributor and that dashed hopes for at least $750,000.

As for Kimmerly, he had not produced on the stock issue, nor had he gotten the best possible deal from Consolidated. On March 12, Kimmerly resigned from the board, along with Henry Bushkin and G. Edmund King. Kimmerly later explained the move by saying that his new status would enable him to represent De Lorean in lawsuits if the need arose. But trial law would have been an unusual new tack for the tax counsel to take so late in his career.

"The tougher the Consolidated deal looked," one of the financial executives says, "the more John and Roy held it against Tom. During the spring [De Lorean] froze Tom out of the key decisions in the company."

As of March 3, against the advice of all of his lawyers, De Lorean started issuing all company disbursements on his own checking accounts. A new multimillion-dollar credit line at Citibank helped him swing the bigger payments. The move was touched off when Gene Cafiero enjoined the bank accounts of the car company to recover the $180,000 that remained in his contract settlement.

For the skeleton crew that stayed on in California, the company entered a strange period of limbo. Most of the senior staff left with Brown. The two key replacements would be Steven Allred, as the new chief financial officer for the sales division, and J. Bruce McWilliams, the vice president in charge of marketing. Both had tangled with C.R. in the past.

Previously associated with American marketing for Saab, Mercedes, and British Leyland, McWilliams was a gentle and genteel man who could offer De Lorean a welcome diversion from the troubles of the day with erudite talk about international motoring. He had joined the company in 1981 and helped secure the supplier ads like Cutty Sark and Goodyear. His major disputes with Brown came over the minuscule advertising budget. He now believes that De Lorean was a contributing factor to their feud. "John," he says, "was telling each of us different things. He hired me to report to him, yet he had written a memo to Brown that I was to work for Brown—a fact for which John later apologized."

McWilliams would have no expectation of the chaos that followed in the wake of Brown's departure. "My total preoccupation was for keeping the company afloat. I arrived to find a bare-bones staff completely demoralized and confused. Some of them were bringing suit to collect their pay. For a time, people challenged my judgment in spending money on the telephone or the postage to raise orders from dealers.

"As far as bills were concerned, we owed everybody. Creditors were inundating the place. These guys would come in, sit in the lobby, and refuse to leave until they got paid.

TRAPPED IN A TERRIBLE TOWER

"There was one cliff-hanger after another. Every week was a cliff-hanger as to whether we'd get payroll from John, and then it was a matter of finding check-cashing companies that would handle his personal checks so people didn't have to wait two weeks for them to clear.

"Then there was the cliff-hanger of whether we'd sell enough cars to pay off our debts. We'd be on the phone from early in the morning to late at night pushing it through."

McWilliams tried to get his head high enough above water to envisage some rudimentary sales campaign. In one of his first moves he had De Lorean send telegrams marked "Urgent and Important To All Dealers." Claiming that the purchase of just six cars apiece could "save the [company's marketing] program," the telegram asked for "total commitment now by the entire dealer organization." It ended, "Please call or cable what you can do. God bless you all."

One other staff member remembers: "When John saw the copy for that telegram, he said, 'This has got to be the end.' "

"We sent telegrams to 345 dealers," McWilliams says. "Out of all those dealers only one Midwest dealer responded. He wrote back, 'No thanks.' "

Early in May, McWilliams did manage to pull off a more beneficial effort, gathering forty dealers from the southwestern region for a meeting. "Our California dealers were just desperate to know whether the company would survive. John was annoyed that I wanted to organize this meeting. He accused me of panicking. I answered, 'You must do this, John. These people idolize you.' I think he was truly afraid of what he might face. One of the reasons he was so attracted to a man like Nesseth was that he didn't have the stomach himself for confrontations.

"Our regional directors were convinced he wouldn't show. He was late, but he came and he carried it off with some flair. I think he assured the dealers about the company. Of course, John bent the truth. He claimed the twin-turbo engine would be ready by the end of the year, and there was no way that that would happen. When they asked about a shop manual, he said it was coming from the printer.

"But he was so well received, he came up later to thank me for pushing him into doing it."

By June, McWilliams was gone and a major reason was Roy. "I never really knew about Roy until I moved to Irvine," he says. "All John told me about Roy was that he'd do the dirty work. He said, 'Some people are mean from time to time, or mean in some way or other, but that Roy Nesseth was a mean man who enjoyed being mean.'"

McWilliams and his staff were not fully informed about the men Roy brought in or what they were doing. Supposedly, two were ranchers, one was a distributor for a door-to-door sales company, and the other a realtor.

When Roy swept into the Irvine office, pandemonium followed. He was making deals over the phone to sell off cars; he was shouting threats to suppliers; he was constantly arguing with practically everyone in the office. There were still a few lawsuits trailing after Roy and, at times, when the staff got too sick of his bellowing voice, one or the other would call the sheriff to let him know that Roy was back in town.

Life had never been more hectic for Roy. "Roy lived on airplanes," Gus Davis says. "The man didn't think anything of booking three or four different flights in different directions and not deciding where he was going to go until he got to the airport."

Davis had had to deal with Roy's peripatetic habits when he worked with him at Manufacturing in Logan, Utah. "One day we were discussing a contract with a firm in Geneva and, without any warning, Roy just went and took the next flight to Geneva. The next thing we know, he's demanding to speak to the chief executive of our distributor there, who just happened to be out of the office that day. I don't think John was too happy with that trip."

What disturbed McWilliams and Allred the most was the way Roy's son Jeff had the run of the premises. "It got to the point where my salesmen didn't have company cars while four were sitting in the Nesseth family driveway," McWilliams says. "One day Jeff brought one of the cars into the shop to be fixed and Allred wouldn't let him take it out. I think Allred at least asked that one of the other cars be returned in its place. Well, we are in the midst of a critical senior staff meeting when all of a sudden young Nesseth barges in and screams he wants his car. I told him to leave the premises and if I saw him hanging around again I'd call the police. I called John about it, but although he promised action, he did nothing. The next thing I know, Roy corners me to say he'd separate my head from my shoulders."

Those threats, along with three months of no salary and the company's bleak outlook, sent McWilliams back home to the East Coast. De Lorean was not in a position to crack down on Roy. Between his deals with suppliers and his new methods of finance, Nesseth was keeping the company afloat. The major hitch with the Consolidated contract was that Shenk required cash before he delivered a title. But the car company couldn't get cash from the dealer until it delivered the car. Roy's solution was to use his dealer friends for the bridge financing. They'd advance him $13,500 to get the title from Consolidated, and once he got the money from the dealer, he gave some of the profit back to his financier. Contractually, Consolidated required that the cars not be sold for any less than $17,500. But to meet the three-month sales quotas, Roy was often letting cars go for much less—and in some special circumstances for hardly any more than his cost. Among those recipients were Chuck De Lorean and one of Roy's dealer-bankers who did so well selling the De Lorean that he considered buying the company. Word of the special discounts reached some of the company's original limited partner-dealers. One day a group of five paid a call for an impromptu inspection. The invoices they saw confirmed their suspicions. A few suspended their orders before they left and promised they would never buy another car.

With all of Roy's fudging, the company was hitting the Consolidated sales quotas, but not meeting the other payments that were due. To make the first contractual ninety-day tab in July, De Lorean finally dug into his own pocket and came up with $300,000.

By this time, California comptroller Allred had left along with McWilliams. One accounting man from Belfast was brought in to take his place. But soon after, Irvine lost the woman who handled the accounts receivable. She was unceremoniously marched out of the building when she continued to prevent the "henchmen" from filling in additional figures in their settlements with suppliers.

No amount of budget-stretching by Roy was going to save the company. De Lorean had to find a major investor, not only to start production in Belfast, but also to help wrest the existing inventory away from Consolidated.

After Blair dropped out of the picture, the closest De Lorean came to another angel was New York City realtor Peter Kalikow. Back in his college days Kalikow had been bitten with the auto bug, and for a few years he tried producing a line of hand-tooled cars in Italy. He returned to the more concrete world of his family's construction business in Manhattan and became one of the city's most successful developers. A mutual friend introduced Kalikow to De Lorean, and it took the builder only a few weeks in April to come up with a plan. Kalikow says he was ready to sink $35 million into the project, and he admits, "I never drove the car or even sat in it. From what I've read and seen, I thought there was nothing wrong with it that wouldn't be too monumental to solve. My dealing with De Lorean was straightforward. I wanted him to remain involved with dealers and marketing, but I felt he couldn't handle production—that was the company's primary problem. We spent about five weeks preparing a plan. I wanted the British government involved, because I wasn't ready to pour money into their factory. They built it. They put it in a poor location. Why did I have to be responsible for capitalizing it?"

Sir Kenneth Cork sent his associate, Paul Shewell, to talk further with Kalikow, but he didn't find the developer in a mood to haggle over his offer. "I'm not a lawyer," Kalikow says. "When I say ten, I don't mean eight." Realizing that the British would put no more money into the assembly plant, Kalikow ended all negotiations.

Following Kalikow's withdrawal, every few weeks De Lorean heralded the approach of another new backer or group of backers. There were investors from the Far East, and investors from the Middle East. There were investors who were car dealers on the

West Coast, and other dealers who might invest from the Midwest. One potential backer was from Cleveland and rumored to be allied with Chuck De Lorean, although soon after his name appeared in the press, his phone was disconnected and all trace of his company vanished. De Lorean identified another solitary sugar daddy as a California insurance man "worth $60 million."

De Lorean's plethora of promising prospects should have tried the patience of the British officials but, for once, a Commonwealth island other than Ireland was attracting the government's attention. After Argentina invaded the Falklands, the De Lorean Motor Company faded entirely from England's limelight. Besides, in one day, Her Majesty's armed forces were spending as much as the nation's entire $150 million investment in the stainless-steel car.

Both the distraction, and the new financial perspective of the Falklands War offered De Lorean some breathing space, but no real chance for a major investor emerged. Instead he had the time to engage in another sort of deal, which—to his great misfortune—he would eventually consummate.

The genesis of this deal, De Lorean says, went back four years earlier to Pauma Valley, when his son, Zachary, started playing with an older boy who lived down the road. The playmate's father, James Hoffman, was never very specific about how he made his living. Instead, he told his wealthy neighbors vague tales about dangerous escapades in South America. At that time, De Lorean says, his contact with Hoffman was limited to a brief chat on his driveway after their sons had come back from an outing.

They would not meet face-to-face again until July 11, 1982. By then, unbeknown to De Lorean, Hoffman had been caught in a drug deal by federal authorities, and to reduce his sentence agreed to be a confidential informant in other narcotics investigations. Hoffman's version of his subsequent meetings with his onetime neighbor would be part of the eventual indictment for drug trafficking issued against De Lorean by the federal grand jury for the Central District of California. De Lorean would choose *Rolling Stone* magazine as the forum for his side of the story.

It was Hoffman who called him, De Lorean says, and offered

to help raise some money to save the car company. Both men agree they first met to discuss the deal in the stuccoed bar of the Newport Beach Marriott Hotel, only a few miles down the road from De Lorean's Irvine office. Hoffman, De Lorean says, claimed he could come up with $15 million in return for a $1.8 million commission. Narcotics crept into their conversation, but De Lorean contends Hoffman was talking about what he might do with his commission. Still, his talk did not scare De Lorean away. He continued to follow Hoffman around the country to meetings with the bizarre broker's other "investors."

Their negotiations picked up pace in early September. The two got together again in the plush L'Enfant Plaza Hotel in Washington, D.C. Then, De Lorean says, Hoffman insisted that the funds be deposited in an escrow bank account so he could collect commission without the knowledge of the investors he corralled. During this exchange, De Lorean told *Rolling Stone*, he first became frightened about Hoffman's connections and decided to make believe he had a few tough guys in his corner as well. Only months before, De Lorean had complained to British reporters that the IRA terrorists were partly responsible for the demise of his car company. Now he informed Hoffman that the Irish Republican Army was on his side in his search for funds.

Four days later De Lorean again met Hoffman in San Carlos, California, just a few miles south of San Francisco. There he was introduced to a man he thought was an officer of the Eureka Federal Savings and Loan Association. Banker James Benedict was, in fact, FBI agent Benedict Tisa, who was performing in one of the federal government's most cherished sting operations. Eureka was an authentic bank, and the pistol-packing chairman of the board, Kenneth Kidwell (his real name), had been gutsy enough to let federal agents use his operation to lure big-time drug dealers in search of laundries for their cash collections.

Two weeks later, De Lorean was in another hotel, the Bel-Air Sands of Los Angeles, meeting strangers at Hoffman's behest. This time, the guest of honor was William Morgan Hetrick, who did not hide the fact that he had made his fortune as a narcotics smuggler. De Lorean later described him as "an old, fatherly schoolteacher-type." Hetrick is in fact seven years younger than De Lorean. Coincidentally, he had once known Cristina and developed a crush on her. Back then, he was the pilot for her old flame, Fletcher Jones. The two often talked as Hetrick flew her to and from dates with the computer magnate. Shortly after Jones's death, Hetrick tried to date the boss's girlfriend, which didn't sit well with Cristina. According to De Lorean, "She got pissed that the guy would be so callous and insensitive." Still, De Lorean gave his wife a chance to renew her acquaintance with the pilot when he invited her out to dinner with his new associates, including "Benedict" and Hetrick, at a ritzy Beverly Hills restaurant, La Scala. Despite the millions of dollars he had amassed, Hetrick rarely wore anything but a tattered, soiled jump suit. His money was spent in other places, and usually, he had a teenage prostitute in tow. It's difficult to imagine how De Lorean explained the motley dinner companions to Cristina.

De Lorean had one more important hotel meeting, in L.A.'s Westin Bonaventure, before Hetrick left to make his Colombia pickup. This time, De Lorean was introduced to a Drug Enforcement Administration man who identified himself as a drug distributor with Mafia connections. By now, De Lorean had backed away from putting any cash into the transaction. Claiming he no longer had the $1.8 million of commission for Hoffman, he offered stock instead. The shares were from De Lorean Motor Cars, Inc., an umbrella company which could help circumvent creditors if De Lorean ever managed to start manufacturing again. When he turned it over to the purported Mafiosi, the stock was hardly worth the paper it was printed on.

Of course, federal prosecutors and De Lorean have two different interpretations of his role in the Hoffman deal. The authorities say he willingly conspired to eventually bring 220 pounds of cocaine into the country and share in the $60 million of proceeds. Although the stock was worthless, they still charge De Lorean had made a deal with the banker to exchange it for Hoffman's commission of $1.8 million and a potential $15 million share of the narcotics (Hetrick managed to smuggle only sixty pounds of cocaine back to L.A.).

De Lorean maintains he never intended to take an active role in a drug deal—only to find an investor for his company. When he discovered the nature of Hoffman's investors and tried to back out, he says, Hoffman threatened the lives of his children.

Whoever is telling the truth, one point is certain: during the course of his association with Hoffman and the undercover agents, De Lorean acted alone. Kimmerly did not hover in the background to explain the tax implications of the stock transfer. Nesseth didn't appear to hammer out a better deal. The man "who could get things done" had finally taken matters in his own hands.

Even without Hetrick's return from Colombia, the week of October 18 promised to be eventful for De Lorean. Hoffman had not been his only potential source of funds. He was also actively engaged in negotiations with his former Logan division manager, Gus Davis, who had brought together a group of California investors to buy the off-track vehicle plant. A continuing obstacle in their discussions had been De Lorean's insistence that, on top of an $8 million purchase price, he keep the property and get $40,000 a month in rent from the new owners. But suddenly, he changed his tune and offered to let everything go for $10 million. The price was still considered too high by Davis's group, but De Lorean planned to talk further with them after he met Hetrick.

The week was also to mark two deadlines for the car company. One concerned the payment of over $1.5 million owed to Consolidated. Schottenstein had been willing to give De Lorean grace periods in the past, but car sales had lagged far behind the rate necessary to hold up his side of the deal. Don Lander, the corporation president and last heavyweight executive still with De Lorean, stumped the Midwest making one more appeal to the big dealers.

By far, the most important deadline was the one set by the British government. Only a few weeks before, De Lorean had signed an agreement with the receivers giving him control of the plant if he could come up with just $10 million by October 18. But the day would come and go and no money appeared in the company bank account. Although other deadlines had come and gone in the past, this deadline, Secretary of State Prior declared,

TRAPPED IN A TERRIBLE TOWER

was the *final* final deadline. (De Lorean has since charged that American officials warned the British that the auto executive's arrest was imminent, so that Her Majesty's ministers wouldn't be embarrassed if he did indeed raise money in time to secure the factory. However, this theory has one major flaw—why would the narcotics agents jeopardize their sting by removing the honey that they thought was attracting the renegade bee?)

Clearly, De Lorean entertained some hope of getting his factory back when, late in the afternoon of October 19, he walked into the Sheraton La Reina Hotel near the Los Angeles International Airport. Just one day earlier, William Morgan Hetrick had gone to Room 501 there to pick up his pay for the cocaine haul, and had been arrested before the night was over. Unaware of Hetrick's bust, De Lorean followed his footsteps into Room 501. When he was shown the smuggler's handiwork, packed in a suitcase, he appeared jubilant. Grabbing a bag of coke, he proclaimed the words that a hundred newspaper headlines would memorialize: "This is as good as gold," it came "in the nick of time."

Videotape cameras then show him passing around the wineglasses and offering a toast. He was in fact frightened, but still happy, he tells *Rolling Stone*, "what I was toasting was starting up the factory again."

What he was toasting was a Lazarus-like climb back from the grave, and an amazing new addendum to the De Lorean legend. The last two years of product-quality flaws, court cases, poor sales, and British receivers would be forgotten. Once again, John De Lorean had pulled off the miracle when all around expected him to fail.

Moments later the police told him he was under arrest.

At first there would be stunned silence. But when the agents closed his wrists in handcuffs, he finally said, "You have the wrong man."

· 20 ·
Aftermath

For John Z. De Lorean, one dream has been fulfilled. His name will surely take its place among those of the auto-industry pioneers of the twentieth century. But, contrary to his plans, any historical prominence he receives will be tied to the grand scale of his failure—not to his success. Before law enforcement officials slammed his business career to a halt, his rush for glory touched the lives of thousands and cost the British government, investors, and suppliers over $250 million.

Not everyone associated with De Lorean can be called a casualty. Engineers at General Motors still speak fondly of his inspirational leadership—although few want to be quoted. Young executives who worked at the De Lorean Motor Company are obviously more cynical about De Lorean's abilities, but are still grateful for what they call a "once in a lifetime" opportunity to help start up a car company. Fittingly, those who profited most from De Lorean's dream car are the dealers. Company executives know of no dealer who did not recover at least his $25,000 stake before De Lorean's arrest. Most did far better—especially those who didn't stick with the sticker price in those heady days when the cars first appeared in America. While most dealers were

• AFTERMATH •

left with unpaid warranty claims, they found the service charges more than offset by the added showroom traffic the stainless-steel attractions generated.

But when all the ledger sheets of John De Lorean's various ventures are totaled in both human and economic terms, the losses far outweigh the gains. The losers range from De Lorean's own brother Jack, to J. Peter Grace, Jr., Clark Higley and Gerry Dahlinger, to cabinet ministers of two British governments. The most visible and most pathetic victims of De Lorean's shattered schemes are the 2,600 Irish workers at his plant and the thousands more employed by local suppliers. Some, like shop steward Malachy Higgins, gave up precious jobs to get on board. Others, like shop steward Billy Parker, never knew steady employment. For the majority, the paychecks lasted no more than a few months in 1981—deceptively long enough to finance down payments on homes and the few luxury items they had never expected to see in their own living rooms.

Despite the disparaging comments De Lorean later made about Belfast, factory workers do not blame him for the company's demise. They point instead at the Conservative government of Margaret Thatcher. But whatever the Tories' true intentions, De Lorean's extravagance and heavy-handed bargaining tactics provided the perfect argument against future government subsidies of private enterprise.

Among the unsuccessful bidders for the Belfast factory in the summer of 1982 was a group of British suppliers who planned resuming a limited production of the TR7—a sports car discontinued by British Leyland. Technically a proven product, the little car had established enough of a market in the U.S.—annual sales of 8,000—to support the scaled-down operation of the assembly plant with a tidy profit thrown in. The group still needed government subsidies of $10 million, but after De Lorean the British were no more likely to agree to aid a sports-car company than they were to purchase the Brooklyn Bridge.

For the men who ran the De Lorean Motor Company, no other aspect of John De Lorean's debacle is more disturbing than the bad name he's given independent automakers. In spite of De

Lorean, they say, they proved that a revolutionary new product could roll off the assembly line and be marketed in America. In their minds, just a few right calls from the man at the top could have made the whole project viable.

For these executives, De Lorean's involvement with cocaine is the most bitter of denouements. Sharing the blame for the car company's demise was bad enough. But then, one morning in October 1982, they woke up to find their reputations smeared even further by unwitting association with De Lorean and his scandalous funding ploy. In their eyes, De Lorean represents more than a symbol of avarice or incompetence, and it takes an evangelist's son like C. R. Brown to verbalize their collective loathing. "Sometimes when I look at John I see the devil."

For anyone taking a more dispassionate look at John De Lorean and the course of his career, it's difficult not to see him as one more victim of his unrealized dreams. It would be too easy to write him off as no more than a con man. Undoubtedly there was an element of greed and cunning in the many deals he swung—especially with United Visuals and GPD. His unscrupulous attempts to enrich himself cannot be explained away but, then again, the John Z. De Lorean image he had so carefully crafted became an increasingly expensive façade to support.

Yet there's little evidence to suggest that De Lorean ever entered deals solely to bilk people, corporations, or governments. Nothing would have pleased him more than if the sundry ventures he started had truly blossomed to the benefit of everyone involved. Success alone would have been his greatest reward. Most often his unethical practices stemmed from attempts to sort out the chaotic consequences of his managerial incompetence.

If anything, the media taught De Lorean that a good front was all that was needed to cover a variety of sins. Speaking for other car-company executives, C. R. Brown says, "We wanted John to be what he said he was," and evidently reporters were of the same persuasion. Rarely did they look for the substance that lay behind the bold rhetoric. The maverick auto engineer was too compelling a character to be deflated with investigative journalism.

• AFTERMATH •

For De Lorean, the impressive stack of press clippings was a potent weapon. No other entrepreneur in business history used publicity as well in amassing his seed capital, and he found that investors were as unlikely to look behind his hollow hype as reporters. In the skewed double standards of high finance, De Lorean underwent only the most cursory check into his background before he was loaned hundreds of millions of dollars. If there had been anything small-time about De Lorean, the banks and the British government might have persevered in turning up the business failures and court cases that followed his resignation from General Motors.

There was nothing small-time about John De Lorean. The ability of his car company to spring forth fully capitalized remains an unparalleled feat, and yet he never found his accomplishments to be big enough. He pushed his factory into ever higher gear, even when sales in the United States dictated against increased production. It was just one more hype to help sell his $20 million stock issue.

His executives claim that the company could have survived without the stock if De Lorean had lowered his sights and been satisfied with just turning out a few thousand cars a year. Unfortunately, such practical thinking would have never gotten De Lorean off the ground. In today's world of manufacturing, the costs of a plant and equipment make it virtually impossible to build up an assembly line product gradually. Only an artist working on a grand scale could have realized the production of a newly designed car. Only a canvas of the largest dimensions could have swept up the executives, suppliers, and investors needed to finish the picture.

De Lorean, as much as anyone else, became a prisoner of his own outsize vision. Eventually no one became more deluded and daunted by De Lorean's favorable and uninformed press than De Lorean himself. A Wizard of Oz, he scrambled behind the curtain to maintain his credibility, turning the levers over to more dynamic types like Roy Nesseth with no concern about what methods they used to keep his reputation and investment intact.

But finally, De Lorean was left alone in his shrouded booth. If he had been only a con man, he wouldn't have offered to invest $5 million before he'd accept Prior's offer to restructure the debt on the Belfast factory, and he wouldn't have bothered to use his own checking account to keep the car company afloat when all those around him diagnosed its drowning. "How could you tell him it was all over?" one advisor asks. "He had pulled off so many miracles before."

De Lorean remained the last believer in John De Lorean's ability to work miracles, and pride, above all else, dictated his desperate attempts to save his company. Eventually, there were no more hopes for a quick killing in the stock market or another windfall from a gullible investor, but De Lorean was out to salvage his reputation as the ethical businessman who could survive in the savage world of finance and, in his effort to preserve the image, he was ready to destroy the substance. By getting involved with Hoffman and the federal agents he thought were Mafiosi, De Lorean was not playing the part of the devil, but he was knowingly dealing with the devil.

Once again, no words on De Lorean's activity are more damning than his own. He admits to *Rolling Stone* reporter Aaron Latham that when he decided to deal with Eureka Bank, he believed it might have been controlled by Mafia interests. Where, Latham asked, did De Lorean think the bank money came from? His answer: "It could be organized crime. It could be drugs. It could be anything. But as long as it came to us through a recognized financial institution, I really didn't give a shit. To be very candid."

It could be anything . . .

In just those few words, the whole De Lorean façade collapses. If it could have been anything, why didn't he compromise himself and stay at GM? Why did he create the good "corporate citizen" if he was ready to resort to anything to keep it alive?

There are no firm answers. The questions ring only with the hollowness of De Lorean's pretensions. Ironically, in claiming that law-enforcement authorities went to illegal ends to entrap him, De Lorean points to his own exalted reputation as the cause for their malevolent designs. He explains to Latham that he was the lure to hook drug-smuggler Hetrick. "Until they used me and my name, they couldn't get Hetrick to go ahead and get into a transaction." Later he speculates that GM, or even the IRA, via influential American friends, was behind the setup. He concludes his speculation by adding, "I'm a fifty-eight-year-old guy who knows nothing but how to build automobiles. I'm not that important a guy. I don't understand."

De Lorean surely does understand, and his importance came crashing home to him after his arrest. The glamour he had so carefully cultivated made him prime meat for the media. In twenty-four hours he learned how quickly his crystalline reputation could shatter. Periodicals that had been circumspect about his car company were suddenly recycling the few negative stories ever done about him. Industry executives who had once had only kind words or silence about De Lorean were coming out of the woodwork with unflattering anecdotes.

Fame was no longer something that got him the best table at "21." It also brought international shame and degradation. On the front pages of newspapers the world over were pictures of a haggard De Lorean in his open-necked shirt. All the careful cosmetic conditioning fell away. From some angles, the loose flesh on his neck betrayed his age, but for those who knew him especially well, the awkward way he held his head was at the same time reminiscent of the shy, homely adolescent of so many years before.

Worse than the newspaper photos were the television transmissions that followed. One clip, a day after his arrest, showed De Lorean getting on board a transport bus in a blue prison jump suit, manacles on his hands and legs. In England, Colin Chapman, estranged from De Lorean for over a year, would see the scene and cry.

If John De Lorean had not become so important—if he had remained just a guy who knew nothing but how to build automobiles—he wouldn't have been brought to the public pillory. But then again, he probably wouldn't have found himself dealing with narcotics agents.

Perhaps such thoughts cross John De Lorean's mind as he awaits the eventual verdict on his narcotics indictment. As the years have passed, he has become ever more tied to his wife and children. His unwillingness to be away from home for long, his car-company executives say, jeopardized his business. Now, as he faces what could be a life sentence, his attempts to save his business have jeopardized his family.

Shortly after his arrest, De Lorean was seen clutching a Bible on his way to and from the courthouse. A few months before his trial was set to begin, he and Cristina were reported to have taken their vows as born-again Christians. Such behavior, skeptics might say, was no more than posturing—this time to impress a jury. Indeed, a Detroit television reporter learned that De Lorean had written to the director of a suburban camp for disadvantaged children, asking him to send a letter about the auto executive's past service to the charity. The request only backfired when the camp director publicly replied that the real benefactor had been De Lorean's second wife, Kelly Harmon, and not De Lorean himself.

But De Lorean's turn to religion cannot be totally dismissed as a charade. Close friends say he occasionally went to church before his arrest. Prayer often gave him solace during his most difficult business and personal trials. Probably no words in the Bible would have more significance to a contrite De Lorean than the admonition from the preacher in Ecclesiastes, "Vanity of vanities; all is vanity."

Nevertheless, it's hard to imagine John De Lorean closeted in his house poring over a Bible. Once the world saw another John De Lorean. This image was his greatest creation; greater than any car he'd engineered at General Motors or the car he engineered after he left. It was the image of a handsome man of deep moral conviction and great talent building his own car as only he knew how to build it:

We return now to John De Lorean in his office, standing in front of a worldwide map or some other business graph.

He says something like this: "Our dream is coming true, and justifying the calculated risk we took. Sure, I'm a risk taker. And the people who drive our De Lorean car are probably risk takers, too. People who dare to lead other people. . . . People who live life to its fullest poten-

tial. . . . People who enjoy the special exhilaration of making things happen. . . . People who dream of a better world, and do whatever is needed to transform that dream into reality."

John De Lorean is next shown sitting inside his car. He ends by saying, "As hard as I've struggled, I'm one man who can say that my dream has come true. Our difficult efforts have succeeded, life is good, and I'm grateful!"

Then De Lorean closes the car and drives off onto a handsome modern highway with elegant city skyscrapers in the background. Closing music and credits appear over this final radiant scene.

Index

Adams, Tom, 56, 66–67, 74
Alfa-Romeo, 167, 227
Allegheny Ludlum, 163
Allison aircraft engines, 33
Allred, Steven, 310–14
Allstate Insurance Company, 145, 146, 163, 167, 175
All That Jazz (film), 213
American Lawyer, 142
American Motors, 113, 180, 239
Anchor Lock, 112
Andersen, Arthur, & Company, 90, 224–25, 244
Anderson, Robert, 55, 56, 73, 76, 168, 187
Andress, Ursula, 156
Ann-Margret, 55
Arkus-Duntov, Zora, 42, 160–61
Arrington, Stephen Lee, 4
Atkins, Humphrey, 218
Audio Systems, Inc., 297
Automotive Industries, 64
Avrea, Bill, 113–14, 117
Avrea, Shirley, 111–12, 122
Avrea, Walter C. "Pete," 111–23

Bache Halsey Stuart, Inc., 284
Bank of America, 285, 286, 296, 300, 301, 305
Beach Boys, the, 7, 48
Belfast, Ireland, 188–94, 208–13
Belzberg, Morris, 305
Bendix Corporation, 119
"Benedict, James," 316
Bennett, Harry, 14
Bennington, Charles K. "Chuck," 212–14, 255
Bergen, Candice, 156
Bernier, Norm, 113–15
Bertone, Giuseppe, 166
Birmingham, Mich., 46, 57
Birmingham Eccentric, 46
Bitterroot Mountains (Idaho), 68, 124
Blair, Alan H., 293–95
Bloomfield Hills, Mich., 46, 67, 68, 69, 108, 139, 140, 157, 158
Bloomingdale, Alfred, 179–80
Bludhorn, Charles, 226
BMW, 296
Boe, Archie R., 145, 146
Boise Cascade, 96
Bonneville (Pontiac), 49
Brasch, Mike, 149–50

INDEX

Bricklin, Malcolm, 164
Brieant, Charles L., 301
Brown, C. R., 77, 170–71, 177–79, 225, 227, 230, 239–51, 254, 256–59, 285–86, 299–300, 310, 322
Budget Rent-A-Car, 305
Buick, 26, 34, 134, 164
Bushell, Fred, 198, 201
Bushkin, Henry, 176, 224, 245–46
Business Week, 59, 170, 194
Byoir, Carl. *See* Carl Byoir & Associates

Cadillac, 30, 34, 71, 102, 133, 134–39, 159, 169
Cafiero, Eugene A., 243–44, 245–46, 247, 255, 310
Cal Prix, Inc., 78, 107–10
Campbell-Ewald, 56, 66, 67
Campian, Reo, 13, 15, 16, 17, 104, 106
Capin, Roy, 180
Carl Byoir & Associates, 1
Carson, Johnny, 176, 187, 246, 261
Cass Technical High School (Detroit), 16–17, 27, 87, 103
Cavanagh, Jerry, 60
Celanese Corporation, 119
Chapman, A. C. B. (Colin), 198–204, 214, 215, 227, 265–68, 325
Charlie's Angels (TV show), 157
Chevrolet, 6, 34, 35–36, 40, 41–42, 61–68, 70–72, 73, 74–75, 113, 118, 126, 154, 160
Cheyfitz, Kirk, 185
Chris-Craft Corporation, 144, 174, 193, 195, 196, 198
Chrysler Corporation, 28, 34, 55, 212, 227, 239
Chrysler Institute, 27–28, 55, 87
Chrysler, Walter, 164–65
Cleveland Diesel, 33
Cohen, Alan, 187, 188, 189, 193
Cole, Dolly, 82
Cole, Edward N., 36, 42, 54, 71, 73–74, 81, 82, 83, 86–87, 105, 161
Collins, Bill, 35, 41, 165–67, 172–74, 177, 182, 197, 198, 199–200, 214, 265

Composite Technology Corporation, 167, 201
Concannon, Don, 190, 192, 216, 217
Consolidated International, 302–307, 309–10, 313, 318
Continental Bank of Illinois, 206–207
Coolant Recovery System, 113
Coopers & Lybrand, 287, 298
Cork, Kenneth, 291, 314
Corvair (Chevrolet), 35–36, 87
Corvette (Chevrolet), 41–42, 87, 160, 172, 264, 265
Crescent City, Calif., 96
Cristina Corporation, 167
Current Biography, 152–53, 154
Curtice, Harlow H., 33

Dahlinger, Gerald W., 133–39, 244, 321
Dahlinger Pontiac-Cadillac (Wichita, Kansas), 133–39, 142, 152
Dahlinger, Ray, 142
Daily Mirror (London), 275–76, 279
D'Arcy McManus, 47
Davis, Ernest "Gus," 229–30, 312, 318
Davis, Sammy, Jr., 286
De Lorean, Charles "Chuck" (brother), 104, 106–107, 313, 315
De Lorean, Cristina Ferrare (third wife), 7, 156–58, 176, 223, 225, 235–36, 247, 248, 271, 295, 308, 317, 325–26
De Lorean Diesel Corporation, 152
De Lorean Dream, The (film proposal), 2
De Lorean, Elizabeth Higgins (first wife), 29, 31, 46, 52, 57, 60, 68
De Lorean, Jack Z. (brother), 103–11, 321
De Lorean, John Z.: automobile styling skills of, 43–44, 63–64; and Walter "Pete" Avrea, 111–23; and bankruptcy of De Lorean Motor Company, 308–19; birth of, 12; British government financing of, 7, 9, 182, 188–94; and C. R. Brown, 239–51, 322; as Chevrolet general manager, 61–68; cocaine deal, involvement in, 3–4, 315–19; as col-

• 330 •

INDEX

De Lorean, John Z. (*Continued*)
lege student, 11–12, 17–24; court cases involving, 7–8, 11–12, 77, 78, 90, 110, 132, 138, 205, 284–85, 301; as critic of General Motors, 6; and Dahlinger Pontiac-Cadillac, 134–39, 205; and De Lorean Motor Cars, Limited, Belfast, 208–21; delusional thinking of, 9–10, 323–24; divorced by first wife, 52; divorced by second wife, 67–69, 76; early years of, 13–17; and the "ethical car," 7, 252–69; extravagant personal expenses of, 222–38; and GPD Services, 195–207, 219; and Grand Prix of America, 103–11; hired by General Motors, 25–26; as Horatio Alger hero, 3, 70; investigation of business practices of, 270–89; in jail, 4–5, 325; lawyers for the defense of, 4, 76, 80, 88–100, 109, 302; leaves General Motors, 6, 70–75, 77, 79–87; "legend" of, 154–58, 323–24; marketing and advertising skills of, 63–64; marries Cristina Ferrare, 156–58; marries Kelly Harmon, 51–54, 61; marries Elizabeth Higgins, 29–30; and Roy Nesseth, 88–100, 101–102, 290–307; and *On A Clear Day You Can See General Motors,* 6, 9, 13, 15, 16, 26, 30, 34, 36, 43, 62, 64, 65, 68, 70, 73, 81, 82, 83, 84, 86, 153, 223, 231, 254, 262, 280; and Packard Motor Car Company, 28–32; patent assignments to, 31–32, 35, 238; and Pine Creek Ranch, 124–32; and Pontiac, 5, 6, 25, 32–38, 40–50; public image of, 2–4, 5, 7–8, 53–54, 58–59, 66–67, 85, 154–58, 308–309; and public relations, 1–3, 54–55, 58–59, 66–67, 83, 252–69, 270–89; and Puerto Rico, financing by government of, 182–84, 193–94; and religion, 326; and Saf-Gard Systems, 114–22; Sixties sensibility of, 2–3, 5–6; sports car, plans to build his own, 159–80; surface appearances, concern with, 5, 19–20, 29–30, 53–54, 56–57; suspicious financial dealings of, 78, 195–207, 222–38; as young engineer, 5, 28–32, 32–38; youth fetish of, 56–57, 61

DeLorean, Katherine Pribak (mother), 12, 14–15

De Lorean, Kathryn (daughter), 236, 325

De Lorean, Kelly Harmon (second wife), 51–54, 61, 67–69, 76, 101, 125, 156, 326

De Lorean Manufacturing Corporation. *See* DMC, Inc.

De Lorean Motor Cars, Limited, 212, 215, 216, 220, 227

De Lorean Motor Company, 1, 7, 9, 10, 77, 89, 101, 143, 157, 167, 168, 170, 175, 176, 179, 181, 197, 204, 206, 216, 225, 227, 234, 241, 246, 270, 271–72, 280, 290, 296, 302, 315, 320–21. *See also* John Z. De Lorean Corporation.

De Lorean Motors Holding Company, 271–77

De Lorean Research Limited Partnership, 184, 195, 196, 202, 286

De Lorean-Ryder Corporation, 152

De Lorean Sports Car Partnership, 168, 169–70, 172–73

DeLorean, Zachary (father), 12–14

De Lorean, Zachary Thomas (son), 67, 157, 236, 315, 325

De Lorenzo, Anthony G., 82

Detroit Athletic Club, 59

Detroit Dragway, 47

Detroit Free Press, 16, 51, 87, 156, 158, 185

Detroit News, 82

DeVito, Anthony P., 186

Dewey, Robert, 62–63, 174, 181, 182, 185, 186–87, 189, 193, 222–23, 226–27

DMC, Inc. (De Lorean Manufacturing Corporation), 10, 206, 216, 220, 228–29, 244, 251, 272

Dow Chemical, 162–63

Drug Enforcement Administration, 4, 317

Drysdale, Don, 96, 98

INDEX

Dubin, Maur, 226, 236, 271
Dunmurry Industrial Estate (Belfast), 209–10
Durant Motor Company, 204
Durant, William Crapo, 26–27, 64, 85, 87, 204

Earl, Harley, 42–43
Elastic Reservoir Molding (ERM), 162–63, 201, 266
Estes, Elliott M. "Pete," 32, 35, 40, 41, 42, 44, 45, 52, 62, 83, 87, 154
Eureka Federal Savings and Loan Association, 316, 324
Evans, Thomas W., 144

Fatjo, Tom, J., Jr., 168–69, 183
Fawcett, John, 18
FBI, 4, 316
Federal Economic Development Administration, 181, 183, 194
Federal Farmers Home Administration, 181, 183
Ferrare, Cristina. *See* De Lorean, Cristina Ferrare.
Ferrari, 45
Fiat, 146
Fifth Avenue (New York City) coop apartment, 157, 174, 196, 223, 295
Fisher Body, 7
Forbes, Malcolm, 237
Ford, Henry, 14, 15–16, 26–27, 35, 85, 87, 142, 164
Ford Motor Company, 12, 13–14, 34, 113, 114, 122, 182
Fortune, 55, 57, 154
Fosse, Bob, 213
Freeman Chemical Corporation, 162–63
Frye, Wheelabrator, 187
Fugazy, William, D., 144

Gallagher Report, 72, 73, 83
Gay, Peter, 7
General Electric, 15, 78
General Motors, 5, 6, 9, 23, 25, 26–27, 32–38, 40–50, 56, 59–60, 61, 63, 64–65, 70–87, 116, 118, 122, 134, 135, 138, 142, 149, 153, 159–61, 170, 182, 192, 215, 232, 235, 238, 254–55, 262–63, 320–21

Georgia Pacific, 96
Gerstenberg, Richard C., 71, 72, 83, 142
Gibson, Marian, 270–79
Gilbert, Ross, 95, 297–98
Giugiaro, Giorgetto, 166–67, 214, 238, 243
Gorf, Ken, 213, 217–18, 224, 281, 285
GPA Systems, 107–108, 132. *See also* Grand Prix of America
GPD Services, 195–207, 219, 269, 277
Grace, J. Peter, Jr., 144–45, 146, 163, 167, 175, 321
Grace, W. R., & Company, 144
Graeffe, Edwin, 21, 23–24
Grand Prix (Pontiac), 44, 49
Grand Prix of America, 72, 73, 103–11, 152, 165, 309
Grant, Cary, 76
Greek Money (horse), 97, 99
Greenbrier, N.C., 82
Gregg, Hamilton, 171–72
GTO (Pontiac), 44–45, 47–49, 154, 165

Haddad, Bill, 60, 84, 197, 212, 218, 230–32, 235, 271–72, 275, 284
Hailey, Arthur, 68
Hammer, Armand, 146, 147
Hanson, Earl, 299
Hard Winners, The (Quirk), 54
Harmon, Elyse Knox (mother-in-law), 51–52, 54
Harmon, Kelly. *See* De Lorean, Kelly Harmon
Harmon, Mark (brother-in-law), 68–69
Harmon, Tom (father-in-law), 52–53, 54, 67, 68, 98
Harte, Shaun, 216–17, 224
Hegedus, Chris, 215, 218
Henkel, Robert, 1–3
Hetrick, William Morgan, 4, 316–19
Higgins, Elizabeth. *See* De Lorean, Elizabeth Higgins
Higgins, Malachy, 260, 282
Higley, Clark, 123–32, 137, 153, 321
Higley, Colleen, 123, 127, 128–29, 130

INDEX

Hilton, Barron, 55
Hilton, Nicky, 51
Hoffman, James, 315–18
Hollywood, Calif., 5, 42, 51–69, 74
Honda, 183
Hookstratten, E. Gregory, 76, 78, 156
Hopkins, Tony, 218, 219, 248
Hunt, Nelson Bunker, 144, 148
Hutton, E. F., 169
Hymes, Myles, 78, 101

Iacocca, Lee, 85
IRA (Irish Republican Army), 191, 211, 259, 316, 325
Irvin, Robert, 82, 154
Irvine, Calif., 249–51
Isuzu Diesel North America, Inc., 151

Jam Handy Corporation, 77
Javits, Eric, 184
John Z. De Lorean Corporation, 140, 143, 147, 151, 167, 175, 206. *See also* De Lorean Motor Company et al
Johnson, Kenneth E., 133, 134–35
Jones, Fletcher, 157, 317
Jordan, Don, 94–95
Juhan, Marie-Denise, 196, 202, 203

Kaiser-Frazer, 164, 167
Kalikow, Peter, 314
Kansas State Bank and Trust Company (Wichita, Kansas), 133, 205
Kerkorian, Kirk, 94
Kidwell, Kenneth, 316
Kimberly, Michael J., 198
Kimmerly, Thomas, 8–9, 10, 90, 91, 109–10, 135–38, 141–42, 167, 168, 174–75, 184, 201, 202, 218, 223, 227, 229, 232–34, 237, 244, 247, 248, 250, 271, 295, 300, 302, 309, 318
King, G. Edmund, 187, 224, 245–46
Kissinger, Henry, 212
Kitch, Paul, 205
Knudsen, Bill, 35
Knudsen, Semon "Bunkie," 32–38, 40, 42, 43, 52, 54, 57, 64–65, 140, 154, 161

Lada (Russian car), 146, 228
Laguna Beach, Calif., 69, 78
Lander, Donald H., 255, 284, 287, 318
Latham, Aaron, 324
Laugh-In (TV show), 49
Lawrence Institute of Technology, 11–12, 17–24, 27, 63, 87
Lawrence Tech News, 18, 22, 23, 24
Lear, Bill, 133
Le Car (Renault), 167
Lehman Brothers, 180
Le Mans (Pontiac), 45
Lentell, J. V., 135
Lighthouse Point, Fla., 71, 102, 103
Lime Rock, Conn., Racetrack, 57
Lisners, John, 274–78
Loasby, Michael, 265, 267, 268–69
Look, 61
Lopez Mateos, President, 96
Los Angeles Dodgers, 96
Los Angeles Times, 75
Lotus Cars, 198–204, 214–15, 219, 227, 265, 266–67, 268
Loving, Rush, Jr., 57
Lucas, George, 232
Lucia, Carroll J., 28–29, 30–31, 32

Mahoney, David and Hilly, 236
Maserati, 159, 167
Mason, Roy, 191–92, 217, 280
Mazda, 162, 170–71, 240, 245
McFarland, Forrest, 29, 32
McKinsey and Company, 245
McLean, Robert F., 33, 43–44, 49–50, 81, 140, 144, 145–46, 147–48, 159, 162
McWilliams, J. Bruce, 310–14
Measelle, Richard L., 225, 227, 245
Mercedes-Benz, 95, 139, 164
Merrill Lynch Pierce Fenner & Smith, 173
Metropolitan Life Insurance Company, 126–27, 129, 131
Michigan Bell, 11–12, 23–24
Midnight Special (TV show), 55
Mini-Theater, the, 74–75, 77
Mint Investment, 78, 101
Misch, Herbert, 32
Mitchell Boys choir, 51
M. L. Associates, 173

INDEX

Modesto, Calif., 75
Monkees, the, 48
Morgan, William A., 177–78, 179, 226, 234, 291, 297, 299
Motor Trend, 58, 60, 164–65
Murphy, Thomas A., 71, 83

Nader, Ralph, 36, 163
Nance, Jim, 28, 29, 32
National Alliance of Business, 79, 142
National Association for Stock Car Auto Racing (NASCAR), 37, 44–45
National Auto Dealers Association (NADA), 157
National Auto Parts Association, 114
National Football League, 77, 151
Navajo Freight Lines, 111
Nederlander, James, 144
Nelson, Mrs. Ricky (sister-in-law), 52, 54
Nelson, Ozzie and Harriet, 53
Nesseth, Donald, 94
Nesseth, Jeff, 312–13
Nesseth, Roy Sigurd, 8–9, 10, 76–81, 88–100, 101, 106–10, 116–21, 126–32, 132–39, 142, 148, 173, 178–79, 227, 228, 230, 241, 244, 271, 290–307, 309, 312, 318
Newhart, Bob, 93, 94
New Issues, 285
News of the World (London), 278
Newsweek, 58, 61, 263
New York Herald Tribune, 230
New York Times, The, 154, 194
New York Yankees, 143
Ninowski, Jim, 104, 105, 108
Noonan, John, 72, 142
North American Rockwell, 55, 72–73, 104
Northern Ireland Development Agency (NIDA), 188–90, 193, 194, 216–17, 218, 219, 220, 224, 227, 242, 247, 272, 273

Occidental Petroleum, 146
O'Connor, Sandra Day, 121
Oldsmobile, 34, 40, 151, 172

On A Clear Day You Can See General Motors (De Lorean and Wright), 6, 9, 13, 15, 16, 26, 30, 34, 36, 43, 62, 64, 65, 68, 70, 73, 81, 82, 83, 84, 86, 153, 223, 231, 255, 262, 280
100 West Long Lake Road (Bloomfield Hills, Mich.), 140–55, 195, 223, 270
Oppenheimer & Company, 184, 189, 193, 196, 219

Pacific International Equipment, 98
Packard Motor Car Company, 28–32, 87
Palm Springs, Calif., 96, 97
Parker, Billy, 208, 220–21, 282, 321
Pasha International, 249, 299
Passages (Sheehy), 6, 154
Patent Office. *See* U.S. Patent Office
Patrick Petroleum Company, 73
Patrick, U. E., 73, 103
Paul, Weiss, Rifkind, Wharton & Garrison, 187, 229
Payne, Thomas, 104, 105, 108, 109–10
Pennebaker, D. A., 215, 216, 238, 265
Penske, Roger, 55, 56, 156, 168, 174
Petroleum Club (Houston, Texas), 168
Phillips, Howard, 193
Pietrykowski, Thaddeus, 17, 21
Pine Creek Ranch (Salmon, Idaho), 124–32, 142, 152, 237
Pininfarina, Sergio, 166
Pizza Hut, 134, 139
Playboy Books, 153
Pomona, Calif., 107, 108
Pontiac, 5, 6, 25, 32–38, 40–50, 64, 68, 93, 133, 134–39, 154
Porsche, 167, 197
Powers, J. D., & Associates, 281
Presley, Elvis, 76
Prior, James, 283, 287, 291, 293, 294–95, 318, 324
Prior, Peck, 74, 77, 78
Private Eye, 279

• 334 •

INDEX

Prussing, Raymond F., 151–52, 166, 183
Puerto Rico, 182–84

Quality Assurance Centers (QAC), 256, 259, 260, 299, 300, 301, 302, 304
Quirk, John, 46, 54–56, 58, 61, 68–69

Ramey Air Base (Puerto Rico), 185
Ran Boys Used Car Lot (Los Angeles), 91
Reese, Emmett, 124–26
Reese, Mrs. Emmett, 124–25, 128
Renault, 147, 167, 215, 282, 286
Republican Party, 46, 60
Reserve Brake Indicator, 112
Road & Track, 264
Roberts, Fireball, 37
Rockwell International. *See* North American Rockwell
Rolling Stone, 315–16, 319, 324
Romero Barcelo, Carlos, 194
Rudd, A. C., 198
Ryder, James, 148

Saf-Gard Products, 113–16, 117. *See also* Saf-Gard Systems
Saf-Gard Systems, 116–22, 132, 138, 142, 152, 309
San Diego Chargers, 55, 72, 151
Schapp, Milton, 183
Schmidt, Julian G., 58–59, 60
Schottenstein, Jerome, 302–307, 318
Scott, Milton Bradley, 74–81, 90, 101–102, 107
Securities and Exchange Commission, 73, 176, 197, 226, 232, 248
Service Parts, 114
Shasta, 144–45
Shay, Arthur, 69
Sheehy, Gail, 6, 37, 154
Shell Oil, 162–63
Shenk, Florence, 303
Shenk, Sol, 302–307, 313
Shewell, Paul, 314
Shriver, Sargent, 60
Siegel, Ann, 236
Siegel, Herbert Jay, 144, 236

Signature, 69
Simon, William, 228
Sinatra, Tina, 156
60 Minutes (TV show), 236
Slavik, Joseph, 104, 155–61
Sloan, Alfred P., 42, 84, 85
Sloan, Allan, 185
Smith, C. W., 148, 227
Snider, Lawrence K., 291
Snyder, Tom, 76
Spooner, Colin, 200, 266
Sports Illustrated, 67
Start-up (film), 215
Steinbrenner, George, 143
Stephenson, Gordon, 131
Stephenson, John, 129, 131–32
Stroock & Stroock & Lavan, 181, 193
Strycker, Walter P., 187–90, 201–202, 204, 206–207, 216, 222, 225, 226, 227, 233, 235, 275
Studebaker, 32
Sugarman, Burt, 55–56, 75, 76
Sunday Telegraph (London), 198, 276
Sunday Times (London), 203
Synor, Jeffrey C., 254, 257–58, 260–61

Taylor, Elizabeth, 51
Technicolor, Incorporated, 75, 77, 80
Tee-Kay International, 237
Tempe, Ariz., 113
Tempest (Pontiac), 36, 44, 165
Terrell, Richard L., 82, 83
Thatcher, Margaret, 217–18, 273
Thiokol, Logan division, 205–206, 207, 225
Thomas, John H., 92, 139
Time, 154
Times, The (London), 191, 275, 277, 279, 280, 288
Tisa, Benedict, 316
Titanic, 209, 243
Tonight Show, The (TV show), 176
Toyota, 95, 100
Trippe, Juan, 172
Troy, Mich., 72, 104, 106
Tucker (car), 164, 167
Turin, Italy, 166

INDEX

Ultramatic transmission, 29
United Visuals Corporation, 75, 77, 78, 79, 80, 90, 101, 102, 132
Unsafe At Any Speed (Nader), 36
Upton, Hazel, 95–99
Upton, William E., 96
U.S. Patent Office, 112, 113, 154

Vacuum-Assisted Resin Injection (VARI), 201, 202, 266, 278, 282
Vacuum Resin Injection Moulding (VRIM), 201, 203
Vega (Chevrolet), 113, 262–63
Volkswagen Rabbit, 166
Volvo, 259

Wallace, George, 183
Wangers, Jim, 47–49
Ward's Auto World, 145
Warner Communications, 104
Webster, Sheffield, 168
Weise, Norman, 103, 106
Wentzel, Fred, 143
Wheels (Hailey), 68
Wichita, Kansas, 132–33, 136
Williams Chevrolet, 76, 93, 101
Williams, George, 65, 93, 99–100, 132–33
Williams, Ted, 30
Winterton, Nicholas Raymond, 273–77
Wood Gundy Limited, 187, 188, 224
Woodward Avenue (Detroit), 39–40
Wright, Frank Lloyd, 136
Wright, J. Patrick, 6, 13, 59, 73, 153, 231
Wulf, Horst, 21–22

Yanitz, Larry, 150
Yates, Brock, 67
Yunick, Smokey, 37–38, 44, 62, 199, 228